Handel und Internationales Marketing
Retailing and International Marketing

Series Editors
Bernhard Swoboda, Trier, Germany
Thomas Foscht, Graz, Austria
Hanna Schramm-Klein, Siegen, Germany

Die Schriftenreihe fördert die Themengebiete Handel und Internationales Marketing. Diese charakterisieren – jedes für sich, aber auch in inhaltlicher Kombination – die Forschungsschwerpunkte der Herausgeber. Beide Themengebiete werden grundsätzlich breit aufgefasst; die Reihe bietet sowohl Dissertationen und Habilitationen als auch Tagungs- und Sammelbänden mit unterschiedlicher inhaltlicher und methodischer Ausrichtung ein Forum. Die inhaltliche Breite ist sowohl im Sinne eines konsumentenorientierten Marketings wie auch einer marktorientierten Unternehmensführung zu verstehen. Neben den Arbeiten, die von den Herausgebern für die Schriftenreihe vorgeschlagen werden, steht die Reihe auch externen wissenschaftlichen Arbeiten offen. Diese können bei den Herausgebern eingereicht und nach einer positiven Begutachtung publiziert werden.

The book series focuses on the fields of Retailing and International Marketing. These two areas represent the research fields of the editors—each of them as a single research area, but also in combination. Both of these research areas are widely understood. Consequently, the series provides a platform for the publication of doctoral theses and habilitations, conference proceedings and edited books, as well as related methodological issues that encompass the focus of the series. The series is broad in the sense that it covers academic works in the area of consumer-oriented marketing as well as the area of marketoriented management. In addition to academic works recommended by the editors, the book series also welcomes other academic contributions. These may be submitted to the editors and will be published in the book series after a positive assessment.

More information about this series at http://www.springer.com/series/12697

Florentine Frentz

The Pursuit of Food Well-Being

The Mechanisms Behind Consumers' Food Well-Being, and Their Relevance for Food Retailing and Marketing

With a Foreword by Prof. Dr. Hanna Schramm-Klein

Springer Gabler

Florentine Frentz
Chair of Marketing and Retailing
University of Siegen
Siegen, Germany

Dissertation, University of Siegen, 2019

ISSN 2626-3327 ISSN 2626-3335 (electronic)
Handel und Internationales Marketing Retailing and International Marketing
ISBN 978-3-658-30365-5 ISBN 978-3-658-30366-2 (eBook)
https://doi.org/10.1007/978-3-658-30366-2

This Springer Gabler imprint is published by the registered company Springer Fachmedien Wiesbaden GmbH part of Springer Nature.
The registered company address is: Abraham-Lincoln-Str. 46, 65189 Wiesbaden, Germany

Foreword

In her dissertation, Florentine Frentz addresses the topic of food well-being by conceptualizing the construct as a whole, while successively analyzing selected aspects and contexts of food well-being in detail, such as related aspects in the context of nutrition and trade or shopping. The construct of food well-being focuses on the well-being of consumers in the context of food and nutrition, describing a positive relationship on a physical, emotional, social, intellectual, spiritual, and self-determined level. Thus, in addition to aspects of nutrition and health (e.g., physical constitution), it also includes, for instance, hedonic elements of wellbeing.

To ensure food well-being is relevant at the individual level of each consumer, but also for society as a whole. This becomes clear when one considers not only the effects of over-nutrition on the health or the physical and mental constitution of each individual, but also the related impact in the context of an entire society, e.g., the effect on the social and health care system, as well as the related economic implications. Therefore, the promotion of food well-being is of high social relevance and is implicitly and explicitly included in the agenda of not only consumers themselves, but also those of companies and consumer policies. Consequently, the fact that this topic is discussed and researched in the context of this dissertation is particularly noteworthy.

In a total of six essays, Florentine Frentz addresses different aspects and facets of food well-being. First, she derives an integrated framework for food well-being, the so-called "Food Well-Being Cycle", within the confines of a conceptual essay. Then, in the second and third essay, she specifically investigates the influence of online food purchases on the development of food well-being and analyzes the reasons or motives for why consumers buy food online. In essay four, she addresses the food well-being of children as a specific consumer group by analyzing the influence of stationary food shopping on this facet of their lives. Furthermore, specific aspects in which the topic of food well-being are implicitly addressed are highlighted in essay five and six, with particular emphasis on impulse behavior. On the one hand, a study is presented that specifically examines eating behavior, and on the other hand, a (replication) study is presented that addresses the topic of in-store slack, while examining the role of mental budgets created by consumers before shopping.

With her work, Florentine Frentz makes a significant contribution to consumer research. She presents significant and novel findings regarding the construct of food well-being, in conjunction with its antecedents and consequences. Her work impresses with its broad spectrum of theory and methods, as well as her conceptual contributions. Furthermore, she derives crucial implications not only for marketing practice but also for politics and consumers.

Florentine Frentz's work represents an outstanding scientific achievement that is convincing in every respect. The theoretical insights and empirical findings represent a significant enrichment for research on food well-being. Since this subject is both topical and empirically relevant, and the implications have a high theoretical and practical applicability, the work is appropriate for wide dissemination, not only in research but also in retail and marketing practice, as well as in consumer policy procedures.

Prof. Dr. Hanna Schramm-Klein

Acknowledgement

My dear parents named me Florentine, which means "the flowering." Therefore, they wisely gave me a name that reflects an essential element of my personality, namely the unlimited will to grow, to develop myself, and to exploit my potential. It is partly because of this desire that I decided to do my doctorate a few years ago.

Another reason for embarking on the doctorate was my passion for food well-being and consumer research. I have been interested in nutrition throughout my life, which was initiated by the cooking sessions with my mother when I was a little girl. My passion for consumer research in this area was awakened, above all, by my studies at Wageningen University. In particular, I remember the inspiring lessons and discussions with Prof. Dr. Hilde Tobi and Prof. Dr. Ellen van Kleef. My internship at the University of Maastricht, during which time I was allowed to assist Dr. Karolien van den Akker with her studies under the supervision of Prof. Dr. Anita Jansen, also strengthened my interest in researching purchase and consumption behavior in a nutritional context.

These interests, combined with my enjoyment of teaching, led to my employment as a research assistant and doctoral student at the University of Siegen. I have learned a lot during this time, not only regarding research and teaching within the context of my doctoral thesis but also about life in general. I have developed and grown in many ways. Now, at the end of this journey, I have a doctoral thesis that reflects my passions and interests, as well as the intellectual development I experienced over the past few years. I am grateful for the opportunity to make this journey, and I know that it would not have been possible without certain people.

First, I would like to thank Prof. Dr. Hanna Schramm-Klein for providing me with the necessary freedom and supervision. She was always prepared to listen and engage in constructive discussions. I learned from her, not only in terms of content and methods, but also regarding life. For instance, she taught me that if something unpleasant happens, to think, "Who knows what it's for?" I would also like to thank Prof. Dr. Gustav Bergmann and Prof. Dr. Giuseppe Strina, who, as my advisory committee members, evaluated my work, encouraged me in my endeavors and, at the same time, showed me new views and perspectives. I am also extremely grateful for the support I received from Prof. Dr. Paul Marx, who, like no other, inspired by breaking down boundaries with courageous ideas and daring decisions.

Furthermore, I am grateful for the inspiring and pleasant collaboration with my co-authors in writing the manuscripts that are presented in this dissertation, namely Prof. Dr. Hanna Schramm-Klein, Dr. Jonathan Blitstein, Prof. Dr. Stephanie Bell Jilcott Pitts, Regina Mukhamedzyanova, Felicitas Mayenschein, Prof. Dr. Gunnar Mau, and Prof. Dr. Paul Marx. Jointly working and writing with these great minds taught me a great deal and resulted in outstanding publications.

It is with gratitude that I think of my colleagues with whom I have walked this path, and without whom this journey would not have been the same: Robér Rollin, Dr. Frederic Nimmermann, Dr. Florian Neuss, Prof. Dr. Sascha Steinmann, Dr. Gerhard Wagner, Carmen Richter, Anne Fota, Tobias Röding, Theresia Mennekes, and Katja Wagner. We have not only supported each other within the framework of our scientific work and our doctoral theses but have also established friendships that will last far beyond the doctorate.

Furthermore, from the bottom of my heart, I thank my family for their support and love. I thank my wonderful parents, Gertrud and Wilfried Frentz, who supported me in my endeavors and who made my studies possible. Since my father is unfortunately no longer with us, I would like to thank my mother, in particular, who gave me strength and always believed in me. I am also delighted that my sister, Cornela Frentz, accompanied me on this journey. I could always count on her to stand by me, no matter what. It is with love that I think of my better half and my rock, Tobias Hamers, who also supported me unconditionally during the last few years.

Finally, I would like to thank everyone who has given me so much over the years: my lovely family, my awesome friends, my inspiring professors, my curious students, and the extraordinary people who have participated in my studies and supported me in completing them. I thank you so, so much for your support, your faith, your inspiring words, your commitment, your honest criticism, and your patience.

Florentine Frentz

Table of Contents

List of Figures

List of Tables

List of Abbreviations

AM	ante merīdiem (before midday)
ANOVA	analysis of variance
AR	augmented reality
ATS	average trip spending
BIS	Barrett impulsivity scale
BMI	body mass index
CA	contingency awareness
CS	conditioned stimulus
CS+	intake-associated environment
CS-	control environment (no food intake)
DS	drug store
DV	dependent variable
F	F-statistic
FWB	food well-being
FWBC	food well-being cycle
HMD	head-mounted display
M	mean
N	number of participants
NPP	number of planned products
ITI	inter-trial interval
OS	organic store
p	p-value
p.	page
PM	post merīdiem (after midday)

R^2	R-squared (coefficient of determination)
RS	revised restrained scale
SD	standard deviation
SL	shopping list
SPSS	statistical package (software) for the social sciences
T	t-statistic
TTB	total trip budget
US	unconditioned stimulus
US	United States
VAS	virtual analogue scale
VR	virtual reality

1 Introduction

1.1 Relevance and Focus

In view of the increasing complexity of food-related life and the challenges it poses (e.g., Block et al., 2011; Scott and Vallen, 2019), such as the overweight and obesity pandemic (Ravussin and Ryan, 2017; WHO, 2018a), this dissertation aims to increase our understanding of the food-related well-being of consumers, and to identify ways in which the various stakeholders affected can exert a positive impact on the maintenance and improvement of this well-being. This emphasis on the food-related well-being of consumers not only serves consumers and, in the long term, the well-being of society as a whole (Block et al., 2011), but also the companies involved, which can thereby gain a competitive advantage (Mittelstaedt, Killbourne, and Shultz II, 2015; Sirgy and Lee, 1996). This dissertation pursues three fundamental objectives in particular: (1) to refine and broaden our understanding of food well-being (FWB) and its development; (2) to identify ways in which consumers can be effectively supported in their development and maintenance of FWB; and (3) to show how companies can use the concept of FWB in marketing strategies to achieve a competitive advantage.

This first chapter sets out the basis for achieving these objectives. First, the underlying problem is outlined to illustrate the relevance of the declared research questions, after which key terms are defined and distinguished from related terms, and the theoretical background is explained; the nature of these elaborations forms the concept of FWB. After that, the relevance of FWB for grocery business operators and food marketing is explained in detail. The chapter ends with an overview of the six scientific essays that constitute the core of this dissertation.

1.1.1 Problem Description: Food-Related Challenges of Modern Society

Food-related life is "that part of a person's life comprising [the] procurement, preparation, and consumption of food and meals" (Grunert et al., 2007, p. 487). In addition, it includes the anticipation of these food-related experiences, as well as their remembrance (Arnould, Price, and Zinkhan, 2002). Like all areas of life, it also does not exist independently and detached from others; it is connected to them, and they partly overlap with and influence each other on a constant basis (Roscoe, 2009; Swan et al., 2018).

F. Frentz, *The Pursuit of Food Well-Being*, Handel und Internationales
Marketing Retailing and International Marketing,
https://doi.org/10.1007/978-3-658-30366-2_1

Food-related life comprises the procurement, preparation, and consumption of food and meals as well as the anticipation and remembrance of these experiences (Arnould, Price, and Zinkhan, 2002; Grunert et al., 2007).

Food-related life can be said to be a complex and difficult issue to unravel (e.g., Guillemin et al., 2016). This is particularly unfortunate in view of the current challenges in this area of life, which affect human beings at the individual, group and societal level (e.g., Block et al., 2011; Thaler and Sunstein, 2008). One current and urgent food-related challenge is the overweight and obesity pandemic, which continues to worsen all over the world (Ravussin and Ryan, 2017). "Nutrition and obesity" constitute "some of the most pressing research topics" of the contemporary era (Mick, 2006, p. 2). In 2016, more than 1.9 billion adults around the globe were overweight (BMI $\geq$ 25), of whom about 650 million were considered to be obese (BMI $\geq$ 30; WHO, 2018a). The trend towards obesity is likely to continue in the future, and with 54% of its population overweight, Germany is no exception (Schienkiewitz et al., 2017). Overweight and obesity are serious physical states that increase the risk of developing diseases such as diabetes, cardiovascular diseases, certain types of cancer, and various psychological illnesses (e.g., Bacha and Gidding, 2016; Mohana et al., 2014; Morrison et al., 2015; Luppino et al., 2010; WHO, 2018b). Furthermore, overweight and obesity often contribute to a higher number of disability-adjusted life years, and a reduction of overall life expectancy (Grover et al., 2015), while the financial consequences for individuals, families, and society can be enormous, especially due to health care costs and productivity losses (Goettler, Grosse, and Sonntag, 2017; Scharff, 2012). Many researchers have suggested that the "obesogenic" environment, i.e., "the sum of influences that the surroundings, opportunities, or conditions of life have on promoting obesity in individuals or populations" (Swinburn, Egger, and Raza, 1999, p. 564), is the main contributor to overweight. Contemporary life promotes a sedentary lifestyle, provides an abundance of easily available high-calorie foods, and supports unhealthy eating choices (Lakerveld et al., 2018; Story, Neumark-Sztainer, and French, 2002).

The **obesogenic environment** is "the sum of influences that the surroundings, opportunities, or conditions of life have on promoting obesity in individuals or populations" (Swinburn, Egger, and Raza, 1999, p. 564).

Although it may seem obvious that the modern physical environment with all its seductions is responsible for people's increased food intake and lower physical activity, given widespread access to, for instance, supermarkets and fast food restaurants that lure customers with favorable offers, comparatively little is known about the precise causal mechanisms involved. This being so, if we are to address the overweight pandemic, it is imperative to understand its formation processes and the contribution of the various stakeholders involved.

Even though the overweight and obesity pandemic appears to be particularly important at the moment, additional food-related challenges exist that threaten the food-related well-being of individuals and of society as a whole. For example, many people are vulnerable as a result of personal characteristics or life circumstances that causes them to experience disadvantages in the market (Andreasen and Manning, 1990), in particular in exchange relationships that impair their food-related life and well-being. For example, due to the gradual ageing of many countries' populations, there is an increasing proportion of elderly and frail people who experience difficulties buying and preparing their food, and who have an increased risk of developing under- and/or malnutrition (Andersson and Sidenvall, 2001; Donini et al., 2013; McKie, 1999). Another issue is that families with children - especially those with only one parent - are increasingly facing financial constraints that force them to pay more attention to price and quantity than to quality when purchasing food (Burns, Cook, and Mavoa, 2013; Grier et al., 2007). The health-related consequences for the children of these families are particularly critical (Broyles et al., 2015). Overall, the contemporary world offers many nutritional traps to which children and adolescents can fall prey. One dangerous development is the spread of eating disorders such as anorexia nervosa, bulimia nervosa, and the binge eating disorder (Ágh et al., 2016; Keski-Rahkonen and Mustelin, 2016). Particularly alarming is a comparably new disorder that is increasingly observed among adolescents, and that holds a mirror up to modern society: the double burden of malnutrition, which involves the simultaneous presence of undernutrition and overweight or obesity (Caleyachetty et al., 2018).

These are just a few of many food-related challenges that modern society is facing, and that demonstrate the complexity of food-related life; they show that this life area entails risks that can have serious health and financial consequences both for the individual consumer and for society as a whole. As a result of the complexity and associated risks, a holistic and integrated approach that takes the individual, group, and societal levels into account is necessary to enable the improvement and maintenance of consumers' food-related well-being. This holistic perspective is a relatively new approach; in recent years, a change in thinking can be observed from a rather functional, medicinal, and narrow view of food towards a holistic, integrative, and positive way of thinking (Block et al., 2011). This paradigm shift is embodied by the term "food well-being," which has only recently been introduced, and which portrays food as an important contributor to well-being and quality of life (Block et al., 2011). In the following chapter, this paradigm shift is described in detail, and the overall thematic and theoretical framework for this dissertation is presented.

1.1.2 A Holistic Perspective on Food in Consumers' Lives and Well-Being

Over the years, our understanding of the importance of food for the well-being of consumers has changed drastically. In this chapter, this new role of food will be illuminated in detail. First, the concept of consumer well-being is outlined, along with spillover theory, which explains the influence of the experiences one has as a consumer on overall life satisfaction and well-being. The concept of FWB is then described, in addition to the corresponding framework, and finally, based on these elaborations, an overarching conceptual framework is presented that forms the basis of this dissertation.

1.1.2.1 The Concept of Consumer Well-Being

Because FWB is based on the more general concept of consumer well-being, the latter notion is explained first. In previous research, consumer well-being has been conceptualized and measured in various ways. In some studies, it has been examined one-dimensionally, such as being conceptualized as satisfaction with the purchase of a certain good (the acquisition model of consumer well-being; e.g., Meadow, 1983; Lee and Sirgy, 2004; Sirgy, Lee, and Rahtz, 2007), or with the material possession of a certain product (the possession model of consumer well-being; Nakano, MacDonald, and Douthitt, 1995; Sirgy, Lee, and Rahtz, 2007), while in other studies, it has been conceptualized as a two-dimensional concept referring to satisfaction with the acquisition and possession of consumer goods and services (the two-factor model of consumer well-being; Leelakulthanit, Day, and Walters, 1991; Sirgy, Lee, and Rahtz, 2007). However, most definitions contain a broader scope of consumption-related experiences, ranging from acquisition through consumption to disposal (the consumption process model of consumer well-being; e.g., Lee et al., 2002; Sirgy, Lee, and Rahtz, 2007). Despite the extensive research that has been conducted in this field of study, the term "consumer well-being" still lacks a common definition (Ares et al., 2014; Ares et al., 2016; Sirgy, Lee, and Rahtz, 2007). In the scope of this dissertation, consumer well-being is broadly understood as a multi-dimensional construct that encompasses how people experience the situations in which they take on the role of consumer (e.g., the acquisition and consumption of products, the perception of marketing campaigns, and the experience of a service), and how this influences them on different levels (physical, emotional, social, intellectual, and spiritual; Hettler, 1980; Roscoe, 2009), and eventually affects their overall satisfaction, well-being, and quality of life (Sirgy, Lee, and Rahtz, 2007).

Consumer well-being refers to how people experience the situations in which they take on the role of consumer, how this influences them on the different overarching levels of well-being (physical, social, emotional, intellectual, and spiritual), and how this in turn affects their overall satisfaction, well-being, and quality of life (Roscoe, 2009; Sirgy, Lee, and Rahtz, 2007).

One example can be that of a young woman with a broken coffee machine who returns to the store from which she bought it. The shop assistant is very friendly, and suggests that she leaves the machine in the store until the next day, so that it can be repaired immediately. Since the damage to the machine is very slight, it will cost only a few dollars, and the young woman is relieved about and happy with the great service. This experience has a positive influence on her mood but also strengthens her trust in people, and especially in shop assistants, and encourages her to proactively ask for help in the future. It has been a positive experience in the consumer life domain, but also contributes to the young woman's emotional well-being and relationships with other people, and these effects in turn have an influence on her overall well-being.

This chain reaction is based on the spillover theory of life satisfaction (Headey et al., 1985; Lee et al., 2002; Sirgy, Hansen, and Littlefield, 1994; Sirgy et al., 2001), which suggests that life satisfaction is influenced by a hierarchy of domain and subdomain satisfactions (see Figure 1). One's level of satisfaction with particular events and experiences within a specific life domain (e.g., personal health, work, and family) influences one's overall satisfaction with respect to this domain, and satisfaction in a specific domain (in the example, in the consumer life domain) can in turn spill over horizontally to neighboring domains (e.g., the consumer domain affects the social equivalent) or vertically (bottom-up) to superordinate life satisfaction and quality of life. On the other hand, overall life satisfaction can exert an influence on one's satisfaction with individual domains, as well as on the perception of specific experiences, the so-called vertical top-down spillover (Headey et al., 1985; Lee et al., 2002; Sirgy, Hansen, and Littlefield, 1994; Sirgy et al., 2001).

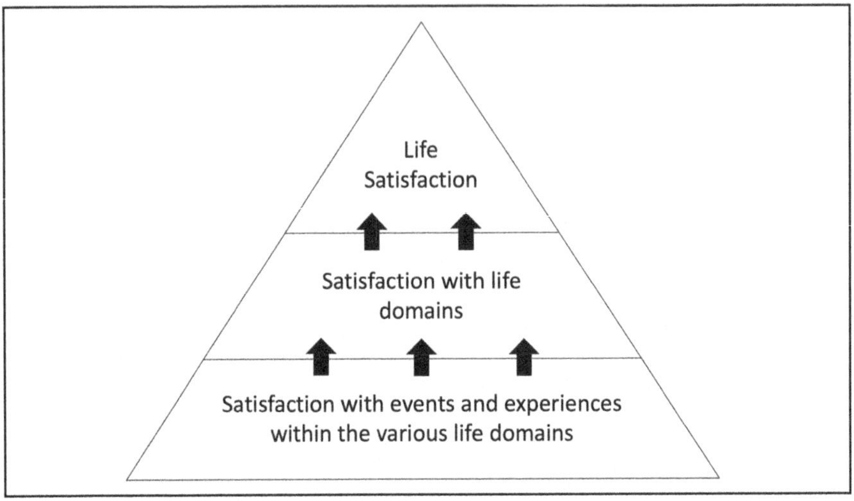

Figure 1: Satisfaction hierarchy based on the spillover theory of life satisfaction (Lee et al. 2002)

1.1.2.2 The Concept of Food Well-Being

In the past, the impact of food on consumer well-being was often perceived as limited to physical repercussions; based on the biomedical model of health, which focuses on the origins and causes of diseases, eating was mainly viewed as a physiological act aimed at fulfilling nutritional needs and maintaining physical health (Biltekoff, 2010; Eriksson and Lindström, 2008; Swan et al., 2018). In recent years, however, research findings have repeatedly demonstrated that food plays a broader role in well-being (e.g., Ares et al., 2016; Block et al., 2011; Bublitz et al., 2013; Guillemin et al., 2016; Martin and Hill, 2012; Rozin, 2005). Grunert et al. (2007) assert that one's satisfaction with food-related life is a major requisite for a high overall quality of life, and this insight inspired them to develop a scale that measures satisfaction with food-related life (Grunert et al., 2007). The far-reaching consequences of food-related experiences are also evident in the results of various studies. For example, Ares et al. (2014) assigned participants the task of listing the words that they associate with well-being, and 39% mentioned food-related terms. Food-related experiences seem to influence overall well-being by affecting various life dimensions, according to a number of studies (e.g., King et al., 2015; Swan et al., 2018). The focus group study results of Guillemin et al. (2016), for instance, suggest that food-related experiences can influence consumers' physical, emotional, and social well-being.

Although Block et al. (2011) were not the first researchers who have proposed a broader role of food in well-being (e.g., Boelsma et al., 2010; Grunert et al., 2007; McMahon, Williams, and Tapsell, 2010; Rozin, 2005), they were pioneers in that they officially suggested a different and more holistic approach in this research area, and introduced and defined the term FWB. According to these authors, food should no longer be seen as mainly functional and medicinal, in that it contributes to health when selected, prepared, and consumed properly (Eriksson and Lindström, 2008; Swan et al., 2018), but should rather be viewed positively and in a consumer-oriented manner, in the broader light of well-being. In particular, Block et al. (2011) proposed a shift from the traditional, health-oriented, and narrow view to a more positive, holistic understanding of the role of food in consumers' overall life and well-being, and based on this train of thought, they introduced the term FWB, which is intended to epitomize the proposed paradigm shift.

Food well-being is "a positive psychological, physical, emotional, and social relationship with food at both individual and societal levels" (Block et al., 2011, p. 6).

There are two crucial aspects in this paradigm shift. First, there is the holistic nature of the approach, which considers food in a broader context, and acknowledges its impact on different areas of life; in this regard, Block et al. (2011) mention the psychological, physical, emotional, and social dimensions of FWB. Second, there is the positive way of thinking. Although Block et al. (2011) do not explicitly mention the issue, the positive approach corresponds to positive psychology, which is "the study of the conditions and processes that contribute to the flourishing or optimal functioning of people, groups, and institutions" (Gable and Haidt, 2005, p. 104). It unites two approaches to well-being: the hedonic approach, which relates to high levels of positive and low levels of negative affect, and the eudaimonic approach, which concerns a sense of fulfillment and meaningfulness in life, based on personal growth and the exploitation of one's unique potential (Deci and Ryan, 2008; Diener et al., 1999; Ryan and Deci, 2001; Ryff and Keyes, 1995).

1.1.2.3 The Food Well-Being Framework

Based on their postulated paradigm shift, Block et al. (2011) present an overarching FWB framework, the so-called FWB pinwheel (see Figure 2), which is intended to support an integrated analysis and understanding of "all health and social challenges associated with the types and amounts of foods and beverages people consume, in addition to the production and consumption contexts of food

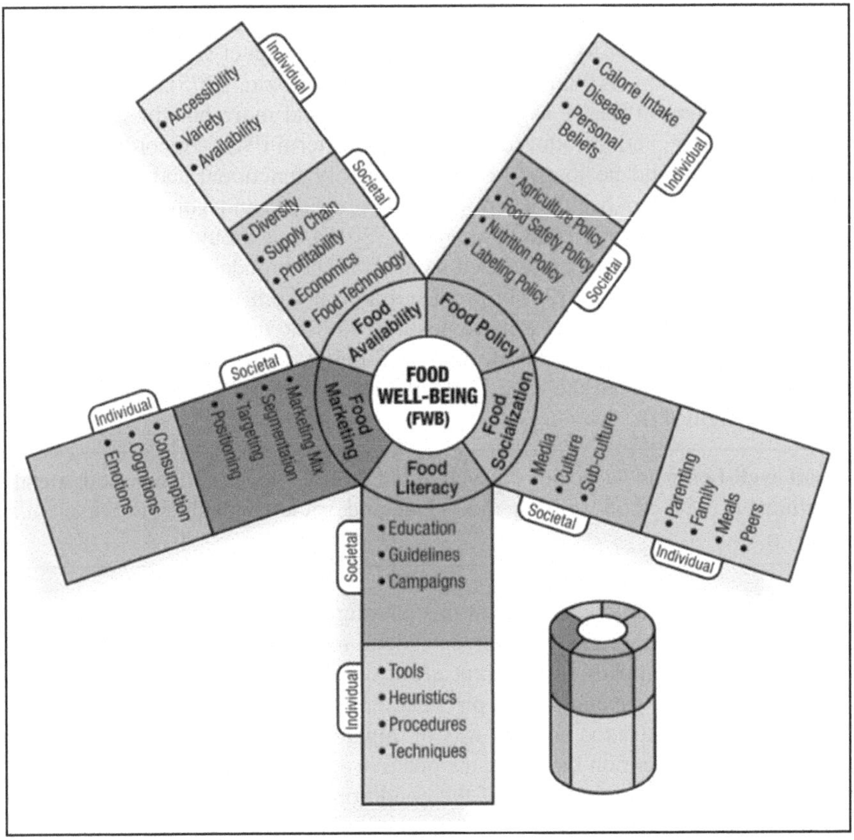

Figure 2: The food well-being pinwheel (Block et al. 2011)

(…)" (p. 6). The framework reveals the need for a holistic and integrated approach by showing how FWB is influenced and formed by the interplay between actions of different stakeholders. It also demonstrates the decisive role of food marketing, which forms part of the higher dimensions in this framework.

The framework has the shape of a pinwheel, and when closed, the figure reflects a "unity of strength," while when it is opened, it metaphorically stands for a "fluid, nonstatic interchange of ideas and influencers" (Block et al., 2011, p. 6). At the heart of the pinwheel are five dimensions of FWB, each of which has an individual and a societal level: socialization, literacy, marketing, availability, and policy.

Food socialization refers to the process through which consumers learn about food and its role in their lives (Block et al., 2011). Food socialization begins during early childhood. The members of a child's family act as socialization agents, and explicitly or implicitly teach the child by exemplifying food-related activities and by living food-related cultural values, rituals, and traditions. But also external influences, such as the media and public institutions, shape the children's food-related development (Block et al., 2011; Mochis, 1985; Moore, Wilkie, and Lutz, 2002). *Food literacy* refers to the knowledge that one has with respect to food and nutrition, and the degree to which this knowledge is used to promote FWB goals. More specifically, it concerns the possession of food-related conceptual knowledge (the learning and preservation of factual knowledge) and procedural knowledge (the application of factual knowledge in practice) and the ability, opportunity, and motivation to use this knowledge in various contexts (Block et al., 2011; Bublitz et al., 2011; Vidgen and Gallegos, 2014). *Food marketing* entails marketing measures that are applied by marketing practitioners to influence consumers' attitudes and behaviors that are relevant to FWB. Within the FWB pinwheel, food marketing contains only three "Ps" (product, promotion, and price) because the fourth P (place) is part of food availability (Block et al., 2011). *Food availability* refers to the degree of accessibility of food in consumers' different life situations and circumstances; in this way, it concerns the variety of food that a consumer can access at home, at work, on the go, or in any other relevant situation (Block et al., 2011; Bublitz et al., 2019). Finally, *food policy* is designed to structure, regulate, and control how food is produced, processed, distributed, and purchased by consumers. In other words, food policy regulates the entire food distribution system, from production to consumption. Different policies in, for instance, the agricultural, food safety, nutrition, and food and nutrition labeling policy realms are implemented at the local, state, national, and international level (Block et al., 2011; Lang, Barling, and Caraher, 2001).

To summarize, the pinwheel demonstrates that many stakeholders can exert an influence on consumers' FWB, and that a high level of FWB can only be reached when all stakeholders involved both individually and jointly work on the enhancement of FWB, at the individual and societal levels. Stakeholders operating in the food industry such as retailers and food marketers play an integral role in this.

1.1.2.4 Conceptual Framework and Research Gaps

Based on the concept of FWB and the corresponding framework, as well as the spillover theory and the approach of positive psychology, a comprehensive and strong framework emerges that forms the basis of this dissertation (see Figure 3). This framework is outlined in the following section, beginning at the bottom level.

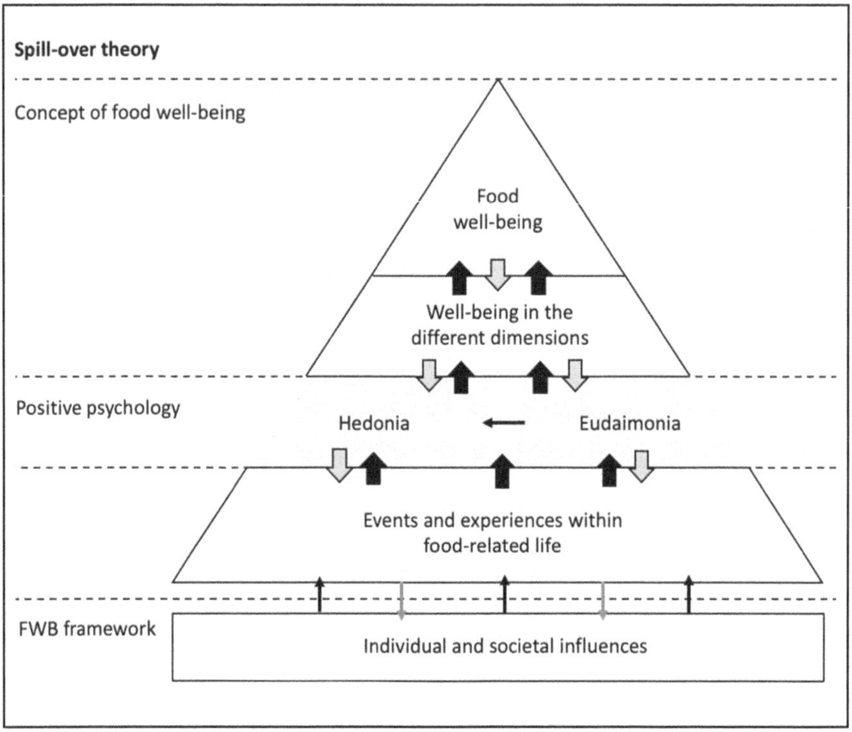

Figure 3: The hierarchical model of food well-being

The FWB pinwheel of Block et al. (2011) makes it clear that the food-related events and experiences that one goes through are determined by influential factors at the individual and societal level, such as the marketing activities that shape the retail environment in which consumers make their grocery purchases (societal), and the self-control strategies that consumers are able to apply to resist these marketing measures (individual). The experiences that consumers have in their food-related life influence the various well-being dimensions, which encompass the psychological, physical, emotional, and social spheres (Block et al., 2011). The influence that such events and experiences have on these dimensions can be based on feelings and emotions (hedonic well-being) and/or personal growth and the fulfillment of their own potential (eudaimonic well-being; Deci and Ryan, 2008; Diener et al., 1999; Ryff and Keyes, 1995). For example, a grocery shopping experience could positively influence the emotional dimension by decreasing stress (hedonic) or the intellectual dimension by enhancing product knowledge, which also contributes to personal growth (eudaimonic). Hedonic and eudaimonic well-being can influence the FWB dimensions separately, but eudaimonic well-being can also influence them by first affecting hedonic well-being. The well-being in the individual dimensions can also spill over horizontally into other dimensions; for example, stress-reduction in the emotional dimension could for instance also lead to physical relief, while the well-being in the dimensions spills over bottom-up into overall FWB. Based on the concept of vertical top-down spillover, overall FWB can in turn exert an influence on well-being at the individual dimensions, as well as on perceptions of specific experiences and events.

This conceptual model depicts the various aspects that contribute to overall FWB, as well as the interrelated structure that they form. However, the framework and literature on which it is based also possess knowledge gaps that pave the way for the essays presented in the course of this dissertation. Several researchers have noted their agreement with the paradigm shift suggested by Block et al. (2011), and have partly adopted the latter's definition of FWB and/or the FWB pinwheel (e.g., Bublitz et al., 2019; Schnettler et al., 2016; Scott and Vallen, 2019), while some have mentioned the need to improve and/or extend the understanding of FWB (Bublitz et al., 2011; Mugel, Gurvize, and Decrop, 2019; Voola et al., 2018). Furthermore, it is striking that some recent research in the field of FWB does not refer to Block et al. (2011) at all, such as Ares et al. (2016), Guillemin et al. (2016), and King et al. (2015), but is rather based on general wellness and well-being theory (e.g., Roscoe, 2009). This indicates that there is no common understanding of the nature of FWB, and how related issues need to be approached, revealing an urgent need for a universal understanding. There also seems to be disagreement with regard to the number, composition, and content of the relevant FWB dimensions (e.g., Ares et al., 2014; Block et al., 2011; King et al., 2015), while neither the elements that form part of FWB, nor the interactions between these elements and the underlying mechanisms of actions, have yet been fully identified (e.g., Bublitz et al. 2011; Mugel, Gurvize, and Decrop, 2019; Voola et al., 2018). Against this background, further research is required to extend the understanding of FWB and its development.

1.1.3 The Relevance of Food Well-Being for Food Retailing and Marketing

In view of the food-related challenges facing modern society such as the continuing overweight and obesity pandemic (Ravussin and Ryan, 2017; WHO, 2018) and the decrease in trust towards the food industry (e.g., Huck, Pezzei, and Huck-Pezzei, 2016; Tonkin et al., 2017), food retailers and food marketers should engage more actively in the improvement of consumers' FWB to help both consumers and society, and simultaneously, to build up a competitive advantage.

Retailers and food marketers tend to be known most of all for their negative influence on consumers' FWB. The overweight and obesity pandemic is said to have been largely driven by grocery business operators and food marketers, who have played a decisive role in shaping the obesogenic environment (e.g., Charlton et al., 2015; Cobb et al., 2015; Monteiro et al., 2013; Virtanen et al., 2015). Various studies have shown the strong influence that retailers and marketers have on consumers' nutrition; for instance, they can influence the demand for food (Huang and Yang, 2013), people's food-related judgements and decisions (Andrews, Burton, and Kees, 2011), and their sensorial expectations of foods (Elder and Krishna, 2009). Given their outsize influence on the consumption behaviors of consumers, food retailers and marketers must ask themselves whether they want to continue to pursue their previous strategies, or are prepared to use their influence to contribute to the improvement of consumers' FWB. The need for action on the part of food retailers and marketers has been recognized by international organizations, public policymakers, and researchers, who have repeatedly called on them to accept their moral and social responsibility by contributing to the creation of a leptogenic environment (e.g., Hawkes, 2013; Hutter, Hoffmann, and Mai, 2016; Schrempf, 2014), i.e., an environment that promotes healthy food choices and encourages physical activity (Swinburn, Egger, and Raza, 1999). Action recommendations for retailers and marketers include improvements to the availability and affordability of healthy food products for consumers, the design of sustainable supply chains, and the implementation of marketing measures in favor of customers' well-being (e.g., Hawkes, 2013; Hutter, Hoffmann, and Mai, 2016; Schrempf, 2014). At the same time, consumers themselves are paying increasing attention to their well-being, and want to see it respected and strengthened by grocery business operators (Havas Group, 2017). Many current consumer trends reflect this preference for the development and maintenance of well-being (Grunert, 2017; IGD, 2018), suggesting that the orientation towards FWB complies with the contemporary zeitgeist. The integration of FWB into marketing efforts not only serves an altruistic and moral purpose, but is also "a source of innovation and competitiveness for food retailing" (Hémar-Nicolas and Ezan, 2018, p. 433) and marketing (Meiselman, 2013). This perspective is also in line with the contemporary quality-of-life marketing concept (Lee and Sirgy, 2004; Sirgy, Samli, and Meadow, 1982; Sirgy and Lee, 1996) and the concept of positive marketing (Gopaldas, 2015; Mittelstaedt, Killbourne, and Shultz II, 2015). According to these concepts, marketing efforts should focus on the enhancement of well-being and the reduction of negative side effects for target groups and other stakeholders; by following such a sustainable and well-being-oriented approach, long-term profitability shall be obtained by building lasting relationships and using economics of scale and scope (Mittelstaedt, Killbourne, and Shultz II, 2015; Sirgy and Lee, 1996). The notion corporate social responsibility (CSR), which is currently enjoying great popularity (e.g., Glavas, 2016; Schramm-Klein et al., 2016; Zentes, Morschett, and Schramm-Klein, 2016), is based on a very similar philosophy in that it also emphasizes the responsibility that a business bears "to society and a broader set of stakeholders beyond its shareholders" (Wang et al., 2016, p. 534). An FWB-oriented approach corresponds to the contemporary zeitgeist, and can lay the foundation for the creation of a win-win situation for companies and their customers.

Some companies have already begun to integrate consumer well-being into their strategic marketing efforts, and to actively communicate this realignment to the outside world. They demonstrate their well-being-oriented approach, for instance, by offering healthier products and supporting environmentally friendly and socially responsible food systems. However, knowledge regarding consumer FWB and how it can be actively supported is still limited, which restricts companies' target-oriented scope of action. This being so, a well-thought-out definition of the term FWB and a comprehensive framework that points the way to a high level of FWB, confirmed by empirical research, is likely to be a valuable basis for a more target-oriented and successful integration of well-being into companies' missions and marketing strategies. This dissertation offers vital added value not only from the perspective of researchers and consumers, but also from the point of view of food companies and food marketers.

1.2 Structure of the Essays and Individual Contributions

1.2.1 Focus of Essays

The aim of this dissertation is to develop a deeper understanding of FWB, and to test and expand this knowledge by means of empirical studies in various contexts and with respect to different phenomena. In addition, action recommendations will be advanced for the stakeholders involved. These aims are achieved by means of six essays, which first take a general and theoretical look at the topic and then increasingly go into detail.

FWB is examined theoretically in the first essay, while an extensive literature research reveals the weaknesses of the current definition of FWB, and allows for the formulation of a more precise and complete definition. Furthermore, an enhanced framework, the so-called FWB cycle, is presented that comprehensively reflects the structures underlying the development of FWB. In the second essay, these theoretical elaborations find a practical application by means of three studies that investigate the extent to which the digitalization of grocery shopping changes the food-related life and well-being of consumers. The choice of this question was obvious, due to the contemporary nature of the topic. It can be assumed that in the future, an increasing number of people will buy their food online, therefore it should be investigated at an early stage what effects this will have, and what measures need to be taken to steer the influence in a positive direction. Given that consumers' food-related purchase and consumption behaviors are strongly influenced by cultural aspects and the market's local and country-specific structure, the third paper examines consumers' motives to shop for groceries online by conducting two surveys in the United States (US) and Germany. Doing so yields valuable insights into the type of motives that drive consumers to shop online, as well as the importance that they attribute to these motives across countries. The findings show that the differences between countries are notable, and that they must be taken into account when addressing consumers. This also applies to nutrition-related goal achievement. Since previous research has shown that the course for a positive development of FWB should ideally be set in childhood, the fourth essay focuses on children in different stages of development, and how their FWB is influenced by family grocery shopping in different grocery store formats. The retail context was chosen because this is the context in which the foundations are laid for the development of children's food shopping skills, while this context also offers a platform to expand children's food and nutrition literacy. The comprehensive field study presented in this essay gives valuable insights into the influences that affect children's FWB in a grocery shopping context, and how retailers, caregivers, and policymakers can help children to strengthen their FWB in this specific environment. Differently to the first four essays, the fifth and sixth each focus on one specific mechanism of action. The fifth essay investigates environment-based and conditioned eating behavior; this is a rather invisible mechanism that is all the more important, when one considers its consequences for consumers' diets and physical health. The conditioning process can be induced by consumers themselves, such as by the regular consumption of chips in front of the TV, as well as by the obesogenic environment around them, such as the all-too-common bag of popcorn in the cinema. The essay makes use of an experimental study conducted in a virtual reality laboratory to demonstrate how consumers can be conditioned to develop a desire for a particular product in a specific environment; by doing so, it highlights the importance of conditioning in consumers' eating behavior, and presents classical conditioning as a possible tool for implementing a healthier diet. Finally, given that previous research has highlighted the importance of financial factors in food-related behavior, the final essay concerns the utilization of budgets during shopping trips, with a special focus on grocery shopping. Prior research has demonstrated that the shoppers' mental budgets consist of a budget for planned products, the so-called itemized portion, and a budget for unplanned products, the in-store slack. However, the literature has not yet clarified the composition or utilization of the in-store slack, therefore, by means of an extensive field study conducted in four different store types, this essay examines the factors affecting its size and exploitation. The findings give insights into the factors that influence consumers' budgeting and, more importantly, their spending on unplanned and impulsive purchases, which are often unhealthy items.

Table 1 provides an overview of the six essays. For each essay, the research objective is presented, and information provided about the research design and method.

Table 1: Summary of research characteristics of the six essays

	Essay 1	Essay 2	Essay 3	Essay 4	Essay 5	Essay 6
Objective	To refine the definition of FWB and the associated framework	To explore how online grocery shopping affects consumers' FWB, and how providers can contribute to consumers' FWB	To investigate and compare consumers' motives for shopping for groceries online in the US and Germany.	To examine the influence of grocery shopping on children's FWB, and how stakeholders can contribute to their FWB.	To test classical conditioning as a mechanism for context-induced eating, taking into account the moderating role of impulsivity.	To investigate the antecedents of in-store slack size, and the factors that lead to its utilization.
Design	Literature research	26 think-aloud protocols and subsequent interviews; six consumer focus group discussions; and a survey with 103 participants.	Two surveys conducted in the US (N = 154) and Germany (N = 240).	Observational study in two store types (an organic store and a supermarket) with 100 observations.	An experiment with a within- and between-subject design, conducted in a virtual reality laboratory with 70 participants.	A field study (observation and survey) conducted in four store formats, with 406 participants.
Analysis	Content analysis	Theory-confirming and hypotheses-testing mixed methods content analysis by means of MAXQDA; a T-test with SPSS.	Bottom-up content analysis with emergent coding, using SAS.	Theory-confirming and hypotheses-testing mixed methods content analysis by means of MAXQDA.	Repeated measures ANOVA, student's t-test, and linear regression by means of SPSS.	Multiple linear regression analysis and ANOVA by means of SPSS.

A variety of research approaches and designs, as well as different consumer groups, are used to explore FWB in detail and from different perspectives. Each essay touches one or more aspects of FWB, and advances our understanding of the complex and holistic relationship between food and well-being. The studies carried out across the essays allow for an illumination of FWB and its mechanisms of action, in relation to the various phenomena examined in different contexts and from multiple perspectives. Overall, this dissertation offers comprehensive theoretical as well as practice-based insights into FWB, and in this way, extends knowledge in this field of research. The findings also provide valuable hints concerning what grocery business operators, marketers, public policymakers, and consumers can do to strengthen their FWB.

The following sections summarize the purpose, research questions, and methodology employed in each essay.

1.2.2 Essay 1: Food Well-Being: The Development of an Integrated Model

Given today's food-related problems, such as the overweight and obesity pandemic (Ravussin and Ryan, 2017; WHO, 2018a), a change in thinking and a new approach to food-related phenomena is urgently needed (Block et al., 2011). For a long time, the impact of food on consumer well-being was viewed as being limited to the fulfillment of consumers' nutritional needs and the maintenance of their physical health (Eriksson and Lindström, 2008; Swan et al., 2018). However, within the last two decades, researchers in various disciplines have increasingly emphasized the notion that food actually plays a broader role than previously recognized, influencing more and different life domains (e.g., Ares et al., 2016; Bublitz et al., 2013; Guillemin et al., 2016; Rozin, 2005). In their pioneering paper, Block et al. (2011) described this paradigm shift and introduced the term FWB, which examines the new role of food in consumers' overall well-being, and presented the first FWB framework: the so-called FWB pinwheel.

It is possible that the postulated paradigm shift and the associated new way of approaching food-related problems will contribute to the development and maintenance of the food-related well-being of individual consumers and of society as a whole. However, despite the work of Block et al. (2011) and extensions by later researchers (e.g., Bublitz et al., 2019; Mugel, Gurviez, and Decrop, 2019; Voola et al., 2018), there is still no uniform and unambiguous understanding of FWB. This being so, in the current essay, the findings on food-related well-being from different disciplines are collected, structured, and combined, and based on these insights, the definition of FWB is enhanced to make it more complete and precise. The definition has been extended as follows: it is a subjective and objective evaluation of people's physical, emotional, social, intellectual, and spiritual relationship with food.

Furthermore, based on an extensive literature research, the development process of FWB is reconstructed, and the individual phases of this process illuminated in detail. A total of four relevant overarching phases can be identified. The first consists of levels of influence, and is divided into individual, social environmental, physical environmental, and general environmental influences. These determine what kind of food-related experiences a person makes at which place and in what time, and how the person perceives these experiences. Through these experiences, which form the second phase, a person is able to develop specific competences that are necessary for living a fulfilled food-related life; i.e., food and nutrition literacy. The building of these competences is the third phase. Eventually, all previous phases (levels of influence, experiences, and learning processes) influence the fourth phase, in which the individual FWB dimensions, i.e., the physical, emotional, social, intellectual, and spiritual dimensions, are impacted. The fulfillment and interaction of these dimensions form the overall FWB. These dimensions can in turn exert an influence on the levels of influence and the experiences one has, and thereby start the FWB cycle anew. Based on this causal chain, this essay presents an improved FWB framework: the so-called FWB cycle.

The FWB cycle offers an overview of the development and composition of FWB. In this way, it points to opportunities for future research such as the development of a measurement instrument for the assessment of FWB, and allows researchers to place research problems and findings more easily in the larger context. Furthermore, there are several possibilities for its practical use, such as in marketing, where the FWB cycle could be used to inform the creation of services and products that contribute to FWB. In public policy, it could help to identify opportunities for creating goal-oriented policies and interventions that can improve consumers' FWB.

1.2.3 Essay 2: How Online Grocery Shopping Influences Consumers' Food Well-Being Compared to Offline Grocery Shopping

It is important to investigate the impact that fundamental changes in the food industry such as the digitalization of grocery shopping have had on consumers and their food-related life and well-being in order that negative consequences can be prevented and positive ones promoted. This should not only be a concern for consumers, policymakers, and consumer protection, but also for online grocery providers. Based on the marketing concept of quality of life and recent trends and developments (Grunert, 2017; IGD, 2018; Sirgy and Lee, 1996), it can be assumed that the consideration of consumers' FWB in grocers' marketing efforts reinforces the latter's relationships with their current customers, and paves the way for new relationships, thereby strengthening their business model over the long term. This being so, a focus on improving consumers' FWB is relevant and beneficial for all parties involved.

The concept of FWB forms the theoretical basis of this essay, which implies that food-related activities including the purchase, preparation, and consumption of food influence various life domains and dimensions and overall well-being and quality of life (Block et al., 2011). In particular, based on this perspective, grocery shopping is deemed able to influence consumers' food-related well-being through five dimensions: physical, social, emotional, intellectual, and spiritual (Ares et al., 2016; King et al., 2015; Roscoe, 2009).

To investigate the consequences of FWB for these dimensions and overall FWB, an exploratory, mixed-methods research approach has been applied. The use of data and method triangulation supports the development of a comprehensive understanding of a phenomenon and adds rigor to research (Denzin, 2012), and therefore three studies were conducted by means of different methods and heterogeneous samples: (i) 26 think-aloud protocols of consumers documenting their completion of online grocery shopping tasks, followed by in-depth interviews; (ii) six consumer focus group discussions; and (iii) a questionnaire with mainly open-ended questions answered by 103 consumers.

The findings suggest that online grocery shopping affects four of the five FWB dimensions identified in the literature search: the physical, emotional, social, and intellectual dimensions. The fifth dimension, the spiritual sphere, did not show itself to be relevant because spirituality and/or religiosity in general seems to play a subordinate role in the lives of the participants. The findings rather point to the existence of an additional factor termed the self-determined dimension. This new dimension, which extends FWB theory, was created because self-determined and independent decision making was found to be highly relevant for many participants, and it does not fit into any of the other dimensions.

In general, the findings show that online grocery shopping can have both positive and negative consequences for consumers' FWB, and that the extent to which it can have a positive influence significantly depends on invidviduals' own preferences and life circumstances. For many participants, a well-balanced combination of stationary and online shopping seems to be the best solution. For online grocery shopping to be beneficial for consumers' FWB, a number of measures still need to be taken. For example, our research shows that shopping online entails that children are no longer involved in the shopping process, which interrupts their food socialization process. Furthermore, many consumers are afraid that shopping online will harm both urban infrastructure and community life, while the selection, storage, and transportation of goods does not always meet their quality standards, and can be inadequately controlled. These are just a few examples of the findings, but they clearly show that researchers, online grocery operators, public policymakers, and consumer protection experts would do well to take action to make online grocery shopping more well-being-oriented.

These findings contribute to our understanding of the relationship between online grocery shopping and consumers' food-related lives and well-being, and thereby allow the derivation of valuable recommendations for the various stakeholders involved. Moreover, this essay extends the theoretical understanding of FWB by deepening our understanding of the FWB dimensions identified in the literature search and by introducing a new dimension.

1.2.4 Essay 3: Fifty-One Reasons Consumers Shop for Groceries Online: A Mixed-Method Examination of Motives for Online Grocery Shopping in the United States and Germany

Cultural differences (e.g., Ares et al., 2016); regional traditions, rituals, and behaviors (e.g., Voola et al., 2018); and regional- and country-specific market structures (e.g., Booth et al., 2001) can lead people in different countries to display divergent food-related purchase and consumption behaviors. Therefore, the goal of this paper is to examine and compare the motives of consumers to shop for groceries online in the United States (US) and Germany. In particular, we strive to extend our understanding of motives behind online grocery shopping across countries, and to investigate the role that nutrition-related goal achievement and healthy eating plays in consumers' channel choices.

To achieve these research goals, two cross-sectional surveys about grocery shopping habits and dietary practices were conducted in the US and Germany. These surveys included an open-ended question that asked participants to report why they opted to shop for food online, as well as comparable questions on participants' characteristics and demographic data. The data were collected via the Internet (US) and a mixed methods approach (via the Internet and intercept surveys in Germany). A convenience sample of respondents (US = 154; German = 240) was used, with a mean age of 33.5 years; there were slightly more females (55.3%) than males. To take part in the study, participants were required to be at least 18 years of age, and had be at least partly responsible for the grocery purchases in their households. For the data analysis, a bottom-up, content analysis approach with emergent coding was employed.

The synthesis and coding yielded 51 benefits of online grocery shopping, clustered into eight motivation categories. The identified superordinate categories confirm previous research findings, and also extend existing knowledge by showing the benefits of which the motives are composed, and how important US and German consumers perceive the individual benefits and motives to be. It is interesting to note that the two consumer groups show essential differences in the perceived importance of some benefits. For instance, German respondents mentioned comparably more often the benefit of saving money, while the US respondents were more interested in saving time. Furthermore, the increased availability and accessibility of products and brands was an important motivation among German respondents, while the US participants emphasized the reduced number of stressors in the online grocery shopping environment, compared to stationary shopping. Support in meeting nutritional objectives was barely mentioned by any participants in either of the two groups; less than 2% of the US participants addressed this issue, and only 10.8% of the German participants said that they can strengthen their food-related knowledge and competences when buying groceries online.

The findings add to the current literature by providing a taxonomy of motivations for online grocery shopping from close to 400 individuals from the US and Germany. The detailed breakdown of the eight motives into the 51 benefits, as done in this essay, is unique in this form, and therefore offers new insights and possibilities for research and practice. Future research can build on these findings, and follow-up studies can be conducted that include more countries. Such studies could measure a higher number of influential factors, such as the chosen delivery type. Furthermore, the findings give initial indications as to how healthy food choices could be promoted and presented in online grocery stores in the United States and Germany. For example, German consumers are more likely to positively react to discounts, while US consumers tend to react positively when healthy choices are made as easy as possible.

1.2.5 Essay 4: Better Marketing for More Food Well-Being: How Retailers and Marketers Can Contribute to Children's Food Well-Being in the Food Retail Context

The overweight and obesity pandemic is an increasingly global problem (Ravussin and Ryan, 2017); by 2016, 1.9 billion adults were overweight, of whom 650 million were obese (WHO, 2018a). However, the growing proportion of overweight and obese children is particularly shocking; as of 2016, almost every fifth child is overweight (WHO, 2017; WHO, 2018b).

To counter this trend, this essay proposes a holistic approach based on the concept of FWB (Block et al., 2011). To achieve the best effect, the habits that promote a healthy development of FWB should be set in childhood (Baur and Garnett, 2019; Lumeng et al., 2015; Ravanbakht, Skinner, and Perrin, 2017), therefore this essay suggests that the FWB of consumers should be strengthened from earliest child age in the physical, emotional, social, intellectual, and self-determined dimensions (Ares et al., 2016; King et al., 2015; Roscoe, 2009).

Even though the purchasing contexts are often denigrated as obesogenic environments that are harmful to consumers' FWB (e.g., Cobb et al., 2015; Monteiro et al., 2013; Virtanen et al., 2015), the latest research also suggests that grocery shopping can be important for the development of children's FWB (e.g., Hémar-Nicolas and Ezan, 2018; Marshall, 2014). This context, and the fact that families and children are regularly confronted with modern-day grocery stores, is the focus of this essay, which looks at how children's FWB is influenced by stationary food shopping, and what the various stakeholders involved can do to positively impact this influence.

To answer these questions, an exploratory, observational study was conducted in two quite different grocery stores: a supermarket and an organic grocery store (it was assumed that store types have variable influences due to their different business philosophies and store characteristics). A total of 100 family purchases were recorded, and their influence on the FWB of the children involved documented. The families were first observed inconspicuously as they were shopping, and then questioned using a short survey.

The results show that the participating children's FWB is influenced in all five dimensions by grocery shopping, and that this influence is particularly determined by (1) the characteristics of the store format, encompassing its layout, product assortment, marketing activities, options for play, and learning opportunities; (2) caregivers' knowledge, abilities, and motivation to involve and educate children; and (3) children's current developmental stage.

All stakeholders can contribute to children's FWB, but caregivers have the most important role because they have the greatest influence over children. However, for caregivers to take on this role, they need to be aware of their influence, possess the necessary knowledge of their children's food-related needs, based on their developmental stage, be able to act accordingly, and have the motivation to do so. This being so, public policymakers should introduce consumer-awareness education campaigns that inform caregivers that shopping with children can in many ways be a meaningful experience, and that it serves the long-term development of their children. Manufacturers and grocers must also be educated so that they are enabled to create shopping environments that stimulate children's FWB through positive external stimuli such as learning stations, tasting stands, child-friendly staff, and shopping trolleys for children. This focus on children's FWB will likely generate a significant competitive advantage because it will attract families, which are a strong consumer group, and foster long-term relationships with young consumers.

While this observational study provides relevant insights into the relationship between food shopping and children's FWB, and allows the formulation of relevant implications for practice, further studies are needed to substantiate the results, and to explore individual influences and the associated possibilities for action in more detail.

1.2.6 Essay 5: Impulsivity Makes More Susceptible to Overeating After Contextual Appetitive Conditioning

The overweight and obesity pandemic continues to spread (Ravussin and Ryan, 2017). Those affected often suffer from a range of illnesses, and have more disability-adjusted life years and a lower life expectancy (e.g., Bacha and Gidding, 2016; Grover et al., 2015). This is compounded by productivity losses and health care costs (e.g., Goettler, Grosse, and Sonntag, 2017; Scharff, 2012). Often, the obesogenic environment is deemed responsible for this development; cues in the direct physical environment continuously signal the availability of high-calorie food, and make it difficult to maintain a healthy diet (Lakerveld et al., 2018; Story, Neumark-Sztainer, and French, 2002; Swinburn, Egger, and Raza, 1999). Classical conditioning has been claimed to be an important mechanism that can explain why it is so difficult for some people to stay in control and ignore these cues (Jansen, 1998; Jansen et al., 2010; Wardle, 1990). By means of classical conditioning one easily learns to view an originally neutral cue as a predictor of intake, and to associate it with actual eating. Virtually any cue has the potential to become associated with eating, and to elicit preparatory responses of the body such as increased salivation (Jansen, 1998; Nederkoorn, Smulders, and Jansen, 2000). Classical conditioning studies with animals suggest that even contexts can function as cues associated with food intake (Boggiano et al., 2009; Petrovich et al., 2007). The current essay strives to test classical conditioning as a mechanism for context-induced eating in humans, taking into account the moderating role of impulsivity.

An experiment was conducted with 70 female participants in a virtual reality laboratory. The conditioning was performed by repeatedly exposing participants to two virtual environments (conditioned stimulus; CS). In one of these environments, the participants always consumed a small cup of milkshake (intake-associated environment; CS+); while in the other, milkshake intake was forbidden (control environment; CS-). It was expected that after the conditioning, the CS+ environment would elicit a stronger desire for a milkshake, increased salivation, and a greater intake during a bogus milkshake taste test, compared to the CS- environment, while it was also assumed that the CS+ environment would be liked more, and that impulsivity would generally facilitate conditioning. The results show that contextual appetitive conditioning in females exists; the participants showed conditioned context-induced cue reactivity in form of increased salivation, a greater desire for milkshakes and higher intake expectancies. Furthermore, a within-subject assessment showed that contingency-aware participants preferred the CS+ environment, and that highly impulsive participants consumed more milkshakes when present in the CS+ environment compared to the CS- environment.

These findings contribute to the existing knowledge on the underlying mechanisms of the obesogenic environment. In addition to isolated food cues, complex non-food-related environmental stimuli can evoke a desire to eat, and trigger preparatory responses in the body. Humans seem to be able to easily and rapidly associate a specific environment with food intake, and highly impulsive people appear to be particularly susceptible to conditioned context-induced overeating. Future research should examine the role and consequences of impulsivity in more detail, and whether environment-based food cue exposure therapy could be beneficial for impulsive people who suffer from overweight and obesity. Augmented and virtual reality could assist in this regard by recreating the contexts in which the participants usually overeat, which then can be paired with healthier eating behavior by means of conditioning.

1.2.7 Essay 6: Understanding Planning for Unplanned Purchases: Antecedents and Exploitation of In-Store Slack

Research has shown that consumers usually have a specific mental budget for every shopping trip that helps them to regulate their purchase behavior, reach shopping goals, and enhance self-control (Kahneman and Tversky, 1984; Thaler, 1985; Heath and Soll, 1996). This budget consists of a part reserved for planned products, the so-called itemized portion, and a part intended for unplanned products, the in-store slack (Stilley, Inman, and Wakefield, 2010a). The in-store slack is used to buy forgotten products, to maintain financial flexibility, and to be able to give in to impulses (Babin, Darden, and Griffin, 1994; Stilley, Inman, and Wakefield, 2010b). So far, few studies have been conducted on the antecedents of in-store slack and its exploitation (Stilley, Inman, and Wakefield, 2010a, 2010b), revealing a need for further research. For example, Stilley, Inman and Wakefield (2010a, 2010b), restricted their work to the US, and only looked at one specific grocery store format. Furthermore, there are no studies that have sufficiently examined the factors leading to the emergence of in-store slack.

Against this background, the current essay examines the emergence and utilization of in-store slack in detail by means of a replication study conducted in different store formats in Germany. The field study involved 406 participants and four store formats: a drug store, an organic food store, a supermarket, and a grocery discount store. Overall, this research follows the procedure outlined in Stilley, Inman and Wakefield (2010a), but the participants were asked more questions about the factors that could have had a relevant influence on their in-store slack size and its exploitation. The participants were interviewed before entering a store, and they specified the amount of money they expected to spend, listed the items they planned to purchase, and the costs of each of these items. They also answered several questions about their shopping intentions, while during the shopping process itself, they were unobtrusively observed. After the shopping trip was completed, the interviewer took photos of the participants' receipts, and asked additional questions about their shopping trip, as well as about their demographics.

The findings reveal that in-store slack exists in all four store formats. The participants showed the proportionately smallest in-store slack in the drug store, for which they also had the lowest total trip budget, the smallest number of purchased goods, and the smallest in-store slack utilization. The shoppers in the other stores were much more similar to each other regarding their mental budget, in-store slack utilization, and number of products purchased. The participants tended to have the greatest in-store slack in the discount store.

An analysis of the antecedents indicates that a higher in-store slack is associated with higher monthly budgets and shopping trip budgets, while in contrast, a higher degree of planning (a higher number of planned products, and the use of a shopping list) reduces in-store slack. The motives to browse and cover an urgent need, a longer shopping duration, higher impulsiveness, and the desire to make savings on unplanned products can increase the utilization of in-store slack. Only paying in cash seems to significantly reduce the use of in-store slack.

The results of this study confirm the existence of in-store slack, and demonstrate its generalizability to international markets and varying product domains. However, the magnitude and utilization of in-store slack varies across different product domains and store formats; for example, it was found that the customers of discount stores tend to plan their shopping trips less precisely, and rely more on in-store slack than customers of other store formats. The research is able to make a number of general recommendations (e.g., that stores combine promotions for planned products with unplanned products), as well as recommendations for specific store formats (e.g., a constantly changing stock in discount stores). Future research would do well to examine in-store slack in more detail, and in diverse shopping scenarios and store formats, and experimental studies could seek to more closely illuminate the underlying mechanisms of action. Furthermore, it is essential to investigate how in-store slack can be used in such a way that it not only meets the goals of the retailers, but also the wishes and needs of customers, so that the utilization of consumers' budgets serves both the fulfillment of their needs and the improvement of their well-being.

2 Food Well-Being: The Development of an Integrated Framework[1]

2.1 Introduction

Food well-being (FWB) is a new holistic perspective on the role of food in consumers' lives. There is the justified hope that this new way of thinking and approaching food-related problems will foster the development of food-related well-being of individual consumers and of society as a whole. Therefore, the aims of this paper are (i) to collect findings on FWB from different disciplines, (ii) to structure and combine these findings, (iii) to extend the definition of FWB, and (iv) to present an improved FWB framework that depicts FWB as completely as possible and is applicable for research and practice.

Over the last few decades, there has been a shift in thinking regarding food-related health and well-being. Based on the biomedical model of health, early research in this area adopted a pathogenic orientation, suggesting that food's impact on consumer well-being is mainly limited to the fulfillment of consumers' nutritional needs and the maintenance of their physical health (Biltekoff, 2010). However, this approach oversimplified the cause-effect relationships that lead to food-related well-being, and detached food-related well-being from its social and psychological dimensions as well as its contextual influences (Engel, 1977). Therefore, researchers started to adopt a more holistic, salutogenic approach based on the assumption that food actually plays a broader role in consumers' lives; influencing more and different life domains and well-being dimensions than previously recognized (Antonovsky, 1996; Grunert et al., 2007; Lindström and Eriksson, 2009). Recent research supports this approach. For instance, when Ares et al. (2014) asked their participants in a qualitative study to list words they associated with well-being, thirty-nine percent of the participants listed words related to food (e.g., "food", "eating", "healthy diet"; p. 64). Furthermore, the results of group discussions conducted by Guillemin et al. (2016) indicated that food-related experiences are strongly connected to the physical, emotional, and social well-being of consumers. And Swan et al. (2018) highlighted in their research that nutrition strategies are related not only to food-specific factors such as cooking skills and nutrition knowledge but also to other

1 Co-author: Prof. Dr. Hanna Schramm-Klein

F. Frentz, *The Pursuit of Food Well-Being*, Handel und Internationales Marketing Retailing and International Marketing,
https://doi.org/10.1007/978-3-658-30366-2_2

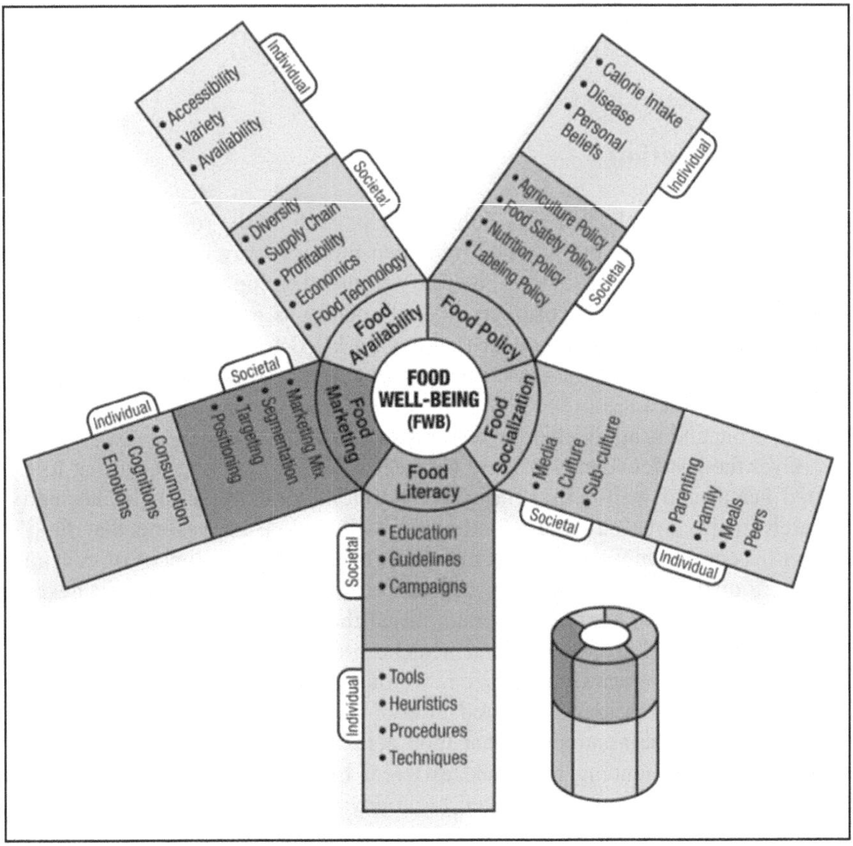

Figure 4: Food well-being pinwheel (Block et al., 2011)

factors such as stress management and empowerment. However, while a gradual change in thinking can be observed, the new perspective on the role of food in consumers' lives is still rather vague. A comprehensive and universally accepted definition and explanation do not yet exist.

Block et al. (2011) launched a first attempt by introducing the term FWB, which they defined as "a positive psychological, physical, emotional, and social relationship with food at both the individual and social levels" (p. 6). They also presented an initial overarching FWB framework, the FWB pinwheel (see Figure 4).

This framework depicts the influences of the cultural, environmental, and legal factors that govern people's food attitudes and behaviors and is meant to support the integrated analysis and understanding of "all health and social challenges associated with the types and amounts of foods and beverages people consume, in addition to the production and consumption contexts of food (…)" (Block et al., 2011, p. 6). The work of Block et al. (2011) is pioneering; they pushed the new revolutionary perspective forward and made it more concrete and tangible. However, the term FWB still needs further explanation and concretization, as has been repeatedly suggested (Ares et al., 2016; Bublitz et al., 2013; Voola et al., 2018). For example, Block et al. (2011) mention the dimensions of FWB in their definition, but they do not explain them in their further elaboration. Furthermore, several elements of the proposed framework require further definition, classification, and/or extension. For example, the individual and societal levels of the individual FWB domains are not fully presented in the FWB pinwheel, nor are their interrelationships with the other elements of the pinwheel sufficiently illustrated. These shortcomings are also not eliminated by later research building on the work of Block et al. (2011), e.g., Ares et al. (2016); Bublitz et al. (2019); Hémar-Nicolas and Ezan (2018); Mugel, Gurviez, and Decrop (2019).

Thus, before the definition and framework of FWB can be effectively applied in research or practice, further specification of FWB and its underlying mechanisms is required. This need is especially relevant given the current food-related problems for which society still lacks effective or feasible solutions. The overweight and obesity pandemic is one of these problems: The prevalence of overweight and obesity linked to non-communicable diseases continues to spread in high-income countries and increasingly in middle-income countries as well (Ravussin and Ryan, 2017). In 2016, more than 1.9 billion adults, 18 years and older, were overweight. Of these, 650 million were obese (WHO, 2018a, 2018b). Worldwide, the number of obese children and adolescents, aged five to 19 years, has risen more than tenfold in the past four decades (WHO, 2017). Research suggests that the economic consequences of food-related ill-health include medical costs, productivity losses, and mortality (Goettler, Grosse, and Sonntag, 2017; Scharff, 2012). For instance, it is estimated that the combined medical costs associated with the treatment of obesity-related diseases alone will increase by $48-66 billion per year in the U.S. and by approximately $2.5 billion per year in the UK by 2030 (Wang et al., 2011). Thus, food-related issues concern not only individuals themselves but also society as a whole.

To be effective in the sense of the salutogenic model, endeavors have to be integrated into one coordinated, coherent movement in every sector of society at the individual, group, organizational and population levels (Lindström and Eriksson, 2009; Martin and Hill, 2012; Ozanne et al., 2016). However, FWB is complex; it reaches into different research areas and therefore requires the input of different disciplines (Mugel, Gurviez, and Decrop, 2019). Hence, in this article, we build on the work of Block et al. (2011) and explain FWB by combining Block et al.'s (2011) elaborations with literature from the disciplines of nutrition and dietetics, psychology, marketing, and public policy. We refine the definition of FWB and outline its physical, emotional, social, intellectual, and spiritual dimensions. Thereupon, we summarize and integrate the literature into a conceptual framework that is designed to offer a good understanding and overview of FWB and how it develops. In this framework, the formation of FWB is regarded as a circuit that is continuously in motion in every person's life, and FWB itself is considered to be constantly moving across a low-high continuum. Finally, the cycle is discussed, and recommendations for research and practice are given.

This paper emphasizes not only the importance of the individual but also the relevance of other stakeholders who are responsible for creating empowering environments in which people are able to identify their internal and external resources, use them in a FWB-promoting manner and find encouragement to learn and grow in order to develop long-lasting FWB.

2.2 Materials and Methods

To receive a comprehensive picture of the current understanding of FWB an extensive literature review was carried out. The review was restricted to English-language, peer-reviewed studies, reviews, and theoretical pieces on FWB and food-related well-being. Searches were conducted in Google Scholar and EBSCO; journals listed in the subject areas "Food Science", "Marketing", and "Public Health, Environmental and Occupational Health" in the Scimago Journal & Country Rank; journals listed in the subject area "Marketing" in VHB Journal Ranking; and reference lists of relevant articles and reviews. Articles were only included in the literature review when they were published between 2000 and 2019. The following key word combinations to search each data base and journal yielded twenty-one relevant abstracts: "food well-being" OR "food-related well-being" OR "food-related life" AND "well-being" or "food" OR "nutrition" AND "well-being" OR "consumer well-being." In all combinations, the word "well-being" was entered in different spellings (well-being, wellbeing) and was also replaced by the word "wellness". Table 2 gives an overview of the relevant articles found.

For the extension of the framework, an additional literature search was carried out, which was based on the individual elements of the framework. Since the framework is extremely extensive and the individual elements in themselves already represent individual research areas, it was not possible to carry out a complete search in this regard. The elaborations therefore do not fulfil the claim of completeness. However, they provide a comprehensive overview of the relevant influencing factors in the scope of FWB and put them into a logical effect relationship, allowing recommendations for practice and the identification of research questions for future research.

Table 2: Literature research on food well-being

Article	Research goal	Theory	Method	Core findings
Bublitz et al., 2019, Journal of Public Policy & Marketing, USA	To extend the FWB paradigm to include people experiencing hunger and to investigate people's relationship with FWB when they experience hunger.	- FWB concept and framework of Block et al. (2011), - Sirgy's (2008) framework on ethical perspectives.	- Case study: Application of the improved FWB framework to several programs of the non-profit hunger task force.	- Block et al.'s FWB framework for understanding the relationship between food and well-being is particularly for people with adequate or abundant access to food. - Food poverty: the progressive experience of hunger at the individual and societal levels. - Critical factors of food insecurity: availability, accessibility, utilization. - Bublitz et al. adapt the framework. They divide the food availability dimension into (1) provision of affordable access to available food and (2) provision of access to nutritious food to thrive.
Mugel, Gurviez, and Decrop, 2019, Journal of Public Policy & Marketing, France	To explore how FWB manifests itself in consumers' lived experiences.	- FWB concept and framework of Block et al. (2011), - hedonic well-being (Kahneman, Diener, and Schwarz, 1999), - eudaimonic well-being (Ryan and Deci, 2000).	- Phenomenological interviews with 29 consumers, - photo elicitation with 62 consumers, - online journaling of 12 consumers. - 12 participants took part in all three parts of the study.	- FWB emerges through multiple processes including consumers' emancipation, immersion in a food experience, sharing of the experience, and sensory processes. - FWB can be loaded with different meanings that match four types of quest: the quest for authenticity in the acquisition phase, the quest for culinary achievement in the preparation phase, the quest for gustatory pleasure in the eating phase, and the quest for sustainability in the post-eating phase. - Certain contextual conditions facilitate FWB: time, product/recipe, physical settings, companionship. - Resulting emotions and moods of FWB might be relaxation/relief, pride, joy/enthusiasm, nostalgia, gratitude.

Article	Research goal	Theory	Method	Core findings
Hémar-Nicolas and Ezan, 2018, International Journal of Retail & Distribution Management, France	To understand what FWB means to children in a food context and to formulate recommendations about the way food retailers may take actions to promote children's FWB.	- FWB concept and framework of Block et al. (2011), - hedonic well-being (Diener et al., 1999), - eudaimonic well-being (Ryff and Keyes, 1995), - social well-being (Keyes, 1998).	- Group discussions about FWB with 25 French children aged 6-11 years. - Among others children drew an advertisement or wrote a story to promote a brand of fruit juice that is supposed to make children happy.	- Children are aware of the impacts of food on the body, feelings and psychological states. - Children's enjoyment is often linked to a feeling of pride and self-confidence, suggesting that well-being stems from self-esteem and self-achievement. - Children's food attitudes and behaviors are predominantly driven by hedonic motivations based on organoleptic pleasure. - Food practices contribute to eudaimonic and social well-being through the fulfilment of inherent human needs, e.g., autonomy, personal growth, social recognition and social integration. - Children emphasized five themes that determine their FWB: sensory taste, health, commensality, empowerment and altruistic behaviors.
Voola et al., 2018, European Journal of Marketing, South India	To investigate the dynamics of food consumption practices in poor families in a developing country to advance the FWB in Poverty framework.	- FWB concept and framework of Block et al. (2011).	- Semi-structured interviews with 25 women (18 had received no formal education, 15 were single parents).	- The paper develops a new version of Block et al.'s framework, called FWB in Poverty framework. In this framework the food marketing dimension and the food literacy dimension are replaced by the food capability dimension which refers to nutritional learning amongst poor families outside mainstream literacy channels. Furthermore, the familial level is inserted between the individual and societal level.

Article	Research goal	Theory	Method	Core findings
Batat et al., 2018, Journal of Business Research, USA	To extend the work on epicurean eating pleasure and FWB by conceptualizing experiential pleasure of food as sustainable journey to well-being.	- FWB concept and framework of Block et al. (2011), - epicurean eating pleasure (Cornil and Chandon, 2016).	- Literature review	- The work on epicurean eating pleasure and FWB is extended by the conceptualization of experiential pleasure. - Experiential pleasure refers to "the enduring cognitive (satisfaction) and emotional (i.e., delight) value consumers gain from savoring the multisensory, communal, and cultural meaning in food experiences" (p. 2). - It is presented as a sustainable journey, consisting of the stages contemplation, connection, and creation, that promotes the savoring of food practices and events to facilitate enduring health and FWB.
Ares et al., 2016, Food Quality and Preference, Brazil, China, France, Portugal, Spain, Uruguay, USA	To investigate cross-cultural differences in perceived well-being of food products and to link those differences to product-specific consumer evaluations.	- General conceptualizations of well-being, - most common well-being dimensions (Roscoe, 2009).	- Development of a questionnaire based on a qualitative study conducted in five countries, - a web-based survey with 1332 participants in seven countries (nine food concepts were presented by means of an incomplete balanced design).	- The results highlight the importance of taking into account cultural differences in the conceptualization of FWB. Consumers evaluate different aspects of FWB differently based on their cultural background. - Consumers use likert scales differently based on their culture-specific consumer values and socioeconomic contexts. - Cross-cultural differences in FWB might be mainly due to differences in the emotional and social dimensions. - Considering the influence of different foods on the different well-being dimensions can provide a more holistic view of their effect on consumers' lives than simple healthiness ratings.

Article	Research goal	Theory	Method	Core findings
Guillemin et al., 2016, Appetite, France	To design the Well-Being and Food Questionnaire (Well-BFQ) to evaluate well-being in the context of diet in a healthy population.	- General conceptualizations of well-being, - most common well-being dimensions (Roscoe, 2009).	- 24 group discussions with 198 subjects, development of a questionnaire, - 29 interviews to test the question naire, interventional study with 444 subjects.	- Development of a conceptual model of food-related well-being with food- and pleasure related well-being and food- and health related well-being at its core. - The questionnaire is generic and can be used with a wide range of food products and aspects. - The questionnaire has five sections which correspond to the main themes of food: grocery shopping, cooking, eating, dining places, and commensality. - Measured benefits were categorized into immediate benefits, direct and short-term benefits, deferred health benefits, and well-being.
Meiselman, 2016, Food Quality and Preference, USA	To give an overview of conceptualizations and measurements of quality of life, well-being, and wellness in general and regarding food.	- No theory/framework mentioned.	- Literature review	- Gives a comprehensive overview of definitions and scales regarding quality of life, well-being, and wellness in general and with respect to food. - All three concepts promise to be important in consumer perception of food and other consumer products. - More attention should be paid to them in sensory and consumer research.
Schnettler et al., 2016, Food Quality and Preference, Chile, Spain	To examine the factor variance of the SWFL scale across two samples of university students from the EU and South America and to compare mean levels of SWFL scores among these groups.	- No theory/framework mentioned.	- 252 university students from Chile and 120 students from Spain completed the Satisfaction with Food-Related Life (SWFL) questionnaire developed by Grunert et al. (2007)	- This study is the first to explore the cross-cultural measurement invariance of the SWFL scale. - The SWFL scale showed to be a valid instrument for the cross-cultural comparison at hand. - The findings demonstrate that the SWFL scale may be used for studying the correlations between the level of satisfaction with food-related life and external variables in several cultural settings. - However, the participants all spoke the same language and the samples were not representative. - In general, the SWFL score was significantly higher in the Spanish sample.

Article	Research goal	Theory	Method	Core findings
King et al., 2015, Food Quality and Preference, USA	To develop a questionnaire that measures consumers' subjective experience of wellness associated with food and/or ingredients.	- Wellness theory (Miller and Foster, 2010).	- Questionnaire created based on various wellness- and emotion questionnaires and terms named by consumers (gathered via 3 internet surveys). - Validity tested with internet surveys. - Stability and capacity tested with experiments.	- General definitions of wellness are used as a basis, but it is explained that there is no commonly accepted definition. - Consumers perceive wellness as positive construct. - The questionnaire is divided into the five dimensions of wellness: physical, emotional, social, intellectual and spiritual. - Results suggest that measuring consumer wellness in relation to foods and ingredients is a viable method of investigation. - The capacity of the questionnaire to predict expected outcomes as well as its stability showed to be high. - All five dimensions of wellness responded to foods/ingredients in different ways. Different stimuli may impact different dimensions. No dimension showed to be dominant over the others. - The authors suggest that further dimensions may play a role in food and wellness that are currently not included.
Ares et al., 2014, Food Quality and Preference, Brazil, France, Portugal, Spain, Uruguay	To explore how consumers perceive well-being in a food-related context.	- Various approaches to well-being (e.g., Diener and Ryan, 2009), - various attempts to the division of well-being into dimensions.	- 755 consumers answered a questionnaire with five open-ended questions about food and well-being.	- More than 19% of the participants mentioned terms related to food when thinking of well-being. - Well-being in a food-related context is perceived as a multidimensional construct, related to a positive condition of physical health, body functioning and emotional state; the spiritual dimension was not salient. - Cultural-based differences were found in the relative importance of the different aspects of well-being in a food-related context. - There are significant differences among countries in the frequency of mentions of foods positive and negative to well-being.

Article	Research goal	Theory	Method	Core findings
Ares et al., 2013, Appetite, Uruguay	To investigate consumers' perception of well-being in a food context.	- Various approaches to well-being, - various attempts to the division of well-being into dimensions.	- Study with 120 participants using three qualitative techniques: word association, open-ended questions, and free listing.	- 39% of the participants elicited words related to food when thinking of well-being. - Food-related well-being is a complex construct, which is strongly associated with physical health, quality of life, emotional well-being (e.g., pleasure, mood, humour, energy) and intellectual well-being (e.g., mental performance, alertness, anxiety, rest, concentration). - Spiritual and social aspects were not salient. - Characteristics of foods that affect well-being are sensory characteristics, nutritional composition, ingredients and manufacturing processes.
Bublitz et al., 2013, Journal of Business Research, USA	To identify ways how consumers can be empowered to advance their FWB.	- FWB concept and framework of Block et al. (2011), - stages of change model (Prochaska and DiClemente, 1982), - information processing model (MacInnis, Moorman, and Jaworski, 1991).	- Conceptual paper	- The understanding of FWB is advanced by (1) discussing how the awareness of functional, symbolic, and hedonic consumer goals and the consumers' motivation and readiness to change could help to understand their preparedness to advance their FWB, and (2) deconstructing the automatic and deliberative influences on food decision making into cognitive and emotional information that guide food choices and can be used by consumers to advance their FWB. - Bublitz et al. highlight 10 variables to promote positive health behavior change towards FWB: food literacy, emotional knowledge, social environment, self-reevaluation, social liberation, counter-conditioning, helping relationships, reinforcement, willpower, stimulus control.

Article	Research goal	Theory	Method	Core findings
Meiselman, 2013, Food Quality and Preference, USA	To present predictions for future changes in food-related sensory and consumer research.	- No theory/framework mentioned.	- Conceptual paper	- The changes that the field must have are among others more emphasis on health and wellness, age (life transitions), measuring beyond liking, and moving beyond the laboratory. - Meiselman regards health as the biological/physiological condition of the body as evidenced by biological measures. Wellness is the subjective side of health and defined by the consumer. - "The emerging view is that every food and beverage company is a health company; every personal care product company is a health company, and so on" (p. 209).
Bublitz et al., 2011, Journal of Research for Consumers, USA	To formulate a vision for developing a comprehensive measure of an individual's level of FWB to facilitate investigations of how to motivate consumers to improve their FWB.	- FWB concept and framework of Block et al. (2011), - Theory of Change (Prochaska and DiClemente, 1982; Prochaska, Wright, and Velicer, 2008).	- Conceptual paper	- They expand the FWB construct to reflect the complexity of a consumer's relationship with food. - Five core areas influence placement on the FWB continuum: social factors, economic issues, food literacy, emotional knowledge, as well as physical and psychological traits. - Consumer need to have the motivation, willingness, ability, and opportunity to change. - Consumers are affected by internal and external automatic influences as well as deliberative influences.
Block et al., 2011, Journal of Public Policy & Marketing, USA	To propose a radical restructuring of the paradigm from "food as health" to "food as wellbeing."	- (Consumer) socialization (Mochis, 1985; Ward, 1974), - health literacy (Ratzan, 2001, Nutbeam, 2008).	- Conceptual paper	- A paradigm shift is suggested from the paternalistic and health-oriented view of food to a holistic and positive perspective. - They introduce the term FWB, which is defined as "a positive, psychological, physical, emotional, and social relationship with food at both the individual and societal levels" (p.6). - They create a FWB framework, the so-called FWB pinwheel, which is based on five dimensions: food marketing, food literacy, food socialization, food policy, and food availability. Every dimension is divided into an individual level and a societal level.

Article	Research goal	Theory	Method	Core findings
Boelsma et al., 2010, Appetite, The Netherlands	To identify and evaluate measures of postprandial wellness, i.e., the subjective appreciation of food after intake.	- Dimensions of wellness (Diener, Suh, and Oishi, 1997).	- Randomized, cross-over, double-blind experimental design with 21 male participants. - Single intake of two meals that differed in the ratio of protein and carbohydrates.	- Food intake influences consumers psychologically, physically and mentally and affects their appreciation of life. Subjective appreciation relates to sensory and cognitive processes and hedonic perceptions. - Dimensions of wellness after food intake: sense of pleasantness, satisfaction, relaxation, physical energy, alertness, and sleepiness. - Subjects reported increased feelings of satisfaction, pleasantness, postprandial wellness, and lower feelings of sleepiness and showed to have a higher CCK response, lower ghrelin concentrations and lower glucose responses after consumption of the HP/LC meal compared to the LP/HC meal.
McMahon et al., 2010, Perspectives in Public Health, Australia	This paper reviews how the terms wellness and well-being are being used in various disciplines and describes implications for adult food choice.	- Various definitions of well-being from different disciplines (psychology, economics, sociology, marketing).	- Conceptual paper	- There is no consensus about how well-being can be identified, measured and achieved. - Different disciplines apply different definitions and approaches. - Psychology: cognitive and affective evaluations of one's life, including happiness and satisfaction. - Economics: quantification of well-being through for instance national income, produce accounts, gross domestic product. - Sociology: political, social, economic realities of groups; emphasize is on proactive positive behaviors. - Food Marketing: focus on ingredients and food choice. - Well-being describes good health that goes beyond the mere absence of illness. It is about a holistic health that comprises all areas of life, such as the physical, mental, and social areas. It comprises subjective and objective elements.

Article	Research goal	Theory	Method	Core findings
Dean et al., 2008, Appetite, UK, Poland, Portugal, Germany, Sweden, Denmark, Italy, Spain	To explore how resources, perceived levels of resources and goal relevance of these resources affect older people's satisfaction with food-related life.	- Satisfaction with food-related life (Grunert et al., 2007).	- 80 in-depth interviews, - A survey answered by 3291participants above 65 years in eight European countries.	- Among others, satisfaction with food-related life is predicted by income, health measures and living circumstances. - Goal priorities were enjoying healthy and varied food and meals. - To achieve these goals participants saw good dental and overall health, mobility, ability to taste and smell, good storage facilities and family support as relevant resources. - Thus, food-related goals are not only linked with health matters but also relate to the enjoyment of food in terms of variety, social networks and surroundings. - The congruence between perceived level and relevance of a resource adds to people's satisfaction.
Grunert et al., 2007, Appetite, Denmark, UK, Germany, Italy, Poland, Portugal, Spain, Sweden	To develop a measure of satisfaction with food-related life.	- Quality of life theory (e.g., Andrews and Withey, 1976; Moons et al., 2006), - satisfaction with life theory (Diener et al., 1985).	- A scale with five items was developed, partly based on the Satisfaction with Life scale. - Data was collected as part of three studies of the Food in Later Life project, conducted in eight European countries.	- Food is an important life domain that should be considered when evaluating quality of life. - Food-related life: that part of life that comprises procurement, preparation and consumption of food. - The measure of satisfaction with food-related life is unidimensional and is applicable across different European countries.
Rozin, 2005, Journal of Nutrition and Behavior, USA	To compare the US and France on eating and well-being and to derive recommenddations for the US.	- No theory/framework mentioned.	- Conceptual paper.	- Foods provide us with necessary nutrients, but they also have emotional, social and symbolic value and can be a form of aesthetic expression. - The US can learn from France with respect to eating and well-being. - For example, US citizens could eat slower and smaller portions, snack less, focus more on quality, enjoy the experience of eating more (consciously) and share this experience more with others.

2.3 Adjusting the Concept of Food Well-Being

Although Block et al. (2011) were not the first researchers to study the broader role of food in well-being (e.g., Grunert et al., 2007; Rozin, 2005), they were pioneers in that they suggested a concrete shift in thinking from the traditional, health-oriented, and narrow view to a more positive, holistic understanding of the role of food in consumers' overall well-being, and, morcover, they introduced the term FWB.

Because Block et al.'s (2011) definition of FWB is the only existing clear-cut definition of the newly understood role of food in consumers' lives, we use this as the basis from which we try to get closer to the core of the concept. In the following, we discuss the definition of FWB, as formulated by Block et al. (2011), in light of the literature of the different disciplines and, based on this, we formulate our understanding of FWB.

First, Block et al. (2011) describe a person's relationship with food as "a positive (…) relationship" (p. 6). Literature implies, however, that it might not be appropriate to regard FWB as a positive relationship end state (Mugel, Gurviez, and Decrop, 2019). Instead, the life course perspective suggests that well-being is fluid and changes based on the experiences one has (Sobal et al., 2006), thus implying a continuum ranging from very low (a negative and/or weak relationship with food) to very high levels (a positive and strong relationship with food) of well-being (Bublitz, Peracchio, and Block, 2010; Bublitz et al., 2013). By defining FWB as a continuum, a consumer's different states of FWB are fully reflected. Instead of relating the word "positive" to one's relationship with food, we suggest using this term to refer to someone's desirable general approach towards food (well-being). In this way, we align with the underlying idea of positive psychology, which combines the hedonic and eudaimonic approach to well-being, i.e., a striving for positive emotions and life satisfaction as well as for a sense of fulfilment and meaningfulness (Deci and Ryan, 2008; Gable and Haidt, 2005; Garcia, 2014; Kashdan, Biswas-Diener, and King, 2008).

Second, in their definition, Block et al. (2011) include four superordinate dimensions. Including these dimensions supports the salutogenic approach by emphasizing that the role of food in consumers' lives goes far beyond physical well-being (Antonovsky, 1996; Eriksson and Lindström, 2008; Swan et al., 2018). However, for reasons of completeness, consideration should be given to adjusting the number of dimensions and their focuses. Though several studies indicate a connection between food-related life and one or more dimensions of well-being, little research has been conducted that specifically focuses on the full set of dimensions relevant to FWB. The number and type of dimensions that need to be included varies in the literature. Block et al. (2011) include psychological, physical, emotional, and social dimensions in their definition of FWB.

Ares et al. (2014) identify physical health, emotions, quality of life, and intellectual well-being as relevant dimensions and, in later work, they identify physical, psychological, and social dimensions (Ares et al., 2016). However, the most recent food-related well-being literature uses the five dimensions that are also most commonly used in the more general well-being literature (Roscoe, 2009): physical, emotional, social, intellectual, and spiritual dimensions (Ares et al., 2016; Guillemin et al., 2016; King et al., 2015; these dimensions are explained in more detail in the chapter "Dimensions of Food Well-Being").

Third, Block et al. (2011) differentiate in their definition between the individual and the societal level. The subtopics which Block et al. assign to the two levels in their FWB pinwheel could be both measurable indicators of individual and societal FWB or determinants of the development of a high degree of FWB. If the levels are meant to categorize the determinants, we suggest to further break them down into (i) individual influences, (ii) social environmental influences, (iii) physical environmental influences, and (iv) general environmental influences (Bronfenbrenner, 1994; Story, Neumark-Sztainer, and French, 2002; Lindström and Eriksson, 2009). This categorization gives a well-structured and detailed overview of the determinants and processes that have an impact on FWB and allows a goal-oriented approach towards improving FWB (the levels are explained in greater detail in the chapter "Levels of Influence"). Because the determinants are not part of FWB, but lead to FWB, we would not include them in the definition, but integrate them into the framework.

Fourth, based on Block et al.'s (2011) definition, it is not clear whether FWB is evaluated subjectively, objectively, or both. Although (food) well-being is sometimes presented as a purely subjective construct resting on the perception and satisfaction of the individual (Ares et al., 2016; Schnettler et al., 2016), we suggest viewing it as a construct with subjective (e.g., hedonic experiences, perceived health) and objective components (e.g., the body's biological/physical condition) to capture it in its entirety (Moons, Budts, and De Geest, 2006). After all, well-being is a holistic view of life comprising a person's health and wellness, which are by definition objective and subjective (Meiselman, 2013).

To conclude, based on the preceding considerations, we suggest the following as an adjusted understanding of FWB: FWB is a multidimensional, synergetic construct represented on a continuum and defined as a subjective and objective evaluation of people's physical, emotional, social, intellectual, and spiritual relationship with food.

2.4 Dimensions of Food Well-Being

Human beings naturally strive for a harmonic state of well-being through the fulfillment and conformity of a number of life dimensions (Roscoe, 2009). This statement holds true not only for well-being in general but also for FWB more specifically (Block et al., 2011; Guillemin et al., 2016; Swan et al., 2018). To cover all relevant cause-effect relationships, we suggest focusing on the five dimensions that are historically most common in the well-being literature (more than 80% usage in wellness models; King et al., 2015) and that are likely to be relevant for food-related life: physical, emotional, social, intellectual, and spiritual dimensions (Hettler, 1980; Miller and Foster, 2010; Roscoe, 2009). Although these dimensions have been explained multiple times in the general well-being literature, their conceptualization in the context of food-related life and well-being is still missing. Therefore, in the following we briefly explain and adapt every dimension in the context of FWB.

2.4.1 Physical Dimension

The physical dimension generally encompasses the physical state of individuals; their attention to physical self-care, nutritional needs, and physical activity; and the use of medical services to be and stay physically healthy (Hettler, 1980). With respect to FWB, the physical dimension is about the implementation of healthy dietary choices and eating habits and the maintenance of a healthy diet to achieve good physical health (Hettler, 1980; Renger et al., 2000; Roscoe, 2009). This dimension also includes high body awareness and a good understanding on how the own body reacts to different foods, eating habits, and behaviors. This comprises immediate responses, such as digestive discomfort, allergic reactions, and athletic performance, as well as long-term consequences, such as growth, weight control, and illness management (Sobal et al., 2006). Thus, the physical dimension comprises all food-related activities that have a direct effect on one's body and, thereby, on one's physical health and well-being.

According to Crose et al. (1992), the physical dimension is also related to one's body awareness and body image. However, body image encompasses "one's body related self-perceptions and self-attitudes, including thoughts, beliefs, feelings, and behaviors" (Cash, 2004, p.1-2), and is thus a combined product of the emotional, intellectual and physical dimensions. For instance, in the Third National Health and Nutrition Examination Survey that was conducted in the USA, 38.3% of women at normal weights implied that they were overweight (Chang and Christakis, 2003), indicating a negative self-perception and body image. Thus, one can be physically healthy but not feel well and can feel well but be physically unhealthy. This contradicts the old way of thinking that the objectively measured physical state alone gives a sufficient indication of well-being (Biltekoff, 2010; Meiselman, 2016).

2.4.2 Emotional Dimension

The emotional dimension is generally related to an individual's awareness, constructive expression, and management of emotions (Hettler, 1980); self-assessment; self-concept (Adams, Bezner, and Steinhardt, 2016); and coping styles and patterns that are applied in emotionally challenging situations (Crose et al., 1992; Roscoe, 2009). Emotional FWB refers to experiencing, expressing and dealing with emotions that are associated with food-related activities.

The relationship between emotions and one's overall food-related life and well-being is reciprocal. On the one hand, the purchase, preparation, and consumption of food is - most often unconsciously - influenced by the consumers' moods and emotions. On the other hand, those food-related activities also affect consumers' moods and emotions (Köster and Mojet, 2015). Emotions and moods, such as boredom, loneliness, or anxiety, can influence when, what, and how much food people purchase and consume and in which manner (Hawks, Goudy, and Gast, 2013; Van Strien, Schippers, and Cox, 1995). Meyer and Waller (1999), for example, showed that women who are exposed to an abandonment cue (lonely) eat significantly more than women who are exposed to a neutral, positive cue or an appetitive cue. The food industry has long known about the power of emotions and, therefore, uses them in advertising campaigns and on product packages and displays - often without consumers' conscious recognition (Bublitz et al., 2013). However, consumers also often consciously choose their food based on their mood status, e.g., they use it as a reward, a comforter, an energizer, or a stress-reducer (Rozin, 2005). Research on the effect of food on the emotions is comparably young (Köster and Mojet, 2015); however, awareness of the importance of this research field is constantly increasing (Ares et al., 2016; King et al., 2015). One example is the research of Boelsma et al. (2010), who demonstrated that a liquid breakfast with a high protein/low carbohydrate ratio induces higher levels of satiety and specific parameters of postprandial wellness (satisfaction, pleasantness) compared to a liquid breakfast with a low protein/high carbohydrate ratio.

A person who scores high on the emotional dimension of FWB is able to reflect on their own behavior and to effectively cope with stressors that challenge FWB by applying and combining coping strategies and cognitive and emotional knowledge gathered through life experiences in both childhood and adulthood (Bublitz et al., 2013; Swan et al., 2018). Thus, the emotional dimension cannot exist on its own. For instance, to be able to effectively cope with stressors at the emotional level, one also has to have declarative (factual) and procedural (action-related) knowledge (Vidgen and Gallegos, 2014), which is part of the intellectual dimension.

2.4.3 Social Dimension

The social dimension, in general, concerns the individuals' relationships with others and with the environment (Hettler, 1980), and their motivations, intentions, actions, and perceptions regarding these relationships (Roscoe, 2009). With respect to FWB, the social dimension is about how these relationships are expressed and considered in food-related purchasing and consumption behavior. Often, eating is a social event such as having lunch with colleagues at work or having dinner with friends. Food is also part of many social rituals and traditions that are passed from one generation to the next and that are shared and experienced with others (e.g., Thanksgiving; Thomson and Hassenkamp, 2008; Wallendorf and Arnould, 1991). These food-related events, traditions, and rituals originate in, for example, a specific culture, a religion, or a social fabric and are used to show where and to whom we belong and who we are (or who we are not). Accordingly, food can also work as a status symbol for example showcased at business lunches or during dinner parties. Thus, by means of food we can strengthen our sense of our common bond and at the same time differentiate ourselves from other groupings. In accordance with that perspective, food allows us to make social distinctions (Rozin, 2005). In a study by Darmon and Drewnowski (2008), for instance, the diets of people with lower socioeconomic statuses were on average of a lower quality compared to the diets of people with higher socioeconomic statuses. In some ways, food is also a sign of closeness and intimacy because people usually do not cook for and share their food with just anybody in everyday life. People deliberately consider the interests and well-being of other people in the food-related decision making to build, repair and maintain relationships (Sobal et al., 2006).

Because this dimension also concerns the responsibility that one feels for other people, future generations, and the environment (Hettler, 1980), sustainable and society-friendly food-related consumer behavior is also part of this dimension. For instance, a person who is aware of and pays attention to the consequences that their own behavior has for society and the environment may tend to purchase products that have been produced in a fair, environmentally friendly and sustainable way (Paul and Rana, 2012). This topic is highly relevant because sustainable food production and consumption is among the most important management and marketing issues that the food industry currently faces (Meyer-Höfer, Wense, and Spiller, 2013). Another example is a person who wants to support their own community, including its small shops, and therefore refrains from purchasing from big online providers, even though it might be more convenient.

2.4.4 Intellectual Dimension

The intellectual dimension is about the degree to which people engage the mind in creative and stimulating activities, use resources to expand knowledge, are committed to learning and sharing knowledge, and use their skills and abilities to achieve a more satisfying food-related life (Hettler, 1980). Thus, people score high on the intellectual dimension of FWB when they develop and apply the knowledge, skills, and motivation that support a healthy and balanced diet and positive food-related experiences, and when they perceive food-related experiences as inspiring and cognitively stimulating.

Especially in modern times, when many young consumers no longer learn how to feed themselves properly (Caraher and Lang, 1999; Garcia et al., 2013), it becomes clear that the proper handling of food, which includes for instance information search, product selection, skillful preparation, and well-being-oriented consumption, is a craft that takes time and effort to develop (Campbell, 2016; Stitt, 1996). People have to be taught this craft from a young age and must be inspired to develop a personal interest in it, thus ensuring that they are motivated to maintain and expand their knowledge and skills in later life (Hartmann, Dohle, and Siegrist, 2013). Depending on an individual's personal interests and preferences, the purchase, preparation, and cooking of food may be not just a necessity but a hobby, i.e., a creative and stimulating activity (Daniels et al., 2012), especially when new recipes and new methods of preparation are used (Caraher and Lang, 1999). For many people, the role that food plays in their day-to-day life also depends on their current life circumstances and situational factors. For example, while grocery shopping can be an annoying necessity during the week because of time limitations, it can be an inspiring and fun activity on the weekend (Seitz, 2014).

Again, the relationship is reciprocal. Consumers' intellect and skills influence their food-related experiences, and these experiences again influence the consumers' intellect and thinking. Gómez-Pinilla (2008), for instance, described how gut hormones can enter the brain or are even produced in the brain, where they influence one's cognitive ability; furthermore, regulators of synaptic plasticity can function as metabolic modulators and respond to peripheral signals such as food intake. However, as with the placebo sleep that affects cognitive functioning (Draganich and Erdal, 2014), the belief in the effect of a specific food or a food-related ritual, such as the obligatory chocolate bar prior to an important test, might also affect cognitive functioning.

2.4.5 Spiritual Dimension

Hawks (1994) defines a high level of spiritual well-being as a "high level of faith, hope and commitment in relation to a well-defined worldview or belief system that provides a sense of meaning and purpose to existence in general, and that offers an ethical path to personal fulfillment which includes connectedness with self, others, and a higher power or larger reality" (p. 6). In terms of FWB, one has high spiritual well-being if one's relationship with food and one's diet and consumption behavior are in harmony with one's own convictions and religious views and also support the feeling of being at peace with oneself. In addition, one's food-related life should support the mind-body connection and the connection of oneself with a larger whole.

Spiritual and/or religious traditions and rituals that contain food-related elements, such as Christmas or Thanksgiving, are embedded in almost every consumer's life. Often, food also has a symbolic meaning, such as breaking the bread and sharing the wine in a Catholic mass. Additionally, religious convictions can directly shape the food-related lives of consumers (Casidy and Arli, 2018; Fischer, 2016; Mathras et al., 2016), such as the Muslim rule that pork should not be eaten because of its impurity, the Jewish rule that the food has to be "kosher", or the recommendation in the Christian religion that for the sake of fasting fish should be eaten on Fridays. However, just as spiritual behaviors and convictions influence FWB, spirituality itself also influences it. Holt et al. (2005) found, for instance, that urban African-American women with strong religious beliefs consume more fruits and vegetables than those with weaker beliefs. Hawks, Goudy, and Gast (2003) demonstrated that lower levels of spiritual well-being correlate with higher levels of emotional eating among college women; and Berrett, Hardman, and Richards (2010) showed that spirituality can have a positive influence on eating disorder treatment and recovery. Furthermore, spirituality can influence how respectfully people treat their food and the environment, how consciously they eat, how grateful they are for food, and how thoughtful they use available resources (e.g., Rosen, 2011).

2.4.6 Interconnection of the Dimensions

The five dimensions exist not only side-by-side but also in interaction with each other. They inevitably overlap, merge into one another, and influence each other to some extent. Especially when evaluated subjectively, the dimensions will, to some extent, be arbitrary (Grunert et al., 2007; King et al., 2015). For example, an environmentally friendly behavior can be part of the social dimension because the person feels responsible for the world around him or her, but it can also be part of the spiritual dimension because the person feels connected with nature or because spiritual convictions make him/her act that way.

Meiselman (2016) describes the five dimensions as "positive" (p. 1); however, with regard to the overall FWB construct, we recommend to not give the dimensions this connotation because that limits their meaningfulness and applicability and gives the dimensions a direction that they simply may not have for some individuals. Thus, as with the FWB construct in general, the dimensions should also be defined rather neutrally.

2.5 The Food Well-Being Cycle

To be able to effectively influence FWB, we have to understand how it evolves and which internal and external factors influence it in which manner. To do so, we structure the findings from the literature search in an integrated model, the so-called FWB cycle (FWBC; see Figure 5).

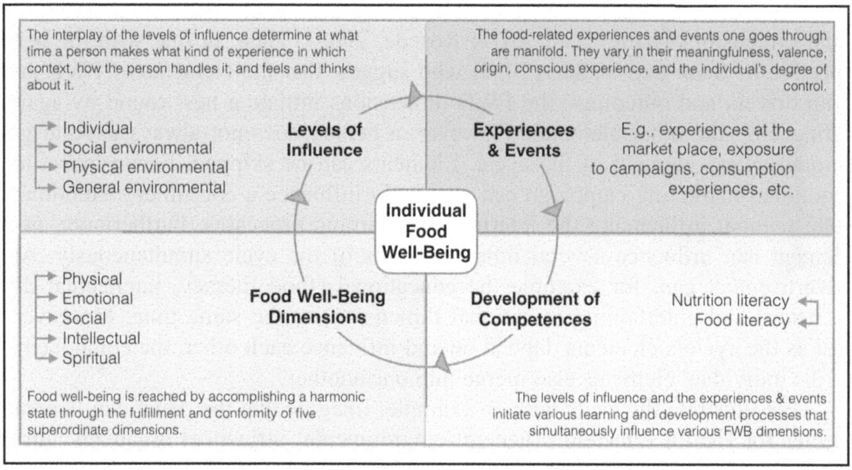

Figure 5: Food well-being cycle

The FWBC presents crucial parts of the development process of FWB and how they are structured and related to each other. Four elements are integrated in the cycle: (i) levels of influence, (ii) experiences & events, (iii) intermediate learning processes, and (iv) FWB dimensions. In this section, we give a basic overview of the FWBC's structure and operating principle. In the subsequent sections, we explain the elements that contribute to FWB one by one. The FWB cycle is based on the life course perspective, which suggests that people develop and change over time. People arrive at their current state of FWB within trajectories that are developed over the course of their lives, shaped by internal factors, external influences and the experiences they have (Sobal et al., 2006). Thus, FWB is dynamic and continuously in motion. The model is presented as a cycle because people repeatedly go through similar experiences and learning processes influenced by a set of recurring factors. The cycle starts with the levels of influence: the individual, social environmental, physical environmental, and general environmental influences (Bronfenbrenner, 1994; Story, Neumark-Sztainer, and French, 2002; Lindström and Eriksson, 2009). These levels of influence directly or indirectly influence all other elements of the cycle. First, they lead and shape food-related experiences and events by determining what type of experiences one has at which time and in which context and how one feels and thinks about these experiences. Each new experience and each new event adds to a person's food-related life course and shapes FWB. The experiences and events can directly influence the intermediate learning processes of FWB, which are divided into food literacy and nutrition literacy (Block et al., 2011; Nicklas et al., 2009; Vidgen and Gallegos, 2014). The intermediate learning processes again affect the five FWB dimensions, i.e., the physical, emotional, social, intellectual, and spiritual dimensions (King et al., 2015; Roscoe, 2009). Then, in line with the perspective of Scott and Vallen (2019) who suggest that the elements of FWB are both drivers and outcomes, the FWB dimensions initiate a new round by again influencing the other elements. However, a person does not always have to go through every element of the cycle. Elements can be skipped. For instance, an emotional marketing campaign can positively influence a consumer's emotional state without influencing the intermediate learning processes. Furthermore, one element can influence several other elements of the cycle simultaneously. An advertisement can, for example, be educational (food literacy, intellectual dimension) and entertaining (emotional dimension) at the same time. Moreover, just as the cycle's elements depend on and influence each other, the components of the individual elements also merge into one another.

We illustrate the cycle with an example. Imagine that the American Federal Center for Health Education (general environmental influence) organizes nutrition courses for pupils in public schools. The pupils take part in this course (experiences & events). They improve their knowledge about nutrition (nutrition literacy) and simultaneously enjoy the time with their peers (emotional dimension). By applying the newly acquired knowledge about food and nutrition in their day-to-day lives, they contribute to their own physical, emotional and intellectual well-being (FWB dimensions). Now, the cycle begins anew because the dimensions in turn influence the other elements of the cycle. A pupil who experienced the nutrition course positively, for example, is likely to have an open-minded attitude toward further interventions and similar experiences (influence of the individual). Other influencers can react as well. For instance, when many pupils improve their food literacy because of the nutrition course, the Federal Center for Health Education might build on this success and offer more courses (general environmental influence).

2.6 Levels of Influence

Based on the ecological model (Bronfenbrenner, 1994), FWB is viewed as affecting and being affected by multiple, interdependent levels of influence (Vidgen and Gallegos, 2014). Inspired by the work of Bronfenbrenner (1994), Story, Neumark-Sztainer, and French (2002), and Lindström and Eriksson (2009), we suggest breaking down the levels into individual, social environmental, physical environmental, and general environmental influences. By doing so we refine the division of Block et al. (2011), who only made a distinction between the "societal" and the "individual" level. By using our categorization, we can develop a structured and detailed overview of the determinants and processes that have an impact on FWB and the resources that are available to consumers at the different levels. This categorization supports the identification of starting points for interventions, the determination of accountable stakeholders who can drive change, and the formulation of goal-oriented recommendations for action. In the following, the levels of influence are described.

2.6.1 Individual Influences

The individual influences provide the basis for a person's unique development of FWB. The individual is complex and comprises various factors: physiological factors, psychological characteristics, knowledge and competences, as well as demographic variables and personal resources (Bublitz et al., 2013; Bublitz et al., 2011; Góngora, 2014; Sobal et al., 2006). The physiological factors include biological (e.g., sensory perception, hunger) and genetic (e.g., Fabry syndrome) aspects that influence one's food-related behavior and thinking (Lindström and Eriksson, 2009; Story, Neumark-Sztainer, and French, 2002). A study by Arner et al. (2011), for example, showed that individuals with a genetic predisposition toward type 2 diabetes are particularly sensitive to the environment and caloric excess. Furthermore, psychological characteristics have been shown to influence whether and to what extent a person pays attention to his or her own eating behavior and overall FWB; such characteristics include, for example, life satisfaction, self-efficacy, attitudes, preferences, interests, motives, goals, moods, and phobias (Story, Neumark-Sztainer, and French, 2002). Swan et al. (2018), for instance, demonstrated in their research that healthful eating involves specific mental and social capacities relevant to coping, including, among other capacities, critical self-awareness, flexibility, and fortitude. Knowledge and competences refer to those means and tools that people learn and develop during their childhood and adulthood and that can be applied to handle food-related situations in favor of FWB (Block et al., 2011; Nicklas et al., 2009). However, other individual characteristics, such as demographics (e.g., age, gender, education) and personal resources (e.g., money, equipment, transportation, time) also play a crucial role (Dean et al., 2008; Rodríguez-Arauz, Ramírez-Esparza, and Smith-Castro, 2016; Sobal et al., 2006; Story et al., 2008). For instance, less educated people with a low income are more likely to eat unhealthily than better educated people with a higher income (Janssen et al., 2006).

2.6.2 Social Environmental Influences

People are embedded in many social relationships that influence FWB. Family, friends, educators, community networks and other social units provide opportunities for constructing the relationship to food as well as food-related thinking and behavior through mechanisms such as modeling, reinforcement, social support, and the perception of social norms (Blum, McNeely, and Nonnemaker, 2002; Lindström and Eriksson, 2009; Sobal et al., 2006; Story, Neumark-Sztainer, and French, 2002; Swinburn, Egger, and Raza, 1999).

Of course, the family plays a crucial role in one's development of FWB. From the very beginning of one's life, the family exerts influence by providing food, being role models, teaching knowledge and skills, and passing on values and ideals (Brown, 2004; Swan et al., 2018; Voola et al., 2018). However, because eating and other food-related behaviors are an important form of socialization and recreation, the impact of other people at the group level is also far-reaching. One reason is the fact that humans naturally strive for a high degree of conformity of their own behavior with the behavior of others and group norms (Story, Neumark-Sztainer, and French, 2002; Story et al., 2008). Christakis and Folwer (2007) observed, for example, the spread of obesity in a large social network for 32 years and found that a person's chances of becoming obese increased by 57% if the person had a friend who also became obese in a given interval. Other research shows that the presence of others in a consumption context can trigger impression management motives that influence what, how much and when a person eats (Vartanian, 2015; Vartanian, Herman, and Polivy, 2007). Burnkrant and Cousineau (2018), for instance, found that people who are susceptible to the influence of others tend to eat food whose consumption they believe others would evaluate positively. Additionally, specific characteristics of others, such as size and gender, have been shown to influence the type and quantity of the food consumed (Allen-O'Donnell et al., 2011; McFerran et al., 2010).

2.6.3 Physical Environmental Influences

The settings in which consumers live and consume, as well as the resources that are available and the influences that affect consumers in their physical surroundings, shape their FWB. Previous research demonstrates that the tempting or "toxic" environment in which people in high-income countries – and increasingly in middle-income countries – live contributes significantly to unhealthy eating behavior, especially excessive intake of empty calories, and discourages physical activity (e.g., Hill, 1998; Lakerveld et al., 2018; Swinburn, Egger, Raza, 1999). In this obesogenic environment the food industry plays a crucial role because they make an abundant amount of unhealthy foods available and easily accessible in the consumers' direct physical environment through, for instance, vending machines, restaurants and convenience stores (Charlton et al., 2015; Cobb et al., 2015; Monteiro et al., 2013; Story, Neumark-Sztainer, and French, 2002). They are even accused of deliberately 'seducing' consumers with marketing strategies and campaigns to consume high amounts of unhealthy foods (Howlett, Davis, and Burton, 2015; McMahon, Williams, and Tapsell, 2010; Meiselman, 2016). On the other hand, the food industry sometimes also seems to contribute to restrained eating. Food advertising has been shown to contribute to the primary precursors of eating disorders (body dissatisfaction and the drive for thinness and dieting) in women by suggesting restricted diets and the consumption of diet products (Wilson and Blackhurst, 2011).

However, the food industry can also improve FWB. The presence of food stores, restaurants, cafés and similar facilities increases the availability of healthy foods and can contribute to healthy eating patterns. Especially vulnerable consumer groups who experience disadvantages in the market due to physical impairments, stress, or difficult life circumstances can benefit from new developments and innovations in the food industry, such as online grocery shopping (Elms, de Kervenoael, and Hallsworth, 2016; Hand et al., 2009; Schnellbächer, Behr, and Leonhäuser, 2015). Additionally, goal-oriented interventions in grocery stores, canteens, and restaurants have been shown to be able to support healthier consumption behavior (Ball et al., 2015; Story et al., 2008). For example, a community-academic partnership developed and implemented a healthy eating program in restaurants and supermarkets in a rural, Midwest community in the U.S. The program included the offering of healthier choices to restaurant and supermarket customers. The intervention proved to be successful and was positively valued in the rural community (Escaron et al., 2016). Thus, the influence of the food industry is not per se good or bad; it depends on how the industry's resources are used.

Other industries also influence consumers' FWB by shaping the physical environment. The fashion industry, for instance, stimulates under-consumption by presenting underweight men and women as beautiful and ideal (Block et al.,

2011), while the fitness industry promotes the achievement of supposedly healthy bodies by losing extreme amounts of body fat and increasing muscle mass with risky training and eating plans (Monaghan, 2001). Additionally, the film, media and cosmetics industries play an important role in promoting body ideals and eating behaviors (Tiggemann, 2014). But industries that are not directly related to food or the body in general have a strong influence as well. In particular, the technology sector, which focuses on the development of technological innovations and the further development of products and processes, has a significant influence. One example are mobile phone applications whose number grew exponentially in the last decade. They are used, for instance, to organize purchases (Flaherty et al., 2017), to share and redistribute food (Harvey et al., 2019) to track the own food intake (Griffiths, Harnack, and Pereira, 2018), or to manage food-related illnesses such as diabetes (Conway et al., 2016).

2.6.4 General Environmental Influences

The general environment is highly important because it determines the broader setting in which an individual develops and maintains FWB. This environment comprises, among other components, the activities of the government, ministries, public institutions, parties, politicians, and non-profit organizations. Ideally, these stakeholders should ensure that the consumers' physical surroundings are as safe as possible for their health, for example by implementing policies and regulations for the food supply chain. Furthermore, they should promote health and well-being by enabling people to gain control over the determinants of their well-being and to use them in the best way possible so that they can enjoy a good quality of life (Lindström and Eriksson, 2009; Shah and Marks, 2004). Thus, raising the awareness of the population and enhancing its empowerment should be important objectives (Lindström and Eriksson, 2009). To reach these objectives, it is important for the stakeholders to identify the salutogenic factors, i.e., the health and well-being resources that are available and the mechanisms that can support a positive FWB development (Antonovsky, 1996). Based on this, a comprehensive picture can be formed from which action recommendations can be deduced. These recommendations could include, for instance, behavioral interventions, the distribution of information material and the offering of courses or counseling services (Pearce and Witten, 2010). Examples are the Healthy Cities Network at the national level in the U.K. and the International Union of Health Education at the international level (Lang and Caraher, 2012). Influence can be directly exerted on the individual, such as the prescription of the compilation of school lunches, or indirectly, for example by teaching parents about their responsibilities for their children's FWB (Story et al., 2008). Furthermore, the activities do not necessarily have to be directly related to food, such as the

French law that came into effect in 2017 requiring fashion models to provide a doctor's certificate confirming they are healthy and not underweight (Ministère des Solidarités et de la Santé, 2017).

Moreover, the general environment comprises culturally shaped norms, behaviors, and expectations (Booth et al., 2001; Story et al., 2008). Here a distinction must be made to the social environmental influences. While the norms there refer to certain social groups whose members usually know each other, the norms at the general environmental level of influence are overarching and generally valid for entire regions or countries. Bessenoff and Snow (2006), for example, demonstrate in their research how cultural norms and the perceived society's expectations influence women's self-perceptions and body shame. Another example is the research of Pike, Hoek and Dunne (2014), who highlight the interrelation between culture and eating disorders by referring to – among others – the increasing rates of eating disorders in the Arab region and the growing prevalence of binge eating and bulimia nervosa in Hispanic and Black American minority groups in North America.

2.7 Experiences and Events

The interplay of the different levels of influence creates manifold FWB-related experiences and events. These experiences and events can be very small and short, such as seeing a food advertisement or talking about favorite foods with a friend, and also very meaningful, like the repeated perception of slim beauty ideals in the media, which cause young people not to feel beautiful anymore and to lose weight. The experiences can be positive, such as cooking a nice dinner, and negative, such as a painful food allergy. Some of the experiences are externally driven, such as the breakfast that a mother serves her child; some are internally driven, such as the decision to attend a cooking workshop; and some are both, such as the joint decision of what to eat for dinner (Herman and Polivy, 2008; Salvy et al., 2012). Consumers can experience these events consciously, such as the deliberate decision to enjoy a piece of cake, or unconsciously, such as the influence of the different marketing activities that consumers are confronted with when shopping for groceries (Wansink and Sobal, 2016). Finally, the degree of control one has about a certain experience or event can vary greatly, such as successful restrained eating in opposition to the unconsciously conditioned insuperable desire to eat in a specific context (van den Akker et al., 2013), e.g., the desire to eat chips while watching TV.

2.8 Intermediate Learning Processes

The levels of influence and the experiences and events one goes through initiate learning processes that impact the five FWB dimensions and other elements of the cycle. The learning about food and nutrition starts early in childhood through food socialization. Food socialization is the part of consumer socialization that is focused specifically on food and involves the processes through which one learns about the purchase, handling, and consumption of food and, moreover, develops food-related beliefs, attitudes, and preferences in one's social milieu (Nicklas et al., 2009). From an early age on, close others such as caregivers, family members and friends as well as institutions such as kindergartens and schools each play a role in the socialization process of children by offering exposure to a variety of foods, as well as by providing a "path for learning about and forming a relationship with food through everyday incidental exposure" (Bublitz et al., 2019, p. 143; Voola et al., 2018). Cultural norms as well as socially and culturally shaped traditions and rituals play an essential role in this process (Block et al., 2011). Families in particular typically use food, especially the joint preparation and consumption of meals, as a means to transmit cultural values and traditions from one generation to the next (Bublitz et al., 2019). However, food-related learning continues far beyond childhood. Throughout their lives, people find themselves in a continuous learning process in which they develop and improve nutrition literacy and food literacy. Nutrition literacy is about the ability to access, interpret, and use nutrition information. Important skills in this regard are, for example, the knowledge of macronutrient intake, food groups, and food compositions, as well as the ability to translate this knowledge into positive dietary choices (Vidgen and Gallegos, 2014). Food literacy is "a collection of interrelated knowledge, skills and behaviors required to plan, manage, select, prepare and eat food to meet needs and determine intake" (Vidgen and Gallegos, 2014, p. 54), i.e., it encompasses declarative types of knowledge as well as procedural knowledge (Block et al., 2011; Bublitz et al., 2011). A high level of food literacy empowers people to protect the quality of their diets and strengthens their dietary resilience (Vidgen and Gallegos, 2014), whereby resilience is defined as "a reduced vulnerability to environmental risk experiences, the overcoming of stress or adversity or a relatively good outcome despite risk experiences" (Rutter, 2012, p. 336).

2.9 Food Well-Being as a Journey

After having identified the need for an integrated approach to FWB, we have, so far, combined and structured the existing knowledge of different disciplines to (i) refine the definition of FWB, (ii) explain its components in (more) detail, especially the dimensions of FWB, which have not been extensively defined before, and (iii) emulate its development process. Based on our elaborations, we created an integrated conceptual model of FWB: the FWBC.

To make the FWB concept as we understand it more tangible and easier to understand, we would like to make a comparison in the form of a journey (see Figure 6): Imagine an individual who starts a journey equipped with a backpack that is filled with personal qualities and prerequisites such as his or her physical state, character, and current state of FWB. Along the path, the individual goes through experiences such as grocery shopping trips or family meals that are co-shaped by his or her environment, including the influence of family members, shopping possibilities in the nearby surroundings, or the laws that are supposed to protect the individual as a consumer. The way the individual perceives and goes through these experiences depends on his or her equipment. The experiences again influence his or her FWB directly, for example through emotions or physical state, or indirectly through learning processes, such as the development of cooking skills. This in turn influences the composition and size of the backpack and, thereby, the experiences that follow and how the individual goes through them. Thus, it is an interactive process that is always in motion.

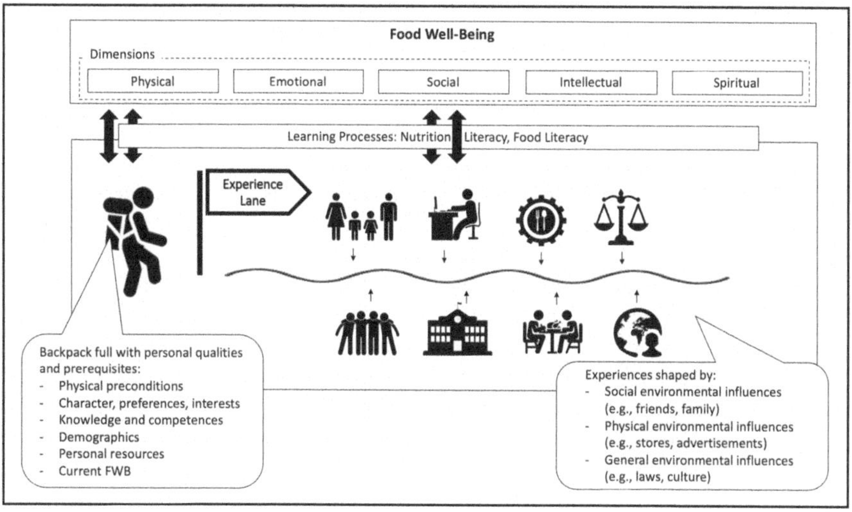

Figure 6: Food well-being as a development process

2.10 Implications and Recommendations

The FWBC is an excellent source of information and provides an analytical structure that different parties can use to make decisions. In the following, we provide some examples of how the FWBC can be used by food business operators and policy makers to enhance the FWB of consumers and society's well-being as a whole. Moreover, we discuss the limitations of the FWBC's current status and provide implications for further research.

2.10.1 Implications for Food Business Operators

The orientation towards the well-being of the consumer and, accordingly, an approach that is meant to serve both the company and the consumer, is in line with today's zeitgeist. Many current trends are about well-being and/or environmentally and society-friendly behavior (Grunert et al., 2017; IGD, 2018), and thus entail the underlying idea of FWB. Providers and marketers who follow the current zeitgeist and trends could, therefore, profit from knowledge and application of the FWBC. Furthermore, the use of the FWBC is in line with the contemporary societal marketing concept which stipulates "that the organization's task is to determine the needs, wants, and interests of target markets and to deliver the desired satisfactions more effectively and efficiently than competitors in a way that preserves or enhances the consumer's and the society's well-being" (Kotler, 1986, p. 16). Sirgy and Lee (1996) developed the idea further and introduced the idea of quality-of-life marketing, which is aimed at enhancing well-being, reducing negative side effects for target groups and other publics, and reaching long-term profitability by building long-term relationships and using the economics of scale and scope (Sirgy and Lee, 1996). Thus, food business operators who (want to) apply one or both strategies will find the FWBC valuable.

Food business operators can use knowledge about FWB and apply the FWBC in several ways. For example, the dimensions of FWB can be used as gateways to create services and products that are meant to feed into specific dimensions. The dimensions could, for example, be starting points in a values hierarchy (a tool to support ethical decision-making) in which design requirements are derived from values and norms to create a technological innovation meant to support FWB (van de Poel, 2013), such as an app for individual consumers to track their own FWB. The cycle could also be used the other way around, i.e., the cycle may enable re-tracing the path of the influence that a service or a product has on the intermediate learning processes and FWB dimensions. Furthermore, especially when the food environment changes or new developments and innovations come into being, the framework could be applied very early in the process to steer it in a more positive direction. For example, online grocery shopping is still a comparatively new way of grocery shopping, and if the FWBC is transferred to online grocery shopping now, online grocery shopping could be further developed and expanded with consideration of the improvement of consumers' FWB.

2.10.2 Implications for Policy Making

Based on the ecological model (Bronfenbrenner, 1994) and the ecological public health model (Lang and Caraher, 2012), it is clear that policy-making at local, regional, national, and international levels strongly influences consumers' FWB by shaping and co-creating their physical environment (Lang, Barling, and Caraher, 2001). Because there is an "interconnectedness of the different levels, as policy outcomes at each level are impacted by, and part of, the dynamics at the other levels" (Lang, Barling and Caraher, 2001, p. 544), a joint, coordinated and integrated approach of the levels is required. Actions and interventions are already underway. The EU platform for action on diet, physical activity and health, for instance, is a forum for European-level organizations, including food business operators, consumer organizations, public health NGOs, and scientific and professional associations that aim to improve the physical health of EU citizens (European Commission, 2018). We would like to encourage stakeholders to continue along this path, to work even more closely together and to introduce projects that are explicitly aimed at improving FWB as a whole rather than just the physical well-being of consumers.

Policy-makers in different policy areas, such as health, environment, social and economic policy (Lang, Barling, and Caraher, 2001), and policy-makers at different levels, might find the FWBC valuable in approaching this undertaking. The FWBC might be able to help policy makers by assisting in the identification of opportunities for exerting positive influences and the creation of goal-oriented policies and interventions that aim at improving FWB domains and/or dimensions. At the local or national level, one example is the goal-oriented implementation of nudges to help consumers make well-being-oriented decisions (Quigley, 2013). At the national or international level, one current example is the establishment, enforcement and control of laws and regulations for the storage and transportation of food ordered over the Internet (e.g., van der Veer, 2017). Although initiatives at every level are necessary, we would like to emphasize the importance of initiatives at the local or regional level because they are comparably easy and fast to implement (compared to those at the national or international level), are developed and integrated in the direct presence or even with the citizens, and can be adapted to local and regional customs and traditions, making them more attractive and acceptable for the target groups.

In general, public institutions, such as the Federal Ministry of Food and Agriculture, should educate consumers and make them aware of FWB and the underlying mechanisms, for example by means of awareness campaigns and FWB courses. Consumers need to understand what FWB is; what influences it; and, most importantly, how they can influence it themselves. Consumers also have to be informed about the importance of the environment for their own consumption behavior so that they can deliberately create an environment, for example at home or at work, that supports their FWB. Consumers can also use the knowledge to help and support each other. After all, human beings are not responsible for themselves alone but also for others, especially for those who cannot care for themselves, such as children, the elderly, or people with disabilities. Consumers have to be sensitized to this social responsibility and be educated about the consequences that their actions might have for the FWB of others. As McMahon, Williams, and Tapsell (2010) formulate it, "the current use of the term well-being can, by its very nature, be elitist and by default marginalize those who do not have sufficient skills and support" (p. 284).

2.10.3 Implications for Research

Given the importance of the FWB construct and cycle, we suggest two steps in the effort to elucidate it further. First, the levels of influence, intermediate learning processes, and dimensions, as well as their interdependent relationships, need to be further explored and empirically tested. For example, larger components of the explanations with respect to the dimensions had to be based on research that is focused on well-being in general and not on FWB because the research in the latter area is too limited. Thus, empirical research is required to confirm the proposed FWBC and to deepen the understanding of the different elements. To strengthen the general validity and applicability of the cycle, it should be investigated in light of and transferred to different phenomena, contexts, and cultures to make it more widely applicable. The FWB framework was created and advanced in developed countries. Due to serious and pressing food-related problems in developing countries, it is imperative to conduct research in the light of the framework in those countries as well (e.g., Voola et al., 2018).

Second, a measurement scale for FWB should be developed (Bublitz et al., 2013). The increasing interest in food-related well-being has led to the creation of several valuable instruments in this area; however, none of these yet covers FWB in its totality. For example, King et al. (2015) developed a questionnaire that measures consumers' subjectively experienced wellness induced by specific foods or ingredients. This questionnaire presents a valuable contribution; however, the questionnaire is limited to the direct effect of the consumption of specific foods or ingredients. Ares et al. (2016) similarly created a questionnaire focusing on the consumers' perceived well-being induced by specific foods. Grunert et al. (2007) introduced the satisfaction with food-related life (SWFL) scale, which is quite relevant for FWB; however, this instrument, which has only seven items, offers only a general insight into consumers' satisfaction with food-related life. Guillemin et al.'s (2016) Well-being related to Food Questionnaire (WELL-BFQ) is comparably comprehensive and captures both short-term and long-term effects. However, it does not reflect the entire construct of FWB because relevant aspects, such as the spiritual dimension or sustainable and responsible consumption, are not included in the questionnaire.

FWB assessments will assist in further exploring and confirming the construct of FWB as well as in capturing it in the individual consumer. However, it will be difficult to capture such a complex and fluid construct, especially because of its (at least in large parts) subjective and personal nature (King et al., 2015). Although well-being is often seen as a purely subjective construct based on an individual's perception and satisfaction (Ares et al., 2016; Schnettler et al., 2016), we suggest the creation of a measurement tool that includes subjective (e.g., hedonic experiences) and objective components (e.g., health status) to capture the full picture (Meiselman, 2013). Furthermore, it is important to pay attention not only to the absence or presence of the elements but also to the importance that individuals attribute to these elements, e.g., a person could score low on the spiritual level but may not care about it because he or she has other priorities. Moreover, a distinction should be made between context-dependent, short-term FWB and overall, long-term FWB. In addition, we assume that consumers themselves might not be able to fully capture and express their FWB, making it necessary to measure it at least partially indirectly through latent constructs (Ares et al., 2016). Finally, in addition to a universally applicable measurement tool that captures the general FWB of consumers, measurement tools must be created that are tailored to specific phenomena and problems, e.g., people living in poverty will have different needs and standards than those without financial problems.

Since we have found in our literature search that different disciplines are working simultaneously on FWB (perhaps without calling it that), but often without building on each other, we would like to emphasize the interdisciplinary exchange at this point and propose a stronger cooperation between disciplines.

2.11 Conclusion

FWB is a highly relevant topic because it concerns the human being as a whole and it extends into every area of life. It comprises the food-related life and problems of humans at the individual, group, and societal levels. It relates to the well-being of human beings as citizens and thereby to the well-being of societies and nations. However, it is also about the well-being of humans as consumers and therefore also about the well-being of companies and industries.

In the spirit of positive psychology, we, the authors, are convinced that we as a society can create an environment in which people can develop the knowledge and skills required to (i) shape and improve their own FWB, (ii) make well-informed decisions that are good for themselves and for society, and (iii) help others achieve a high FWB. A change in thinking is already underway, allowing traditional ideals of health, well-being, and beauty to be scrutinized. However, this change in perspective is still in its early stages and needs to be strengthened and further developed.

A holistic view is indispensable, as are endeavors that are coordinated, coherent, and integrated (Ozanne et al., 2016; Bublitz et al., 2019). Accordingly, it is important to find ways to connect stakeholders and interest groups with each other and to develop common approaches. To do so, we need to understand the antecedents and consequences of consumers' behaviors, feelings, and thoughts with respect to FWB so that the environment can be built in such a way that it is indeed supportive and empowering.

The FWBC is a tool that can be used to help consumers achieve a high level of FWB because its application allows us to analyze and understand consumers' behavior, how it is formed in different life situations and the consequences it has for overall FWB. Moreover, based on the knowledge provided by the FWBC, interventions and strategies can be created and realized to effectively improve FWB. However, further research is required to improve and scientifically substantiate the FWBC and to create instruments with which FWB and its components can be measured. As Meiselman (2013) states, "health and wellness are a tsunami wave of the present and the future; I recommend that we ride this wave and use the skills of sensory and consumer science to do that" (p. 209).

3 How Online Grocery Shopping Influences Consumers' Food Well-Being Compared to Offline Grocery Shopping[2]

3.1 Introduction

The online grocery market is constantly growing as more companies enter the grocery delivery business (Deloitte, 2018). The forecasts are positive and predict further global growth; e.g., Forrester (2018) expects the global online grocery market to double from $150 billion in 2017 to $334 billion by 2022. Despite this rapid development, the online grocery market in most countries is still in its infancy. In Germany, for instance, online grocery sales accounted for only 1.2% of total grocery sales in 2017 (Handelsverband Deutschland, 2018). For retail practice, policy-makers, and consumer protectors, the early developmental stage of the online grocery business offers the opportunity to intervene early and to coshape it in such a way that it benefits both companies and consumers.

This situation is particularly interesting because of the impact that online grocery shopping (OGS) seems to have on consumers' food well-being (FWB), which is a "subjective and objective evaluation of people's physical, emotional, social, intellectual, and spiritual relationship with food" (Chapter 2.3; p. 40). Previous research suggests, for instance, that the shopping experience (Hand et al., 2009), daily food-related routines and rituals (Seitz et al., 2017), and food-related decision making (Huyghe et al., 2017) change when consumers shop for groceries online. Although some previous research findings on OGS have implications for certain aspects of FWB, no research thus far has focused on the influence of OGS on all dimensions of FWB, i.e., the physical, emotional, social, intellectual, and spiritual dimensions (Ares et al., 2016; King et al., 2015), and therewith on FWB as a whole.

Especially in light of current food-related problems that are often influenced by the food industry (Sobal et al., 2006), the influence of OGS on FWB should be investigated in detail. For example, the prevalence of overweight and obesity continues to spread despite increased attention (Ravussin and Ryan, 2017). In 2016, more than 1.9 billion adults were overweight or obese (WHO, 2018a), and the number of obese children and adolescents has risen more than tenfold in the

2 Co-author: Prof. Dr. Hanna Schramm-Klein

F. Frentz, *The Pursuit of Food Well-Being*, Handel und Internationales Marketing Retailing and International Marketing,
https://doi.org/10.1007/978-3-658-30366-2_3

past four decades (WHO, 2017). The obesogenic environment, which is strongly influenced by the activities of grocery business operators, has a major role in this development (Lakerveld et al., 2018; Story, Neumark-Sztainer, and French, 2002). OGS could reinforce these negative effects, for example by making unhealthy foods more accessible and available, by supporting a sedentary lifestyle, and by reducing the social aspect of buying and consuming food. However, OGS could also have positive effects on consumers' FWB. OGS could, for instance, make healthy products more accessible and available, promote the acquisition of food-related knowledge, and help people with physical disabilities to live a self-determined and independent life. Thus, both negative and positive influences seem possible. However, it is not clear yet which effects indeed occur.

Therefore, in this paper we examine the effect of online vs. offline grocery shopping on the different dimensions of FWB from the consumers' perspective. This will allow the derivation of recommendations for grocery business operators on the contribution they can make to consumers' FWB in the context of the digitalization of grocery shopping. By considering FWB in their strategies, grocery business operators would not only improve their image by demonstrating their concern for their customers' well-being but would probably also strengthen their relationships with their customers and, in the long run, their profitability. One reason for this assumption is that an orientation towards FWB is consistent with today's zeitgeist, as many current trends focus on the well-being of the individual consumer and of society as a whole (Grunert, 2017; IGD, 2018; Piacentini, MacFadyen, and Eadie, 2000). Furthermore, such a strategy is in line with the contemporary quality-of-life marketing concept aimed at enhancing well-being, reducing negative side effects for target groups and other stakeholders, and reaching long-term profitability by building lasting relationships and using economics of scale and scope (Sirgy and Lee,1996). Furthermore, research suggests that a high level of FWB induced by a specific retailer can contribute positively to retailer loyalty and positive word of mouth (Hedhli, Chebat, and Sirgy, 2013). As online food retailing is still in its infancy and consumer protection measures are not yet fully developed, our findings will also be interesting for public policy and consumer protection.

Thus, this paper explores (i) what FWB means in the context of OGS, (ii) how OGS affects consumers' FWB compared to offline grocery shopping, and (iii) what online grocery operators, public policy, and consumer protection can do to support the development of FWB in the online grocery retail context. In particular, this paper investigates which positive influences are possible and should be supported and which negative influences have to be counteracted. To answer these questions, three studies are conducted: (i) 26 think-aloud protocols of consumers documenting the completion of some OGS tasks, followed by interviews; (ii) six consumer focus group discussions; and (iii) a questionnaire answered by 103 consumers. Based on the findings, a comprehensive picture of the relationship between OGS and FWB can be presented, allowing the formulation of recommendations for grocery business operators, public policy, consumer protectors, and research.

The remainder of this essay is organized as follows: We first conceptualize FWB and explain its five dimensions which form the theoretical framework of our investigations. Building on this, we give an overview of the current state of research regarding the relationship between OGS and FWB. Then, we present the three studies one after the other. We discuss the findings in light of the current state of research and theoretical background. Finally, we close with implications for research and practice.

3.2 Food Well-Being and Online Grocery Shopping

The FWB concept is based on the idea that a shift in thinking has to take place from the traditional, health-oriented, and rather functional view of food to a more positive and holistic understanding of the role of food in consumers' overall well-being (Block et al., 2011). In the past, research regarding food-related health and well-being often adopted a pathogenic orientation, which implied that the influence of food on consumer well-being is mainly limited to the fulfilment of nutritional needs and the maintenance of physical health (Biltekoff, 2010). However, this approach did not fully reflect the cause-effect relationships that lead to food-related well-being. For example, the role of social and psychological factors as well as the context in which behavior develops has been largely ignored (Engel, 1977). Therefore, researchers started to adopt a more holistic approach (Antonovsky, 1996; Lindström and Erikkson, 2009), in which food is given a greater role. This new perspective manifests in the term FWB that was introduced by Block et al. (2011). FWB embodies an integrated way of thinking, in which food-related activities, including the purchase, preparation and consumption of food, are assumed to influence different dimensions in life and therewith overall well-being and quality of life (Block et al., 2011). In recent years, this approach has been repeatedly confirmed (e.g., Ares et al., 2016; Guillemin et al., 2016; King et al., 2015).

The literature suggests that FWB is formed by the fulfilment and interaction of five superordinate dimensions: the physical, emotional, social, intellectual, and spiritual dimensions (Ares et al., 2016; King et al., 2015; Roscoe, 2009). These dimensions are the theoretical basis of our investigation. Within each dimension, people arrive at their current state and therefore at their current overall level of FWB within trajectories that are developed over the course of their lives. These trajectories are shaped by internal factors, external influences and personal experiences (Sobal et al., 2006). Due to the omnipresent role of food purchasing in consumers' everyday lives (Guillemin et al., 2016), it can be assumed to have a critical influence on the five dimensions and thus on overall FWB (Grzeskowiak et al., 2016). In the following, we provide a brief explanation of every dimension and present results of previous research on the role of OGS in contributing to these dimensions compared to offline grocery shopping. It should be stressed in advance that the boundaries between the dimensions are not sharp, as they influence each other and merge in parts.

Physical well-being is attributable to food-related activities that directly or indirectly influence physical well-being (Hettler, 1980; Roscoe, 2009), such as the implementation of healthy dietary choices or the walk to the grocery store. OGS can contribute to consumers' physical well-being by eliminating or reducing the physical effort that is often associated with in-store shopping (Seitz et al., 2017). This is especially relevant for consumers with physical impairments, health issues, and immobility (Hand et al., 2009), because OGS enables them to conveniently purchase bulky or heavy products without having to carrying them (Elms, de Kervenoael, and Hallworth, 2016). This could also have a positive influence on the product selection as it increases the possibilities of choice. Furthermore, OGS might be able to support healthier food choices due to the large physical and temporal distance to the products and their low vividness during product selection which supports rational decision making (Huyghe et al., 2017). Additionally, OGS offers individuals with allergies or special diets new ways to find and purchase products that meet their nutritional needs (Tukkinen and Lindqvist, 2015).

The emotional dimension covers the experience of having and dealing with emotions that are linked to food-related activities. This comprises, among others, the conscious perception, expression and management of emotions, including for instance the application of coping strategies in emotionally challenging situations (Adams, Bezner, and Steinhardt, 2016; Hettler, 1980; Roscoe, 2009). OGS in this context is believed to reduce stress and anxiety by eliminating the stressors of in-store shopping (Seitz et al., 2017). Especially vulnerable consumers who cannot cope well with stress or excitement could benefit from this (Elms, de Kervenoael, and Hallsworth, 2016). The other side of the coin, however, is that the shopping pleasure experienced during OGS is often low; new products and offers cannot be discovered in the same way as in-store (Hand et al., 2009), and the sensory experience is strongly reduced (Martinez et al., 2018). While researchers are already working on solutions, such as the use of a touch screen and 3D pictures (de Vries et al., 2018), this apparent disadvantage might also be beneficial because the decreased product vividness can support emotional control and, therewith, reduce impulse purchases and foster healthier choices (Huyghe et al., 2017). However, OGS can also increase perceived risk and insecurity due to concerns regarding product quality (Karahsanovic, Holm, and Nejad, 2017), the maintenance of the cold chain (Hand et al., 2009), and the unfamiliarity of the providers (Seitz et al., 2017). Consumers are also afraid of delivery and return problems (Martinez et al., 2018) and describe a reduced perceived responsibility for and emotional connection with food when shopping for groceries online (Ilyuk, 2018).

The social dimension of FWB refers to one's relationships with others and the environment and how these are considered and expressed in food-related purchases and consumer behavior. This dimension also comprises sustainable and environmentally conscious consumption, as this behavior is strongly based on the level of responsibility that one feels for others and the environment (Hettler, 1980; Roscoe, 2009). Previous research shows that social norms play an important role in forming attitudes towards OGS (Sreeram, Kesharwani, and Desai, 2017), and, more specifically, that the attitudes of acquaintances and relatives towards OGS influences one's attitude and intention to use it (Ranadive, 2015). Furthermore, family and household circumstances (e.g., caring for children or other relatives) can support or counteract the intention to use OGS (Harris et al., 2017). However, if shopping in stationary retail stores is, at least sometimes, viewed as a social activity, consumers strive to maintain this ritual (Hand et al., 2009). Culturally-bound customs and traditions that are connected with specific foods or meals are also difficult to leave behind for the sake of OGS. It might also be unpleasant to shop for foods online that have moral or ethical importance or that hold social or symbolic meaning (Elms, de Kervenoael, and Hallsworth, 2016). Regarding social responsibility, OGS could promote food waste by private households due to the increased emotional distance from the products (Ilyuk, 2018).

The intellectual dimension comprises the degree to which people use resources to expand their knowledge, are committed to learning and sharing their knowledge with others, pursue creative and stimulating activities, and use skills and abilities to achieve a satisfying food-related life (Hettler, 1980). OGS can support the organization and execution of purchases and promote food-related skills, such as the planning and preparation of meals. Furthermore, online grocery stores can provide inspiration for purchase decisions and cooking (Tukkinen and Lindqvist, 2015). However, consumers also report an increased effort to plan their purchases, for example due to the greater care required to make the shopping list (Elms, de Kervenoael, and Hallsworth, 2016). Moreover, to use OGS a specific skill set is required regarding internet use and online (grocery) shopping that some consumers do not seem to have yet. In particular, lacking background knowledge of and experience with OGS can prevent consumers from using OGS (Martinez et al., 2018). Fortunately, previous research also suggests that the use of OGS can be learned comparably easy and fast (Anesbury et al., 2016).

The spiritual dimension refers to the extent to which consumers' relationships with food and food-related activities are in harmony with their convictions and religious or faith-related views and support the feeling of being at peace with oneself (Hawks, 1994). In the literature, there is no clear mention of the possible connection between OGS and the spiritual dimension. However, some of the behaviors that are categorized as socially responsible behaviors in the social dimension (e.g., a vegan diet) could also be regarded as elements of the spiritual dimension if the behavior is based on faith-related values and beliefs (Raggiotto, Mason, and Moretti, 2018). However, since the underlying motives are often not known, a clear categorization is hardly possible.

The literature already gives several indications on how consumers' FWB is influenced by the use of OGS compared to offline food shopping. However, the influence on FWB was never examined in its entirety, nor was research done on how online food retailers in particular can positively influence consumers' FWB taking into account all five FWB dimensions. Thus, a holistic and integrated approach is still missing. Therefore, this essay examines what FWB means in the context of OGS, how it is influenced in this context compared to stationary food shopping, and what measures can be taken to strengthen consumers' FWB through OGS

3.3 Empirical Approach

An exploratory, mainly qualitative mixed-methods approach to develop a deeper and more holistic understanding of the relationship between OGS and FWB was chosen (Spiggle, 1994). Even though qualitative research is sometimes regarded as controversial among academia and practitioners (de Ruyter and Scholl, 1998), it is certainly able to uncover essential determinants underlying the consumption and purchase behavior of consumers (Sinkovics, Penz, and Ghauri, 2005) and to provide rich insights into their thinking and perception (Conrad and Blair, 2009). Especially the use of data and method triangulation, which implies the integration of data gathered through different methods and sources (Alam, 2005), supports the development of a comprehensive understanding of a phenomenon and adds rigor to research (Denzin, 2012). Therefore, in our research, we made use of data and method triangulation by conducting (i) think-aloud protocols and interviews, (ii) focus groups, and (iii) a survey with closed and open-ended questions with consumers from several consumer groups. Within this paper, respondents have been given pseudonyms to protect their privacy.

3.3.1 *Study 1: Think-Aloud Protocols and Interviews*

Twenty-six individual think-aloud protocols involving the completion of OGS tasks in a German online grocery store and subsequent interviews with members of the three consumer groups 'students and young professionals', 'parents', and 'elderly people' were conducted. The original subjective of this study was to examine how consumers perceive OGS and how it changes their shopping behavior and experience. However, the findings sparked the idea of focusing on the influence of OGS on FWB.

Think-aloud protocols offer direct access to what happens when people make sense of information and how their thought processes influence the choices they make (Ericsson and Simon, 1998). However, they only give us limited insights into why consumers do what they do. In-depth interviews can counter this disadvantage by encouraging participants to talk about their thoughts, feelings, and motives (Conrad and Blair, 2009).

3.3.1.1 *Sample, Data Collection and Analysis*

Purposeful criterion-based convenience and snowball sampling were used to recruit participants for this study. Because previous research has shown that consumers' life circumstances strongly influence their OGS intentions (Hand et al., 2009), a heterogeneous sample was chosen consisting of three consumer groups who could especially benefit from OGS due to their group-specific life circumstances: students and young professionals, parents, and elderly persons (Grant, Fernie, and Schulz, 2014; Seitz et al., 2017). Participants were inexperienced in OGS, allowing us to examine how shoppers experience the transition from in-store shopping to OGS and to observe what prejudices consumers have and what risks they initially see regarding the impact on their FWB. Table 3 shows the distribution of demographics in our sample. The participants' acquisition and the data analysis were conducted in parallel. Data were collected until saturation was reached.

Table 3: Consumer groups interrviewed in study 1

Consumer groups	Age	Gender		Household size			
		female	male	1	2	3	4
Young people	21-32 years	4	4	6	2		
Parents	22-43 years	5	3			5	3
Elderly people	65-83 years	3	5	2	3	1	

The fieldwork was conducted over a period of six months, with think-aloud protocols and interviews lasting up to 90 minutes. The study was conducted in the participants' homes. The interviewer brought a laptop, a laptop mouse, and a tape recorder with her. Participants first completed three shopping tasks in a German online grocery store (www.mytime.de) while thinking aloud (see Figure 7 and 8 for the landing page and an exemplary product detail page of mytime.de). The tasks consisted of (i) selecting five familiar items that are part of the participant's weekly shopping trip, (ii) selecting five items based on a predefined shopping list, (iii) selecting five items for a barbeque by using different functions/paths at the website. Both familiar and unfamiliar items were included because previous research suggests that the selection process is different for them (Benn et al., 2015). Then, participants were interviewed about this experience, their general grocery shopping experiences and the influences they have on their FWB, and how they think their food-related life may be impacted by OGS. With the respondents' consent, the think-aloud protocols and interviews were audio recorded and the participants' activities within the store were recorded using desktop video recording. The relatively realistic setting (participants were at home and shopped in a real online grocery store) contributed to the study's ecological validity (Cicourel, 1982).

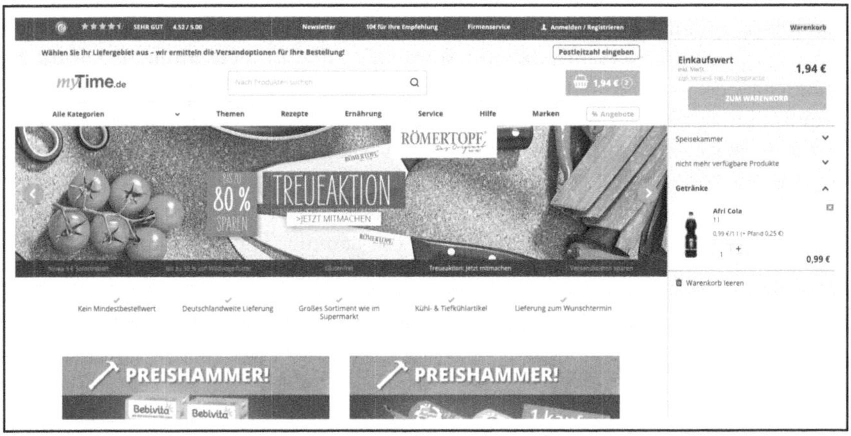

Figure 7: Landing page of the online grocery store mytime.de

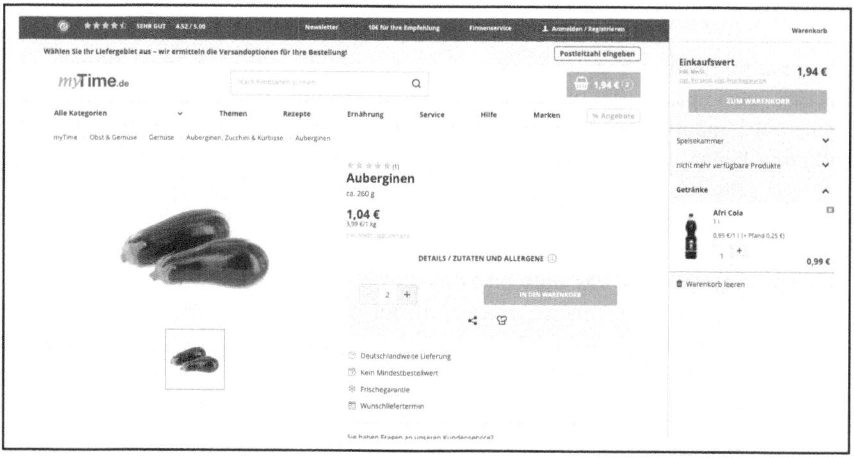

Figure 8: Product detail page of the online grocery store mytime.de

The audio files were transcribed and analyzed using the qualitative research analysis software MAXQDA 18. A coding manual was used in which the codes were listed and operationally defined and the rules for the coding process were explained (Kolbe and Burnett, 1991). The development of the coding list was an iterative process in which the two coders discussed, reviewed and improved the coding list until a shared understanding and usage of the codes was reached and the codes fully reflected the phenomenon under investigation. To increase objectivity, one coder was not an author (Kolbe and Burnett, 1991).

A combination of theory-confirming and hypothesis-generating content analysis was used to examine the data (Cho and Lee, 2014). First, we applied the deductive approach and prepared a provisional list of theoretically-derived codes. The superordinate themes comprised the five dimensions of FWB, i.e., the physical, emotional, social, intellectual, and spiritual dimensions (Ares et al., 2016; King et al., 2015; Roscoe, 2009). These themes were subdivided into mutually exclusive subcategories. During the analysis process, in which the results of all three studies were included, more specific and different themes and categories inductively emerged from the data; requiring an improvement of the overall coding list (Cho and Lee, 2014) (see Appendix I for the final coding list). The subsequent evaluation and interpretation of the coded data was based on a mixed methods approach: the frequency of the codes as well as the frequency of consensus and dissent among the participants on specific topics were quantified and each code was supplemented with a description and exemplary citations (Onwuegbuzie and Dickinson, 2009).

3.3.1.2 Results

The results confirm the relevance of OGS regarding the physical dimension. Several participants thought about the physical relief that OGS could provide. Some participants would use OGS when being ill or not able anymore to do the shopping because of age-related constraints. Participants also thought about the physical relief due to the absence of the need to carrying the food, taking long walks to the grocery store, and being exposed to bad weather. However, some of the older participants regarded this reduction in physical activities as negative. The issue of nutrition was only addressed to a limited extent, which could indicate that this was not a major concern of our participants in the situation under study. Only the provision of nutritional tips and recipe suggestions was praised a few times.

With regard to the emotional dimension, most participants were critical. The majority of participants criticized the impossibility of selecting products according to their personal preferences and quality standards. Some felt that they had been manipulated on the website to select a greater number of (more expensive) products. Furthermore, many participants experienced negative emotions during the shopping process and described OGS, for instance, as "impersonal", "emotionless", and "annoying". Anna (31, employee) said: "It's all there. But it's no pleasure. It's practical and you can find everything quickly, but it's not so much fun." Participants especially missed the opportunity to experience their shopping trips and the selection of the products with all their senses, to browse and be inspired, and to be spontaneous. The fear that the delivery might jeopardize the meal plans, for example because one loses the appetite while waiting or misses the delivery, was also repeatedly mentioned. Some respondents supposed that when shopping online, they would make more target-oriented and planned purchases and fewer emotion-driven purchases. While most of them found this quite pleasant, some found it restrictive. Only very few participants described OGS as a positive and exciting new grocery shopping experience.

Regarding the social dimension, some participants thought that it was disadvantageous that they could not meet other people or ask salespeople for help; however, other participants argued that the absence of other people promotes a relaxed shopping atmosphere. Moreover, some parents emphasized that OGS enables them to take better care of their children while shopping and to have more time for the family. It was even suggested that OGS can have a relaxing effect on family life: "Maybe sometimes I would be more balanced, nicer to the kids (…). that we don't argue. Yes, I think that would be good" (Eva, 34, parent). Obviously, parents often perceive offline food shopping as an unpleasant duty rather than a chance to do something with the family or to teach the children about food. In this respect, OGS would provide a welcome relief. Furthermore, some participants feared that the delivery would harm the environment and that

OGS would jeopardize local businesses, jobs and familiar city life: "Local shops are slowly dying out. Fewer and fewer people will go shopping in the city" (Tobias, 24, employee). Thus, the participants feel a strong sense of social responsibility for their community and wish that their local community does not change negatively because of OGS. This aspect has not been addressed in the literature so far.

The findings regarding the intellectual dimensions were both positive and negative. Generally, participants' OGS-related knowledge was low. A minority of the participants did not know that OGS existed or were not aware that fresh products could be purchased online. Most participants admitted having too little background knowledge, e.g., regarding the operation of the shop, the delivery process, the method of payment, and data protection. Even after using the store, many questions were still unanswered. During the interview, Janosh (28, parent) said: "I want an introductory video explaining the shop and the delivery process. I don't quite understand it yet." It is surprising that even the younger consumers had difficulties to get used to the OGS process.

Obviously, when people shop groceries online for the first time, the habitualized purchase process suddenly becomes a consciously executed and cognitively challenging task. All participants had problems finding their way around the shop. Cognitive challenges included among others assigning products to the right categories, choosing the right key words for searches, and selecting the correct number, size and weight of products. Tobias (24, employee) said "I am forced to fight my way through the categories here. I hate that." Due to age-related sensory limitations, shopping online was particularly difficult for older participants. At least three of the senior participants would not have been able to perform the shopping tasks without the help of the interviewer.

People also change the ways they approach shopping tasks when shopping online. An older gentleman, for example, tried in vain to transfer his cognitive map from the stationary store to the online store before realizing that he had to reorient himself. Anna (31, employee) said: "When shopping in-store you tend to think from one category to the next but here you probably think in meals." Additionally, the sequence and structure of purchase-related activities changes; steps that formerly belonged to the preparation or follow-up of the purchase process are now part of the purchase itself.

Generally, OGS seems to be able to inspire and creatively stimulate people, for example, through product and recipe suggestions. It might also be able to enhance purchasing and cooking skills: "Even a layman can compile a menu based on the suggestions and recommendations. The recipe suggestions are especially helpful for men who have no idea how to cook" (Jan, 65, senior). Furthermore, OGS can support both the careful examination of product information and informed purchase decisions. However, it was also emphasized that the shop in use was generally still expandable and was not yet well tailored to intellectual needs.

The results provide no indication that OGS affects the spiritual dimension of FWB. Previous research on food-related well-being has also not found a connection between FWB and spiritual well-being (Ares et al., 2013; Ares et al., 2014). Therefore, we exclude this dimension from the analysis. However, we include a new dimension of FWB that our findings highlight: the self-determined dimension of FWB. As this aspect was on the one hand extremely relevant for participants of all age groups and on the other hand did not fit into any of the other dimensions, it was decided to create a new dimension. Based on the definition of Murphey et al. (1963), the definition of emancipation in the context of food-related experiences of Mugel, Gurviez and Decrop (2019), and the current study results, an individual with a high level of self-determination is a person who is able and willing to take decisions that depend neither on others nor on external circumstances and acts independently and free. Thus, the individual is in control. In the context of this essay, this also includes making use of the available resources to reach self-determination.

The results show that OGS supports self-determined day planning and promotes independence from place, time, weather, means of transportation, and physical state. In particular, parents would use OGS to be more independent and flexible. Moreover, some participants would use OGS when ill or unable to go shopping because of age-related constraints, thus increasing their independence. Sometimes it seemed that the participants were torn between the self-determination enabled by the possibilities and flexibility of OGS and the certainty made possible by the well-known shopping trips in the familiar stationary retail stores. However, the feeling of self-determination is also decreased by the impossibilities of physically selecting the products and controlling the packaging and delivery process. In addition, the insufficient assortment of some providers as well as high prices and shipping costs can impair perceived self-determination.

At the end of the trials, of the twenty-six participants twelve could not imagine using OGS in the near future and seven would only use OGS if circumstances required it, e.g., if a product is not available in-store or in case of illness. Only seven participants were willing to try OGS. However, ten participants indicated that the OGS experience had improved their attitude towards OGS, highlighting the important role of one's own experiences in forming opinions in this regard.

This first study provides valuable insights into the short-term influences of OGS on the FWB of consumers who try OGS for the first time. However, this study is limited to a comparably low number of consumers who all have a similar level of experience. Therefore, further research is required. To compensate for the limitations of the first study, in the second study, consumers with different levels of OGS experience should be included so that short- and long-term effects of OGS on FWB can be uncovered. Furthermore, discussions between consumers should be facilitated to inspire detailed reflections on experiences and to reveal the perception of OGS in a social and cultural context.

3.3.2 Study 2: Focus Groups

Six focus groups, with appropriate sizes of six to seven people each, were conducted over a period of three months, with discussions lasting up to 180 minutes until data and theoretical saturation were reached (Onwuegbuzie and Dickinson, 2009). During the sessions, participants discussed OGS and its hypothetical or real influence on their food-related lives and well-being. The group setting allowed the collection of qualitative in-depth data from all individuals. The socially oriented environment helped reveal how people develop and change attitudes in a group setting and which social norms and values influence their decisions (Krueger and Casey, 2000). Because grocery shopping is shaped by society and culture, taught and influenced by relatives and friends, and often executed with and/or for other people (Seitz, 2014), focus groups were a suitable method. Moreover, the knowledge level of a group is greater than that of an individual, which was particularly helpful as the general knowledge level regarding OGS among consumers is still comparatively low (Onwuegbuzie and Dickinson, 2009), which was also evident in the first study.

3.3.2.1 Sample, Data Collection and Analysis

The focus groups were newly formed by purposive convenience and snowball sampling (Palinkas et al., 2013). Again, an overall heterogeneous sample was used; however, each focus group was in itself homogeneous to create a common basis for a pleasant and stimulating discussion. Participants lived in their own households and were at least partially responsible for grocery shopping. Table 4 gives an overview of the composition of the focus groups. Participants in the "Parents II" group were all online customers of a local organic store that sells its products both offline and online.

One moderator and two assistant moderators conducted the focus groups. With the participants' permission, the discussions were audio and video recorded. The interview guidelines were semistructured and developed in an iterative process based on the theoretical background, current state of research, and previous findings. After participants had introduced themselves, they individually made a mind map with everything that came to their mind when thinking about shopping for groceries in-store, followed by a discussion within the group. The

Table 4: Composition of the focus groups in study 2

Consumer groups	Age	Gender		Household size				OGS users
	years	female	male	1	2	3	4≤	n
Young adults I	24-38	3	4	2	2	1	2	2
Young adults II	27-36	3	4	2	5			2
Parents I[a]	27-49	5	2			2	5	1
Parents II[b]	34-60	3	4			2	5	7
Older adults I (>50)	52-71	6	1	2	4			1
Older adults II (>65)	66-80	4	2	2	4			2

[a] Children were younger than 10 years; [b] children were older than 15 years but still living at home

same was done with OGS. Then, participants subsequently discussed the influence of OGS on the five FWB dimensions compared to offline grocery shopping. Prior to every dimension-related discussion, the respective dimension was explained by the moderator. For the data analysis, we applied the same coding manual that was used for study 1. In addition, it was observed how and to which extent the participants within each focus group influenced each other and changed their mind in the course of the group discussion.

3.3.2.2 Results

The results show that OGS impacts the physical dimension of FWB by reducing physical exertion and physical discomfort. For parents with young children in particular, OGS seems to bring a great deal of physical relief. However, OGS could also encourage a sedentary lifestyle and be detrimental to people who already get too little physical exercise. In particular, elderly people use food shopping in stationary stores to stay physically active and fear that shopping groceries online could physically harm them in the long run.

Regarding nutrition-induced physical well-being, participants mainly attributed a positive effect to OGS. The customers of the organic online store believed that OGS supports a healthy and varied diet by making healthy, regional and organic foods easily available. "Online shopping means a healthy diet for me" (Gustav, 57, employee). Children's nutrition could also be positively influenced: "If I want to make baby porridge and need special products like parsnips or fennel. (…) Then that [OGS] would be practical. I went to three different stores last week to get the stuff" (Daniela, 27, mother). Furthermore, OGS can increase the availability of products needed by consumers who have health-related issues such as allergies or who follow specific diets. However, some participants also had reservations: "Online you don't have to pass by healthy foods like the fruit and vegetable department, so you may be less admonished to shop healthy. It's easier to sneak past and directly type in cola" (Lena, 28, student). The attitude towards the effect on nutrition seems to depend strongly on the experiences that one has with OGS and the online food stores that one knows or uses.

In particular, the offline shoppers described OGS as "emotionally cold" and "annoying", revealing the relevance of OGS to the emotional dimension of FWB. The negative attitude was aggravated by a fear of contact induced by the unfamiliar shopping environment and a lack of spontaneity and sensory experiences (e.g., the scent of freshly baked bread was missing). Only a few participants thought that OGS could induce positive feelings. Parents in particular saw OGS as an opportunity to shop with less stress and more peace and quiet. Offline shoppers assumed that OGS would, on the one hand, support controlled, rational purchasing but would, on the other hand, also decrease general involvement. However, the multichannel shoppers did not confirm this assumption. Overall, they described a far more positive effect on emotional well-being, which indicates that offline shoppers have at least partly unfounded preconceptions.

The suspicion of OGS among the offline shoppers was profound. Participants feared that online providers would not keep their promises, would withhold important information, and would manipulate customers. Susanne (59, employee) described OGS as "a forum for criminal activities." Even most of the multichannel shoppers explained that they only started to do OGS because they knew the stationary store and its owner beforehand. This reinforces the statement of many other participants that they would only shop online if they already knew the store from stationary shopping. Then, they would also have a place to go if they had a problem. A stationary contact point would also make it more difficult for the business to cover up scandals and other problems. The doubts persisted across all age groups.

The opinions of others informed participants' behavior and thinking, reflecting the social dimension of FWB. Several participants did not want to use OGS because they had learned from acquaintances or the media that OGS was not sufficiently developed or was of poor quality. The group discussions also influenced the participants' attitudes. Especially the multichannel shoppers were able to convince some of the offline shoppers to give OGS a try. Several participants said they would miss social interactions if they were shopping online. "The older you get the more you need the social environment when doing the purchases" (Susanne, 59, employee). Interestingly, some older participants would not even want to use OGS even if it enabled them to be independent; they preferred to be cared for. Furthermore, there was fear that interpersonal interaction generally atrophies when more and more is done online. Only few participants, mainly parents, appreciated the absence of social contact.

Most parents would use OGS to exclude their children from the shopping process, making the shopping process more relaxed and limiting the children's influence on product selection. However, a few parents were concerned about the effect that such exclusion might have on their children's food socialization because the children would then miss out on opportunities to learn not only about foods and grocery purchasing but also about social interactions and the completion of tasks by being with their parents. Daniela (27, mother of a 4-year-old) said: "You have to involve them somehow. (…) They learn to be considerate of others. The more often we shop together the better it gets and the more disciplined he is (...). He would then no longer have the experience to push the trolley, to pack something into the trolley, or to give a coin to the cashier".

Furthermore, many participants feared that OGS itself is not environmentally and socially friendly and that their own behavior would become more socially irresponsible in the long run if they used OGS. Ben (34, employee) stated, "If I ordered online on a regular basis, the garbage collection would have to come twice a week". Moreover, participants were concerned about the working conditions of the employees involved and were apprehensive of negative consequences for local businesses and jobs, the social cohesion within districts, and even the social fabric of the city. Only a few participants saw a positive influence. One participant, for instance, reported that his family purchases more organic products and consumes them more consciously since they purchase them online. It was also discussed whether OGS could reduce CO_2 emissions and food waste through more efficient use of resources.

Regarding the intellectual dimension of FWB, the results show that offline shoppers in particular had an incomplete picture of OGS. Most of them did not know about the market's current state or the existing providers, let alone what kind of business model the suppliers were using or what assortment of products they were providing. They also had many unanswered questions regarding the organization and logistics behind OGS.

Participants believed that they could develop new skills through OGS but also saw the danger of losing their traditional purchasing skills and their sense of responsibility for food and resources over time. "You don't have to think anymore" (Ralf, 33, employee). Moreover, inexperienced participants assumed that OGS is less inspiring and creative than stationary grocery shopping; however, the multichannel shoppers disagreed in this regard. Interestingly, the elderly participants feared losing skills not related to food, such as driving a car. Some also saw grocery shopping as memory training.

Furthermore, it was suggested that OGS could support need- and goal-oriented purchasing; ease purchases based on certain nutritional styles, diseases or intolerances; and enhance cooking skills through recipe suggestions and preparation instructions. The assistance provided online, such as prefabricated shopping baskets and filters, could make shopping easier. Furthermore, in-home shopping enables the review of the current stock and the involvement of other household members. While some participants believed that OGS could support informed decisions by enabling comprehensive information search and acquisition, others thought that informed decisions would be hampered through a lack of information regarding the products as well as the organizational and logistical processes of OGS. These doubts were again expressed mainly by the offline shoppers.

With regard to the new dimension of FWB, the self-determined dimension, the results show that while consumers previously had to adapt their daily routine to their shopping, shopping now adapts to the daily routine, increasing consumers' self-dependence and flexibility. Particularly vulnerable consumers who are disadvantaged by stationary retailing could benefit. However, some participants also felt restricted by the exclusion from the physical product selection process, the limited assortment, the need to be present at delivery, and the impossibility of being spontaneous. Furthermore, our offline shoppers feared poor price-performance ratios for particularly small or large purchases and an inadequate supply of fresh food. Although this was not true from the viewpoint of the organic online store shoppers, it could be true for other store formats.

While the costs associated with OGS were criticized, it was also discussed whether OGS could support an effective use of financial resources, e.g., by helping shoppers to manage expenses and to meet predetermined budgets. However, these were exclusively hypothetical considerations. Most participants assumed that OGS would mean, at least in the long run, less time and effort.

The results of study 2 offer comprehensive, in-depth insights into the perceptions of different consumer groups with varying background knowledge with respect to the influence of OGS on FWB. However, in total, only 15 multichannel shoppers took part in this study, limiting the meaningfulness of the results and justifying another study with a greater range of coverage.

3.3.3 Study 3: Survey

To obtain more comprehensive insights into the perceptions of multichannel shoppers and to verify the findings of studies 1 and 2, we additionally conducted an exploratory survey study about the influence of OGS on food-related life and FWB compared to offline grocery shopping.

3.3.3.1 Sample, Data Collection and Analysis

A convenient and criterion-based sampling approach was applied to recruit the participants for this study. Participants were 18 years or older and had at least joint responsibility for shopping for groceries for the household. In total, 103 consumers (69 female (67.0%), $M_{age} = 34.3$ (SD = 12.9), 20-74 years) took part in this study, of whom 41 (39.8%) were multichannel shoppers. Table 5 presents the sample's demographic characteristics.

Table 5: Participants' demographic characteristics in study 3

Level of experience	Age M(SD)	Gender N(%)		Household size N(%)				Children N(%)
		female	male	1	2	3	4≤	
Offline shoppers	34.0 (12.9)	41 (66.1)	21 (33.9)	9 (14.5)	15 (24.2)	11 (17.7)	27 (23.6)	20 (32.3)
Multichannel shoppers	34.8 (13.0)	28 (68.3)	13 (31.7)	10 (24.4)	11 (26.8)	8 (19.5)	11 (26.8)	13 (31.7)

Of the 41 multichannel shoppers, 4 (3.9%) used OGS weekly, 12 (11.7%) monthly, 17 (16.5%) every few months, and 8 (7.8%) only once at the time of the survey. On average, they had started using OGS 12 months (SD = 13.5) before the survey. The fast majority (40 shoppers) used home delivery. The five product groups that were purchased most often online by the participants were "coffee, tea and hot chocolate", "sweets and nibbles", "vinegar, oil and spices", "muesli and breakfast cereals", and "baking ingredients." Thus, durable food was bought preferentially. Of the 62 offline shoppers, only 11 (10.7%) indicated to be willing to try OGS in the future.

Because of the difficult nature of the topic, most participants were interviewed face-to-face (n = 68). This enabled the interviewer to give more detailed explanations and answer questions if required. The other participants filled in the survey by themselves but in the presence of an interviewer who would answer questions if needed. First, participants evaluated their satisfaction with food-related life by means of a seven-point Likert scale with seven items (Grunert et al., 2007), ranging from 1 (totally disagree) to 7 (totally agree) (see Appendix II for the full list of items). Then, participants described the advantages and disadvantages of traditional grocery retail shopping. If they were multichannel shoppers, they then provided detailed information on their OGS habits. Next, participants described the advantages and disadvantages of OGS in general before explaining their thoughts and experiences regarding the influence of OGS on the five FWB dimensions (see Appendix II for the full list of the open-ended questions with respect to the influence of OGS on FWB). The survey ended with questions on offline grocery shopping habits and the participants' demographics. For the qualitative data analysis, we applied the same categorization scheme that was used for studies 1 and 2. To prevent distortions in the results, a code was only counted once per participant. For the quantitative data analysis, we made use of SPSS (Statistical Package for the Social Sciences).

3.3.3.2 *Results*

An independent-samples t-test was conducted to compare multichannel shoppers and offline shoppers regarding their satisfaction with food-related life (cronbach's alpha = 0.857). Interestingly, the test revealed a significant difference in scores for multichannel shoppers ($M = 5.44$, $SD = 0.99$) and offline shoppers ($M = 4.88$, $SD = 1.07$; $t(101) = 2.68$, $p = 0.009$); suggesting that multichannel shoppers experience a greater satisfaction with their food-related life than those shoppers who purely shop offline.

The answers to the open-ended questions generally confirm the results of studies 1 and 2. Figure 9 shows the distribution of the number of positive and negative mentions in the respective FWB dimensions with regard to OGS. In the following, the results are brought down to the most meaningful findings.

The self-determined dimension was with 246 positive mentions and only 95 negative mentions most frequently highlighted. The "large product assortment and the possibility to purchase more and other products online" was mentioned most often (73%). Furthermore, time savings (63%), and increased self-determination/flexibility (55%) were often commended. One participant, for instance, said: "You reduce the time for this task, you can organize your time better, you can shop comfortably everything you need while sitting at the couch and you are independent of location". While many multichannel shoppers praised the assortment (88%), they disagreed with respect to the prices. This disagreement could also be observed in the two previous studies. The offline shoppers often stressed the reduction in effort (37%). Generally, negatively mentioned was especially the decrease in self-determination due to the inability to select the products, as well as the dependence on the provider and the higher prices.

The emotional dimension was the second most frequently mentioned dimension, but most mentions were negative. Most of the 248 negative mentions related to the lack of spontaneity (79%), the high mistrust (50%), and the poor sensory experience (47%), and are therewith in line with the findings of study 1 and 2. One participant formulated it, for instance, as follows: "Personally I miss the joy because of the missing sensory experience. (…) Spontaneous purchases are also not possible or more unlikely." The missing emotional relationship to food was also criticized: "(…) The relatedness to food could be reduced. By this I mean that we may value food less if we get it with only one click." However, it was also often stressed that OGS makes shopping more relaxed (40%). Compared to the multichannel shoppers, offline shoppers more often mentioned OGS-related emotions negatively. It logically follows that offline shoppers in particular see the potential in OGS to buy more controlled and goal-oriented (39%): "Online, I concentrate more on my nutritional goals. There, I purely focus on the products that are important to me and the diet that I'm following. Quite in contrast to this, in-store I'm often easily seduced to take a 'last snack' before I 'really' start the diet."

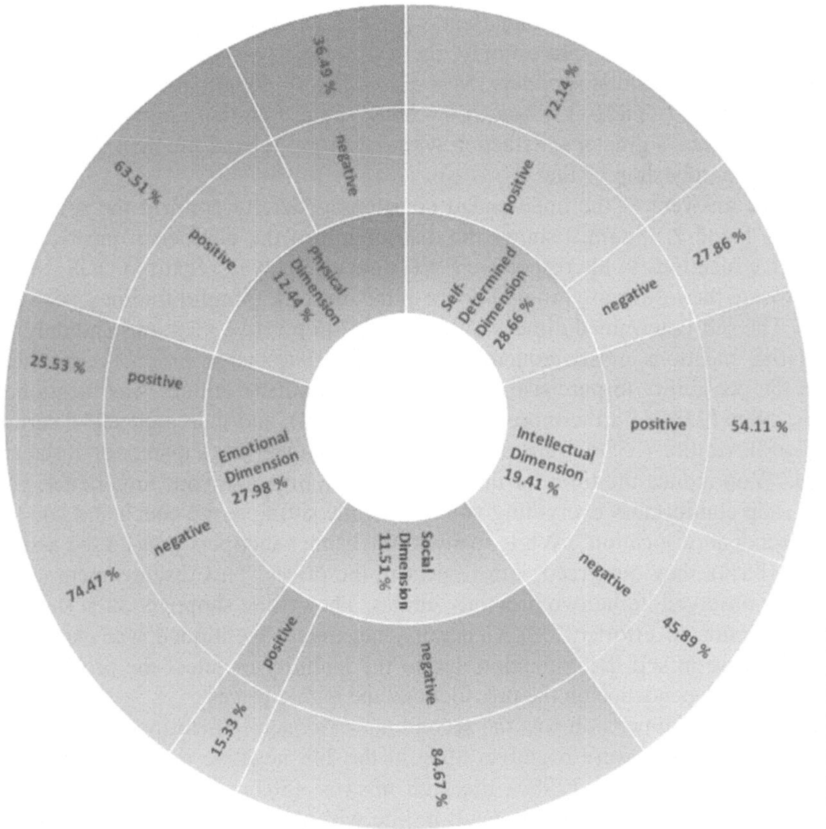

Figure 9: Distribution of the positive and negative mentions in the FWB dimensions with respect to online grocery shopping

The intellectual dimension was with 226 mainly positive mentions in third place. In particular, the multichannel shoppers appreciated the possibility of making an informed and well-founded decision (56%) and experiencing and discovering new things such as new products, shopping opportunities or providers (34%), and therewith confirmed our previous findings. The possible positive consequences for food literacy were recognized by both online and offline shoppers. One participant, for instance, said "The products are better presented and important information is available with one click." However, many participants also felt that they learn less online: "I often buy other products online than offline, because I am simply offered completely different products online. (…) But otherwise I don't feel that I learn a lot about nutrition or the products by shopping online. Actually, I have the feeling that I can get better and more detailed information about products in a stationary store." Opinions on this subject therefore diverged quite widely. Furthermore, some of the parents expressed concerns that the children are not involved in OGS which could inhibit their food socialization process: "From an educational point of view, children learn from their parents [during offline grocery shopping] how and which food to buy and what can be cooked from it. If we only order [groceries] online, that would be omitted."

The physical dimension was addressed less frequently, with 148 citations. While it was often mentioned that OGS can be physically relieving (44%), it was mentioned almost as often that it supports a sedentary lifestyle (42%). This was noticeably often mentioned by the offline shoppers (48%), e.g., "When shopping online, I don't have to leave my house, I don't have to carry the purchases and I don't have to squeeze myself through the crowds. However, I still prefer to go shopping myself, because every kind of movement and every possibility to leave the house is important to me." In particular, multichannel shoppers recognized added value with regard to nutrition (25%). One participant said, for instance, "the probability that I order something that I don't need or that doesn't match my vegetarian diet is much lower there." The same picture was evident in the focus group discussions.

The social dimension was mentioned mainly negatively, with 137 mentions. In particular, offline shoppers believed that OGS impairs social contacts (65%) and negatively affects the time spent with family and friends (16%): "Stationary shopping is a social experience. Buying bread rolls on Saturday mornings and groceries for the weekend is part of the family program." Noticeably, more multichannel shoppers (22%) than offline shoppers (11%) believed that OGS could also enhance social contacts. This distribution is just as comparable with the results of the first and second study as the emphasis on social responsibility. The fear that using OGS could harm the environment, for instance through "the pollution caused by the delivery," and the society, for instance through "damaging the smaller local businesses in the long run," was mentioned slightly more often by multichannel shoppers (32%) than by offline shoppers (27%).

3.4 Discussion and Future Research

Despite the consolidated body of knowledge related to the impact of OGS on consumers' food-related life, surprisingly no research addresses the issue of how shopping groceries online affects consumers' FWB in its entirety compared to offline grocery shopping. This essay addresses this issue by answering three research questions: (i) what does FWB mean in the context of OGS, (ii) how does OGS affect consumers' FWB compared to offline grocery shopping, and (iii) what can online grocery operators, public policy and consumer protectors do to support the development of FWB in the online grocery retail context.

As for the first question (what means FWB in the context of OGS?), the basis of our studies formed the five dimensions of FWB, i.e., the physical, emotional, social, intellectual, and spiritual dimensions (Ares et al., 2016; King et al., 2015; Roscoe, 2009). Our data show that OGS affects the physical, emotional, social, and intellectual dimensions. The spiritual dimension was never addressed by our participants. However, spirituality in general does not seem to play a major role in the lives of our subjects. This should not lead to the conclusion that the spiritual dimension should no longer be taken into account when it comes to food shopping, as the results could be culture- and country-specific. Further research is needed to understand the role of the spiritual dimension in food shopping across countries. Furthermore, our findings point to the existence of an additional dimension: the self-determined dimension. Individuals who score high at the self-determined dimension are people who are able and willing to take decisions and actions independently of others and external circumstances and thereby create a food-related life that is best tailored to their ideas and needs (Mugel, Gurviez, and Decrop, 2019; Murphey et al., 1963).

The finding that the spiritual dimension does not play a role for our participants when it comes to the purchase of food, but that a new dimension, the self-determined dimension, takes on a very relevant role, expands our understanding of FWB considerably and therewith contributes to the current state of knowledge. In the following, we will highlight and discuss relevant influences of OGS on the five FWB dimensions based on our findings and therewith answer the second question (how does OGS affect consumers' FWB compared to offline grocery shopping?). Additionally, we will point out limitations and provide suggestions for future research.

Regarding physical well-being, our findings confirm that OGS can have the effect of physical relief (Tukkinen and Lindqvist, 2015), and improve the availability of healthy and nutritionally necessary foods. However, the current findings also suggest that OGS promotes a sedentary lifestyle. This, combined with a higher availability and accessibility of unhealthy foods and the reluctance to purchase fresh foods online, could contribute to the overweight and obesity pandemic. This possible future scenario has not yet received any attention in the literature. Therefore, future research, especially longitudinal studies, should investigate this possible scenario.

On the emotional level, the mistrust, the perceived control loss, the doubts regarding data privacy, and the low emotional involvement when shopping for groceries online that was found in previous research could be confirmed (e.g., Huyghe et al., 2017; Karahsanovic, Holm, and Nejad, 2017; Martinez et al., 2018). Participants with little or no experience in OGS in particular described these disadvantages. One reason for the negative reactions could be Germany's high store density and short distances to food stores that might make OGS often appear unnecessary to German consumers (Teller, Kotzab, and Grant, 2012). Regardless of its reasons, the observed reactance behavior confirms that OGS is still in its infancy in Germany and that most people have not gotten used to this way of grocery shopping yet (Seitz et al., 2017). It was also striking that participants, especially the participants who took part in the first two studies, stated that engaging in OGS also made them feel less involved in and responsible for food and the exploitation of resources, confirming the findings of Ilyuk (2018). However, it is unclear whether these negative feelings will persist even after prolonged use of online grocery stores (the participants in study 1 and 2 often had little or no experience in online food shopping). The quantitative results of the third study, in contrast, show that multichannel shoppers generally feel more satisfied with their food-related life than offline shoppers. This is an interesting result as it provides a concrete indication that OGS could improve the food-related life of consumers. Since the majority of multichannel shoppers who participated in the third study still mainly shop their groceries offline and only use OGS when needed, it can be assumed that they have learned to use the advantages of both the online and offline channel and thus avoid their respective disadvantages. Our findings confirm, for instance, that OGS is used to avoid the stress and anxiety that is often associated with offline shopping (Seitz et al., 2017). However, further research is needed to identify the factors that cause this increased satisfaction and to investigate what effects this has on FWB.

The detrimental effect of OGS on social well-being, especially on social contacts, has already been observed (Picot-Coupey et al., 2009). However, consumers' concern for the well-being of local businesses and the maintenance of the well-known urban fabric and regional cohesion are new and credible findings. Future studies will have to investigate whether this is a cultural phenomenon. The extent to which these fears are justified must also be examined and, if so, what measures can be taken to mitigate these negative consequences. Furthermore, because our findings suggest that elderly people prefer to be cared for instead of using OGS, it must be investigated whether OGS would indeed be as much of a help for seniors as has been postulated by previous research (Seitz et al., 2017; Tukkinen and Lindqvist, 2015). These studies should also take into account character traits and living conditions.

Regarding intellectual well-being, we could confirm that OGS can help improve food-related competences and can at least sometimes be inspiring and creatively stimulating (Tukkinen and Lindqvist, 2015). However, participants' low background knowledge of OGS and the challenges experienced during OGS were unexpected. Furthermore, it was striking that the purchasing process changes dramatically when shopping online, which at least in the short term makes food shopping a greater cognitively demanding task. In the long run, however, it should lead to cognitive relief; however, the question arises whether this is absolutely positive, as participants stated that when shopping in-store, they train both cognitive abilities and less-obvious competences, such as driving. Furthermore, future research should observe children's changing role in grocery shopping and how this influences their intellectual well-being. While many parents stated that they want to use OGS to purchase groceries without their children, some also had concerns about what the absence of the child during the grocery shopping trip means for the child and its development. Especially in view of current study results which underline the importance of stationary family co-shopping for children's FWB (Hémar-Nicolas and Ezan, 2018), these concerns are justified. Future research should examine the long-term impact of the switch to digital food shopping on children and how children can best be involved to strengthen and enhance their FWB.

The influence of OGS on the self-determined dimension showed to be mainly positive. OGS can support a self-determined and more independent daily routine with a high degree of flexibility (Elms, de Kernevoael, and Hallsworth, 2016). However, there are also detrimental effects on the self-determined dimension due to the perceived loss of control and the dependence on the provider (e.g., Martinez et al., 2018). It seems as if consumers are often torn between self-determination by the unknown and the safety of the familiar when choosing the shopping channel. Our participants mostly decide in favor of the latter, independently of the consequences that this decision might have for their FWB. Furthermore, we found that assortments were considered insufficient and prices too expensive. While some previous studies showed similar results (e.g., Martinez et al., 2018; Melis et al., 2016), others found that consumers are satisfied with the product range and prices of online grocery providers (e.g., Richards, Hamilton, and Allender, 2016) Thus, these findings seem to be provider-, market-, and country-specific. Particularly in Germany, the business models and offers of online food retailers seem to vary greatly.

Overall, while OGS has a few general advantages and disadvantages compared to offline grocery shopping, it can be said that the extent to which OGS can influence a person's FWB positively or negatively depends strongly on the individual's characteristics and life circumstances. While some would profit more from the online channel, others would benefit more from the offline channel. Often, balanced multichannel shopping behavior seems to be a good middle way to use the advantages of both channels and to minimize their disadvantages. Figure 10 presents exemplary cause-effect relationships of how the two channels could support FWB, depending on the situation and personal characteristics of a person.

In general, quantitative and long-term research is required to gather more representative results. These studies should take a closer look at how the behavior and attitude of multichannel shoppers will stabilize in the long run. While the first study, which was conducted with inexperienced online shoppers, showed, for instance, a high reactance behavior and reservation among the participants, the second study indicated that these negative feelings can decrease over time and can sometimes even turn into the opposite. The third study even shows that multichannel shoppers experience a higher satisfaction with food-related life than the offline shoppers. Furthermore, future studies may reveal if consumers conducting their grocery shopping primarily online think differently about food, have different food-related rituals or practices, or generally have a different relationship with food because our findings indeed suggest that the relationship to food can change as a result of OGS. Because grocery shopping is shaped by culture, research should be conducted in different geographical regions and countries. The spiritual dimension did not play a role in our studies, as spirituality and/or religiosity in general play a subordinate role in the lives of our subjects; however, this might be different in regions where spirituality is considered more important. Furthermore, future research should consider the different existing store formats, as our findings showed that they are perceived very differently; leading to varying shopping experiences. Moreover, it must be mentioned that most of our participants had a higher education level and often seemed quite educated in terms of nutrition. Therefore, future studies should include consumers with more diverse backgrounds. Additionally, special attention should be paid to consumers who are facing food-related problems, such as consumers who are overweight or obese. Finally, the studies conducted focused on the subjective perception of the consumers. Future research has to investigate the influence of OGS on FWB also objectively, for instance through taking into account the fitness level and body mass index of participants.

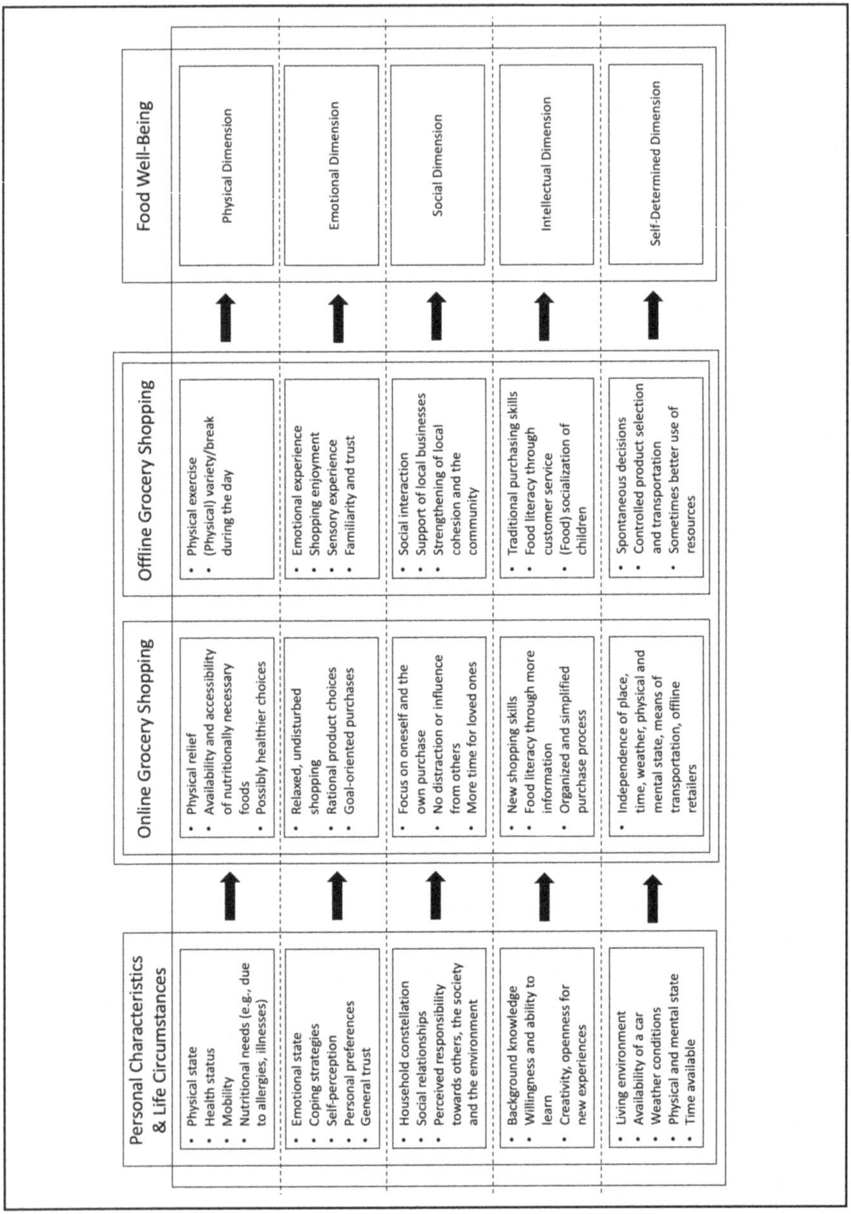

Figure 10: Possible positive influences of online and offline grocery shopping on food well-being, depending on character traits and life circumstances

3.5 Recommendations for Practice

The third research question of this essay deals with the actions that retailers, public policy and consumer protection can take to contribute to consumers' FWB in the online grocery retail context. The following two sub-chapters give an answer to this question.

3.5.1 Recommendations for Online Business Operators

The study results point to various recommendations for action for online business operators that could improve consumer FWB and improve customer-provider relationships:

Reduce information asymmetries: To address information asymmetries, consumers need to be informed about the online grocery market, the existing suppliers and their offers, the processes underlying OGS, and how they can use OGS for their purposes. For instance, for a good overview of the existing suppliers and their delivery radius, a virtual map would be a useful tool. Furthermore, detailed information on products, manufacturers and manufacturing conditions should be made readily available at the online grocery stores' websites. Moreover, when promoting OGS, the advantages for the intellectual and self-determined dimensions should be addressed, as should advantages for vulnerable consumer groups.

Inspire confidence: Because consumers are concerned about the quality of products and their correct treatment during storage and delivery, providers should stress that online grocery retailing is regulated and controlled by official laws and regulations and that consumers are protected by law. Furthermore, an additional stationary store or contact point would make the online store look more trustworthy and approachable. It would also inspire confidence if customers had the opportunity to communicate with other customers, e.g., through a chat function.

Act value-driven: German consumers have a very pronounced sense of values and it is important to them that the suppliers they buy from internalize and implement these values. In particular, retailers should firmly integrate sustainability and social responsibility into their marketing strategies, e.g., by ensuring that transport is as environmentally friendly as possible, that reusable and minimal packaging is used and that production and working conditions are fair. Local infrastructure and businesses must also be taken into account. Where possible, communities should be supported, e.g., though charitable projects in and with the community.

Use personalized content: Through customized profiles, offers, and shopping lists, providers should address consumers individually based on their personal preferences, life styles, and nutrition goals and thereby provide a service that consumers do not receive offline. Furthermore, consumers should receive more filter options and should be enabled to give more detailed instructions regarding the product selection when purchasing for groceries online. This should make it easier for them not only to find desired products but also to ignore unwanted ones. The latter is particularly important for people who have dietary goals but have difficulties meeting them. Research has shown that people find it difficult to stick to a healthy diet when purchasing in-store, because at the point of sale unhealthy products and ready-to-use products are often displayed in such a way that consumers are consciously aware of them and repeatedly have to make the decision not to take them (O'Brien et al., 2014). Moreover, online grocery providers could collaborate with the Federal Ministry of Food and Agriculture and/or nutritionists so that vulnerable consumers, who have for instance food-related illnesses or allergies, receive the food- and nutrition related information they need when shopping online. However, providers must be careful not to threaten the privacy of consumers or to give them the feeling of being patronized, which would lead to distrust and emotional distance.

Support food literacy: Many participants emphasized the fact that OGS could be used to gather general information about products, recipes, healthy eating as well as healthy and correct food preparation. Therefore, online grocery providers should create value-added content in this regard. Furthermore, the introduction of educational content aiming at children and the development of their food literacy and grocery shopping skills could be of great benefit to families. Instead of excluding children from OGS, parents should be motivated to involve them and playfully teach them how to buy food. Online grocery stores could, for example, support an interactive shopping process for both children and parents by means of providing learning material, additional information, educational videos, etc.

3.5.2 Implications for Public Policy and Consumer Protection

Consumers often feel unprotected, for example with regard to the data they reveal during OGS, the intransparent storage and transport of the products, or the seemingly manipulative marketing strategies of the providers. However, consumers often also do not know which laws and policies are already in place for providers. Educational work should be done in this regard. On the other hand, it does indeed seem that providers at least sometimes do not meet the standards and legal requirements and therewith confirm and fuel the fears of many consumers. It is therefore necessary that the existing logistical and organizational structures are (more frequently) controlled by a higher authority and that the noncompliance with laws carries consequences for the providers. Quality labels should be used to reward good providers and to identify them to consumers.

In addition, public policy should pay special attention to the vulnerable consumer groups and how they are influenced by the digitization of grocery shopping. Some might need help with the conversion. Policies to help for instance individuals with impaired mobility to use OGS may be highly beneficial, for example through financial support or OGS courses. In addition, the changing role of children in the grocery shopping process should be monitored and, if necessary, it should be intervened. Public policy and consumer protection should also educate parents about the benefits of keeping children involved in food shopping and of providing opportunities for children to learn about grocery shopping, food and nutrition.

3.6 Appendix I: Coding Scheme

The qualitative results of all three studies were coded using one comprehensive coding scheme (see Table 6). This coding scheme reflected the customer perspective. Its core consisted of five FWB dimensions (physical, emotional, social, intellectual, self-determined), which were each subdivided into four to eight codes. These individual codes were again subdivided into "positive" and "negative", depending on the participants' subjective judgements.

Table 6: List of codes

Codes	Meaning	
	Positive	Negative
Physical FWB		
Physical constraints	Enables convenient shopping for those with physical restrictions such as people who have problems with vision or walking.	Complicates shopping for those with physical restrictions such as people who have problems with vision or walking.
Physical activity	Fosters activities that positively influence physical well-being such as the prevention of overexertion, or taking a walk and getting fresh air.	Fosters activities that negatively affect physical well-being such as too little exercise, overexertion, and too little time outdoors.

Codes	Meaning	
	Positive	Negative
Health-related nutrition	Supports nutrition-related measures that are necessary due to illness or physical complaints such as a restricted diet due to diabetes or allergies.	Impedes nutrition-related measures that are necessary due to illness or physical complaints such as restricted diet due to diabetes or allergies.
Body-related goals	Supports nutrition-related decisions that are supposed to positively influence the body such as vegan and sugar-free diets.	Impedes nutrition-related decisions that are likely to positively influence the body, and supports nutrition-related decisions that are likely to negatively influence the body such as more sweets and fewer vegetables.
Emotional FWB		
Trust	Customers have a high level of trust in the shopping channel in general and/or in providers and their goods and services in particular.	Customers have a low level of trust in the shopping channel in general and/or in providers and their goods and services in particular.
Emotional FWB		
Spontaneity	Customers are satisfied with the number of spontaneous and impulsive decisions, purchases, and consumption experiences that are possible.	Customers are not satisfied with the number of spontaneous and impulsive decisions, purchases, and consumption experiences that are possible.
Emotional control	Consumers are satisfied with the extent to which controlled, rational, and functional behavior is supported.	Consumers are not satisfied with the extent to which controlled, rational, and functional behavior is supported.
Purchase-related emotions	Positive emotions triggered or strengthened by a purchase, such as joy, fun, relaxation. This includes emotions experienced prior to and after shopping.	Negative emotions triggered or strengthened by a purchase, such as stress, frustration, anger. This also includes emotions prior to and after shopping.
Sensory experiences	Positive perceptions of smelling, feeling, tasting, and seeing during the shopping processes.	The absence or decrease of positive perceptions of smelling, feeling, tasting, and seeing during the shopping processes.
Relation to food	The emotional relationship with food is strengthened.	The emotional relationship with food is weakened.

Codes	Meaning	
	Positive	**Negative**
Variety/change	Positively perceived changes in scenery, and breaks in everyday (working) life.	The absence of positive breaks or changes of scenery.
Emotional ritual	Shopping as a positively perceived and cherished ritual/habit.	An interruption of a cherished (daily) ritual, or a disturbance in everyday life.
Social FWB		
Social interaction	Supports positive interactions and contact with other people, and/or reduces negative encounters and experiences.	Reduces positive interactions and contact with other people, and/or increases negative encounters and experiences.
Personal service	A positive perception of a personal service.	A negative perception of or a somehow lacking/insufficient personal service.
Time spent with family and friends	Shopping can support the time spent with family and friends by allowing more time for other activities, or can itself be a social event.	Shopping can negatively affect the time spent with family/friends by taking time away from positive activities, or by negatively affecting the time spent together, such as by increasing stress.
Socialization	Supports the socialization process of children, facilitated by joint family purchases (including preparations and follow-ups).	Impedes the food socialization process of children.
Social responsibility	Consideration of consequences for humans, animals, environment, and the (local) economy.	No or insufficient consideration of consequences for humans, animals, environment, and the (local) economy.
Intellectual FWB		
Shopping competence/ informed decision	Purchasing is simplified and an informed decision supported by, for instance, better (price) comparisons, easier orientation, or more (product) information.	Purchases and an informed decisions are made more difficult by, for instance, cognitive overload or a lack of information.
New experiences	Supports new experiences, such as by fostering the discovery of new products, providers, or ways of shopping.	Impedes new experiences, such as by hampering the discovery of new products, providers, or ways of shopping.
Food socialization	Children's socialization process regarding nutrition and food shopping is positively influenced.	Children's socialization process regarding nutrition and food shopping is negatively influenced.

Codes	Meaning	
	Positive	Negative
Food literacy	The development of nutrition literacy, food literacy, and/or cooking skills is supported.	The development of nutrition literacy, food literacy, and/or cooking skills is made more difficult.
Background knowledge	Background knowledge of the shopping channel is pronounced and supports purchasing.	Background knowledge of the shopping channel is limited and hinders purchasing.
Creative, inspiring activity	Purchasing is seen as a creative, inspiring activity.	Purchasing is not seen as a creative, inspiring activity, and/or inhibits creative, inspiring experiences.
Self-determined FWB		
Self-determination	Promotes self-determination and independence, such as through self-determined product selection, an everyday life tailored to one's own needs and wishes, and shopping independently of one's location.	Dependence on external factors that make it difficult or impossible to make self-determined decisions, and to shape one's own everyday life freely and according to one's own needs and wishes.
Use of time	Saves time.	Wastes time.
Use of money	Supports good budget planning and use, such as by reducing costs and offering attractive prices and discounts.	Inhibits good budget planning and use, such as through high delivery costs or high product prices.
Effort	Purchasing is associated with a low or positively perceived effort.	Purchasing is associated with a rather high and unpleasant effort.
Assortment	A high availability and accessibility of a great variety of products.	A comparably low availability and accessibility of a restricted variety of products.

3.7 Appendix II: Questionnaire of the Survey Study

In the following, questions and scales from the questionnaire of the third study (the survey study) are presented.

Satisfaction with food-related life scale (Grunert et al., 2007; $\alpha = 0.857$)

- My life in relation to food and meals is close to my ideal.
- With regard to food, the conditions of my life are excellent.
- I am generally pleased with my food.

- Food and meals give me satisfaction in daily life.
- Food and meals are positive elements in my life.
- When I think of my next meal, I only see problems, obstacles and disappointments.
- I wish my meals were a much more pleasant part of my life.

Open-ended questions about the influence of OGS on FWB
- What do you like about purchasing groceries online?
- What do you not like about purchasing groceries online?
- What influence does online grocery shopping have on the availability and accessibility of groceries for you?
- What influence does online grocery shopping have on your physical well-being? Please consider both short- and long-term influences.
- What influence does online grocery shopping have on your emotional well-being?
- What influence does online grocery shopping have on your social life and well-being?
  Explanation: Social well-being refers to your relationships and interactions with other people, and also to your relationship with your environment, as well as the responsibilities and attitudes you have towards the environment.
- What influence does online grocery shopping have on your intellectual well-being?
  Explanation: In terms of intellectual well-being, we regard food shopping as an activity in which one must actively apply knowledge, and consciously think and concentrate. For example, when buying food, you need to know recipes and where to find what kind of information. You also need to be able to understand product information. Moreover, online grocery shopping could be stimulating and inspiring to the mind.
- What influence does online grocery shopping have on your knowledge and skills in relation to nutrition in general, and the purchase, preparation, and consumption of food?
- What influence does online grocery shopping have on your compliance with nutritional goals?
- What influence does online grocery shopping have on your spiritual well-being?
  Explanation: Spiritual well-being concerns well-being that relates to one's values, beliefs, and religious convictions.

4 Fifty-One Reasons Consumers Shop for Groceries Online: A Mixed-Methods Examination of Motives for Online Grocery Shopping in the United States and Germany[3]

4.1 Introduction

The overall goal of this paper is to examine and compare the motives for consumers to shop for groceries online in the United States (US) and Germany, while a concrete aim is to extend our understanding of these motives across countries, and to examine to what extent compliance with nutritional goals and healthy eating play a role in the channel choice of present-day consumers. The answers to these questions will help to understand to what extent shoppers in different countries engage in online grocery shopping (OGS) in order to promote healthy eating, and formulate recommendations for future research and practice on the potential of OGS as a tool to promote healthier nutrition choices.

OGS is a growing component of the retail food environment (Deloitte, 2018). Recent surveys have found that globally about one in four consumers currently shops for foods online, with more than half indicating a willingness to do so in the future (Meena, Swerdlow, and Kumar, 2018; Nielsen, 2015). These forecasts are positive, and predict that the number of people who shop for at least part of their groceries online will further increase in the future (Forrester, 2018), giving rise to great interest in why people are shifting to online channels, and moving away from traditional brick-and-mortar stores. Nutritionists and public health professionals are particularly interested in understanding whether this shift could be used to leverage online retailing platforms to promote healthier purchase and consumption habits (Epstein et al., 2016; Pitts et al., 2018; Sacks et al., 2016).

---

3 A slightly modified version of the essay will be published in the Journal of Food Products Marketing; Reference: Blitstein, Jonathan, Frentz, Florentine, Jilcott Pitts, Stephanie Bell. A mixed-method examination of reported benefits of online grocery shopping in the United States and Germany: Is health a factor? Journal of Food Products Marketing, in press.

F. Frentz, *The Pursuit of Food Well-Being*, Handel und Internationales Marketing Retailing and International Marketing,
https://doi.org/10.1007/978-3-658-30366-2_4

There are many possible reasons for consumers to turn to online channels for groceries. The review by Pitts and colleagues (2018) presents a summary of the limited literature on this topic. Initiation of OGS has been tied to major life events and transitions such as caring for a sick relative or the birth of a child (Elms, de Kervenoael, and Hallsworth, 2016; Hand et al., 2009). Other studies have found that time savings and product quality and availability predict intentions to shop online (Zhu and Semeijn, 2015). OGS may also be influenced cultural and geographic factors. A study that looked at consumers' OGS behavior in four European countries found that reasons for OGS varied depending on country of residence (A.T. Kearney, 2012). These differences may reflect market penetration of online grocery retail; structural differences in brick-and-mortar retail markets; and differences in culture, lifestyle, and attitude.

Research has shown that OGS can have both negative and positive effects, with regard to nutrition and healthy eating. Some studies have found that concerns about freshness, bruising, and food safety (Hand et al., 2009; Lennon et al., 2009; Nielsen, 2015) may make consumers less likely to purchase fresh and perishable foods online such as fruits, vegetables, and fish that are essential for a balanced diet (Clark and Wright, 2007; Elms, de Kervenoael, and Hallsworth, 2016). However, a study by Appelhans and colleagues (2013) found that consumers living in an urban food desert who were given a voucher for OGS used at least some of the voucher on fresh and perishable foods. OGS may also help to promote healthier eating by decreasing impulse purchases (Campo and Breugelmans, 2015; Gorin et al., 2007; Huyghe et al., 2017) and facilitating greater access to healthy foods (Appelhans et al., 2013). Because research in this area is still in its infancy, further studies are needed to explore the role of OGS on consumer nutrition and how it could be used to promote healthy eating (Pitts et al., 2018).

The literature describing personal motives for online grocery shopping includes two types of studies. First, quantitative studies used close-ended survey methods to test a priori hypotheses. These studies can be characterized as confirmatory; they assess motivations derived from academic theory and tend to include fairly robust samples. Second, qualitative studies used semi-structured interviews and ethnographic methods. These studies can be characterized as exploratory; they uncover participants' experiences but tend to include a small number of participants.

The present study fills an important gap for public policy practitioners interested in consumers' motivations for OGS. It uses a content analytic approach to derive and quantify a set of motivations and benefits from participants who responded to surveys that included an open-ended question asking them why they shop for groceries online. The surveys were conducted in the United States

(US) and Germany and therefore additionally allow the comparison of consumers' motives between two countries.

4.2 Materials and Methods

4.2.1 Data Collection

Two surveys examining food retail shopping habits provided raw data for this secondary synthesis and analysis. The surveys, one conducted in the US and one conducted in Germany, included comparable questions on participants' characteristics and reasons to shop for food online. Both studies were designed to compare people who shop for at least some of their groceries online to those who prefer traditional brick-and-mortar stores and to understand the factors that influence the decision to shop for groceries online. The study conducted in the US recruited participants through Amazon's Mechanical Turk (MTurk), an online labor market that can be used to collect survey data from a panel that is demographically diverse and represents all 50 states (Buhrmester, Kwang, and Gosling, 2011). Research studies using MTurk have demonstrated that MTurk respondents provide accurate information (Goodman, Cryder, and Cheema, 2012). The study conducted in Germany employed a convenience sampling approach across a number of German towns (e.g., Berlin, Cologne, and Siegen) to reach a heterogeneous and demographically diverse sample. Participants completed either a paper-and-pencil or an electronic version (i.e., online) of the survey. Eligible respondents for the two studies were over 18 years of age, were at least partly responsible for shopping the groceries for their household, and resided in the US or Germany.

4.2.2 Data Coding and Synthesis

The study followed a qualitatively driven, mixed-methods approach (Leech and Onwuegbuzie, 2007; Schoonenboom and Johnson, 2017). Data synthesis employed a bottom-up, content-analysis methodology with emergent coding (Hsieh and Shannon, 2005). Open-ended, verbatim responses to the question "why do you shop for food online?" were downloaded and merged into a single database. Some responses were brief and simple (i.e., one or two words or a single phrase); others were long and elaborate, listing multiple reasons or including detailed justifications. Reponses that included multipart answers were logically parsed; for example, if a participant responded that they shopped online to "save money and time", the response was parsed into two responses: (1) saves money and (2) saves time.

Next, researchers examined the verbatim responses and generated lists of codes representing benefits of OGS. Discussing innovations in general, Rogers (1995) defined benefits as relative advantages that reflect the degree to which an innovation is perceived as being able to provide more benefits than that which is superseded. Because OGS differs considerably from its offline equivalent and can be regarded as a discontinuous innovation (i.e., one that entails a new product or service that induces new behavioral patterns) (Robinson et al., 2007), Roger's definition can be applied to the OGS context where the perceived relative advantages are essential because they are important factors in the decision-making process that is associated with the adoption of the innovation. This has been confirmed by Forsythe and colleagues (2006) who looked at the perceived benefits and risks of online shopping and defined the perceived benefits in this context as consumers' "subjective perception of gain from shopping online" (p. 59).

Through an iterative process, researchers derived and compared lists of benefits and resolved differences through discussion until consensus was reached. This process resulted in a set of 51 benefits organized in eight superordinate categories (i.e., motives), with 2 to 11 benefits nested in each motive. Thus, the overarching motives, under which thematically similar benefits are bundled, emphasize qualities that differentiate the experience of online shopping from shopping at brick-and-mortar stores and drive consumers to shop for groceries online. A ninth category labeled "Other" was included for responses (approximately 2%) that consisted of ambiguous single words or clipped phrases that did not fit into any of the defined categories.

To create the analytic dataset, the researchers double-coded a randomly selected sample of responses (approximately 5%), compared codes, and discussed differences in coding. After two rounds of comparisons, inter-rater agreement of greater than 90% was reached, and the remaining responses were divided between two researchers. Data analysis consisted of quantification and summarization of reported motivations, which was carried out using SAS software. To prevent bias in the results, a benefit was only counted once per participant; this reduced the total number of benefits in the analysis from 1,056 to 1,013.

4.3 Results

The sample included slightly more females (55.9%) than males with a mean age of 33.2 years (see Table 7). Overall, 46.1% of the sample lived in a household

Table 7: Demographic characteristics of the participants

Demographics	Total (N = 388)	US Sample (N = 149)	German Sample (N = 239)
Sex (% female)	55.9%	57.7%	54.6%
Age (mean, standard deviation	33.2 (11.9)	37.1 (11.8)	30.8 (11.4)
Lives with another adult (% yes)	46.1%	63.8%	35.1%
Distance to brick-and-mortar store in miles (mean, standard deviation)	3.0 (4.1)	4.7 (5.1)	1.6 (1.9)
Education			
Less than high school	0.5%	0.0%	0.8%
High school or equivalent	9.0%	12.8%	6.7%
Some college/technical school	39.7%	34.2%	43.1%
College graduate	48.7%	52.3%	46.4%

with another adult; however, living with another adult was more common among US respondents than among German respondents (63.8% v. 35.1%). On average, US respondents reported traveling approximately three times farther than respondents from Germany to the nearest brick-and-mortar grocery store (4.7 miles v. 1.6 miles).

The coding process resulted in the identification of 51 benefits nested in eight motives (see the Appendix for an overview). The most commonly noted motive, "economy", refers to the consumers' belief that OGS provides a benefit in terms of costs and efficiencies. The motive was mentioned by 70.6% of the total sample and included four benefits: saving money, saving time, saving fuel, and the ability to use special coupons. We included both financial and time savings within the category of "economy", noting that time is an important resource (Chatzitheochari and Class, 2012) and that time-poor households may make suboptimal choices due to a lack of flexibility in their daily schedules that affects food acquisition and nutritional quality (Devine et al., 2009; Jabs and Devine, 2006). Overall, the proportions of responses in this category were similarly distributed among the US (67.1%) and German respondents (72.8%); however, more German respondents mentioned saving money and more US respondents mentioned saving time.

The second most frequently mentioned motive was "product availability and variety". This category was mentioned by 50.3% of the total sample and included 11 benefits that described online shopping's ability to provide access to more products, including local and regional foods, new products, and specialty products (e.g., for special dietary needs). Substantially more German (72.0%)

than US respondents (15.4%) mentioned benefits in this category. The German respondents especially highlighted the fact that OGS increases the availability of more and unusual products and brands.

The third most commonly cited motive was "stressors," which emphasized online grocery shopping as a means to reduce or avoid the stresses commonly involved in shopping at brick-and-mortar stores. The 10 benefits in this category included avoiding environmental conditions (i.e., bad weather, driving) and in-store factors (e.g., standing in lines, crowded aisles). This motive was identified by 39.4% of the respondents overall and was mentioned more frequently by US (67.8%) than German respondents (21.8%). Benefits most commonly noted by US respondents included the reduced stress and hassles of shopping, the reduced contact with others and crowds, and the absence of lines.

"Comfort" was the fourth most commonly cited motive, mentioned by 36.6% of respondents. Benefits related to comfort included the convenience of shopping online and the ability to shop from home. The word *convenience* was used frequently, but the code "convenience" was only applied when more specific information was not present in participants' response. When more specific information was mentioned (e.g., home delivery makes it more convenient), the response was coded to the more specific benefit. Responses in this category were similar among US (39.6%) and German respondents (34.7%).

The fifth most commonly cited motive, labeled "innovations", included seven benefits that referred to technological and business adaptions that advantage OGS over brick-and-mortar shopping. Examples of these advantages include ease of payment, the ability to set up recurring orders, transparency/price comparison, and flexibility (i.e., one can shop anywhere at any time). Responses in this category were similar among German (36.0%) and US respondents (32.9%).

Few participants mentioned the remaining three categories, which are labeled "physical/ structural barriers," "food knowledge", and "social image and lifestyle." Physical/structural barriers included mobility issues such as not being able to carry groceries up multiple flights of stairs and not having access to a car; responses in this category were similarly prevalent among the US and German respondents. Food knowledge included the ability to access product reviews, recipes, and tools that support meal planning, and to receive additional information about foods and nutrition. Responses in this category were more common among German (10.9%) than US respondents (2.0%). Social image and lifestyle included seven benefits such as the ability to purchase environmentally friendly products (e.g., less package waste) and more socially conscious (e.g., fair trade) products. German participants were somewhat more likely than US participants to endorse these motives (7.1% v. 2.7%).

4.4 Discussion

The research goal of this paper was to examine and compare the motives behind consumers' decision to shop for groceries online in the US and Germany. We aimed to extend our understanding of consumer motivations to engage in OGS across countries, and to examine to what extent compliance with nutritional goals and healthy eating plays a role in the channel choice of contemporary consumers.

To answer these questions, we made use of two surveys that were conducted in the US and in Germany, and that investigated why consumers shop for groceries online by means of an open-ended question, among others. Because the answers were open-ended and not predefined, we were able to see which benefits were really most significant to participants and had a significant influence on their decisions. To our knowledge, this is the first study to have employed a content analytic approach with bottom-up coding of participant responses to examine consumers' motives for online grocery shopping across countries. Our findings add to the current literature by providing a unique taxonomy of motives for food shopping behavior that are derived from over 1,000 open-ended responses provided by close to 400 individuals from two different countries.

The 51 benefits we identified demonstrate that consumers are grocery shopping online for a wide array of reasons, ranging from economizing to expressing aspects of their social identity. The benefits that were most often mentioned are functional, i.e., they are related to utilitarian needs (Sheth, 1983), such as saving of money and time or the increased availability and accessibility of products. These findings confirm previous research on online shopping in general and OGS in particular that suggest that functional motives are highly relevant in these contexts (e.g., Al-Debei, Akroush, and Ashouri, 2014; To, Liao, and Lin, 2007), including time savings (Harris, Dall'Olmo, and Hand, 2017; Van Droogenbroeck and Van Hove, 2017), lower costs (Appelhans et al., 2013; Jayasankaraprasad and Kathyayani, 2014), and a greater product selection (Melis et al., 2015; Ramachandran, Karthick, and Kumar, 2011).

This paper extends the literature by showing how these motives are put together, and how important the individual benefits, that make up the motives, are for consumers. Furthermore, we demonstrate the diverging importance of benefits for US and German consumers. This is the first time that such a comparison of US and German consumers with regard to their perceived benefits of OGS has been made. It is noteworthy, for example, that German respondents appear more interested in saving money, while US respondents are more interested in saving time. Furthermore, the availability of a wider range of products not available in local, brick-and-mortar stores was an important motivation among German respondents, whereas US respondents found more value in avoiding stressors commonly associated with brick-and-mortar shopping.

These differences in motivation may reflect structural differences in retail food environments. In Germany, the food retail landscape is dominated by discount stores and supermarkets, and characterized by a high store density and short distances to food stores (Teller, Kotzab, and Grant, 2012); however, most stores in Germany offer only a small range of products, compared to their US counterparts. Additionally, the variety of products in German grocery stores is comparably limited, as the number of foreign and unusual products, which might account for German consumers placing more emphasis on the increased availability and accessibility of products through OGS. The desire of US participants to reduce the stressors of in-store grocery shopping by shopping online could also have its origin in existing market structures. In the US, the food retail density is generally lower, while individual stores are bigger, and as a result, the journey to and shopping time within stores are on average longer, the transportation of purchases more difficult, and the stressors within stores, such as crowds and lines, are more pronounced.

Interestingly, the findings indicate that nutritional goals and healthy eating play a minor role in the channel choice of contemporary consumers. Only 2% of the US participants mentioned this aspect of motivation, while 10.8% of German respondents stated that they engage in OGS to improve their food-related knowledge and skills or to meet nutritional goals. The fact that most consumers do not shop online for the sake of their diet may be due to the fact that the benefits are not yet sufficiently pronounced, consumers do not recognize the possible benefits, or nutrition is simply not considered important enough.

Even though few participants reported that they engage in OGS to support a healthy diet, the findings still indicate that consumers in the US and Germany could be nudged into a healthier direction in the online food retail context. For instance, the US participants placed considerable value on escaping the stress of brick-and-mortar shopping, and on being able to shop as efficiently and easily as possible; in response, healthier choices could be made easily accessible, such as by always being placed at the top of the web page and/or presented prominently. As Breugelmans, Campo, and Gijsbrechts (2007) have noted, the probability that a consumer will select a particular product can be increased by placing it at the top of the screen or near focal items. Furthermore, German participants paid especially attention to prices, so healthier products could be advertised with discounts in German online grocery stores.

4.5 Limitations and Directions for Future Research

The findings reported in this paper are subject to the following limitations that underscore the need for additional research. First, as with all content analyses, some coding decisions are inherently subjective. For example, we categorized "avoid impulse purchases" under the motivation "stressors" because respondents tended to see impulse purchase items as a characteristic of the brick-and-mortar store environment. Other may disagree with this approach, preferring to categorize impulse purchasing as a health-related benefit. Second, although the data we combined were captured contemporaneously, we acknowledge that variations in data collection methodology may have influenced our samples. Thus, comparisons between US and German respondents are descriptive only. Third, we did not ask respondents whether their online shopping was based on home delivery or curb-side pick-up (i.e., order online, pick up at store). This difference has not received much attention in research literature but could influence the perceived value of online shopping as well as the types of foods consumers are willing to purchase.

4.6 Appendix: Coding List

Table 8 presents the benefits and overarching motives identified by the bottom-up content analysis, and the (relative) frequencies with which these were named in total and by the German and US samples, respectively.

Table 8: List of codes and their (relative) frequencies

Categories (motives with subordinate benefits)	**Total N = 388**	**US N = 149**	**Germany N = 239**
Economy	274 (70.6%)	100 (67.1%)	174 (72.8%)
Save money/better price	119 (30.8%)	24 (16.1%)	95 (39.8%)
Save time	117 (30.2%)	58 (38.9%)	59 (24.7%)
Coupons and special deals	29 (7.5%)	10 (6.7%)	19 (8.0%)
Save gas	9 (2.3%)	8 (5.4%)	1 (0.4%)
Availability and variety	195 (50.3%)	23 (15.4%)	172 (72.0%)
More products/brands	102 (26.3%)	13 (8.7%)	89 (37.2%)
New/unusual products	28 (7.2%)	0 (0.0%)	28 (11.7%)
High quality products	15 (3.9%)	4 (2.7%)	11 (4.6%)
Larger quantity options	13 (3.4%)	0 (0.0%)	13 (5.4%)

Categories (motives with subordinate benefits)	Total N = 388	US N = 149	Germany N = 239
Special dietary needs (e.g., allergies, vegan diet)	10 (2.6%)	1 (0.7%)	9 (3.8%)
Increased food variety	10 (2.6%)	2 (1.3%)	8 (3.5%)
Access to local/regional foods	5 (1.3%)	0 (0.0%)	5 (2.1%)
Everything located in one place	4 (1.0%)	1 (0.7%)	3 (1.3%)
More organic foods	3 (0.8%)	0 (0.0%)	3 (1.3%)
Rarely/never out of stock	3 (0.8%)	2 (1.4%)	1 (0.4%)
More fresh foods	2 (0.5%)	0 (0.0%)	2 (0.8%)
Stressors	153 (39.4%)	101 (67.8%)	52 (21.8%)
Reduce stress/hassles of shopping	34 (8.8%)	20 (13.4%)	14 (5.9%)
Avoid contact with others and crowds	27 (7.0%)	27 (18.1%)	0 (0.0%)
Avoid lines	23 (5.9%)	16 (10.7%)	7 (2.9%)
Avoid physical effort	22 (5.7%)	3 (2.0%)	19 (8.0%)
Avoid compulsion/impulse shopping	12 (3.1%)	8 (5.4%)	4 (1.7%)
Avoid driving/don't have to travel	11 (2.8%)	6 (4.0%)	5 (2.1%)
Dislike brick-and-mortar shopping	10 (2.6%)	9 (6.0%)	1 (0.4%)
Avoid need to shop with children	9 (2.3%)	9 (6.0%)	0 (0.0%)
Avoid bad weather	4 (1.0%)	3 (2.0%)	1 (0.4%)
Safety (personal)	1 (0.3%)	0 (0.0%)	1 (0.4%)
Comfort	142 (36.6%)	59 (39.6%)	83 (34.7%)
Convenient/easy (w/o additional clarification)	128 (33.0%)	54 (36.2%)	74 (31.0%)
Shop from home	14 (3.6%)	5 (3.4%)	9 (3.8%)
Innovations	135 (34.8%)	49 (32.9%)	86 (36.0%)
Delivery	57 (14.7%)	19 (12.8%)	38 (15.9%)
Flexibility	27 (7.0%)	6 (4.0%)	21 (8.8%)
Easier navigation	23 (5.9%)	12 (8.1%)	11 (4.6%)
Transparency/price comparison	16 (4.1%)	2 (1.3%)	14 (5.9%)
Enjoy/fun online shopping	6 (1.6%)	5 (3.4%)	1 (0.4%)
Use of recurring orders	5 (1.3%)	5 (3.4%)	0 (0.0%)
Easier payment	1 (0.3%)	0 (0.0%)	1 (0.4%)
Physical/structural barriers	45 (11.6%)	18 (12.1%)	27 (11.3%)
No car	12 (3.1%)	6 (4.0%)	6 (2.5%)
Brick-and-mortar store is too far	9 (2.3%)	1 (0.7%)	8 (3.4%)

Categories **(motives with subordinate benefits)**	**Total** **N = 388**	**US** **N = 149**	**Germany** **N = 239**
Illness/mobility/limited ability to carry	19 (4.9%)	10 (6.7%)	9 (3.8%)
Difficult to access home	4 (1.0%)	1 (0.7%)	3 (1.3%)
Age-related constrains	1 (0.3%)	0 (0.0%)	1 (0.4%)
Food knowledge	28 (7.5%)	3 (2.0%)	25 (10.8%)
More information (e.g., customer reviews)	10 (2.6%)	0 (0.0%)	10 (4.2%)
Planning food/meals	7 (1.8%)	3 (2.0%)	4 (1.7%)
Discovery/try new foods	5 (1.3%)	0 (2.0%)	4 (1.7%)
Improving cooking skills/recipes available	4 (1.0%)	0 (0.0%)	4 (1.7%)
Reach personal goals	2 (0.5%)	0 (0.0%)	2 (0.8%)
Reach health-related goals	1 (0.3%)	0 (0.0%)	1 (0.4%)
Social image and lifestyle	21 (5.4%)	4 (2.7%)	17 (7.1%)
More time for other things (e.g., with family)	5 (1.3%)	2 (1.3%)	3 (1.3%)
Environmentally conscious (e.g., reduce waste)	4 (1.0%)	1 (0.7%)	3 (1.3%)
Eco-conscious products (e.g., fair trade)	3 (0.8%)	0 (0.0%)	3 (1.3%)
Modern lifestyle	3 (0.8%)	1 (0.7%)	2 (0.8%)
Exclusivity	3 (0.8%)	0 (0.0%)	3 (1.3%)
Advertising/role models	2 (0.5%)	0 (0.0%)	2 (0.8%)
Support local/small shops	1 (0.3%)	0 (0.0%)	1 (0.4%)
Other	19 (4.9%)	3 (2.0%)	16 (6.7%)

5 Better Marketing for More Food Well-Being: How Retailers and Marketers Can Contribute to Children's Food Well-Being in the Food Retail Context[4]

5.1 Introduction

The research goal of this paper is to examine the influence of grocery shopping on the food well-being (FWB) of children[5] and to identify measures that different stakeholders can take to contribute to children's development of FWB in the grocery retail context. Special attention will be paid to the role of food retailers, marketers, and public policy makers and the positive contributions they can make to children's FWB. We focus on the grocery retail context because it is a context to which children are often exposed and that has the potential to offer many opportunities for children to develop a good relationship with food. In the long run, positive grocery shopping experiences are expected to strengthen children's FWB (Bublitz et al., 2019; Hémar-Nicolas and Ezan, 2018; McNeal, 2007; Wingert et al., 2014) and to contribute to decreasing their risk of becoming overweight and/or developing food-related diseases.

Nutrition and obesity have been described as "some of the most pressing research topics" of the present time (Mick, 2006, p. 2). The rates of overweight and obesity continue to increase (Ravussin and Ryan, 2017). In 2016, more than 1.9 billion adults were overweight, of whom 650 million were obese (WHO, 2018a). The growing number of overweight and obese children is particularly alarming. In the past four decades, the number of obese children and adolescents between five and 19 years old has risen worldwide more than tenfold (WHO, 2017). In 2016, almost 340 million children, i.e., almost one in every five children, were considered overweight or obese (WHO, 2018b). Health-related consequences include increased risks for diabetes, cardiovascular diseases, certain cancers, and various psychological illnesses, resulting in more disability-adjusted life years and lower life expectancy (e.g., Bacha and Gidding, 2016; Grover et

4 Co-authors: Regina Mukhamedzyanova, Felizitas Mayenschein, Prof. Dr. Hanna Schramm-Klein

5 For simplicity, the term "children" is used in the following to refer to children and adolescents up to 17 years of age.

F. Frentz, *The Pursuit of Food Well-Being*, Handel und Internationales
Marketing Retailing and International Marketing,
https://doi.org/10.1007/978-3-658-30366-2_5

al., 2015; Mohana et al., 2014; Morrison et al., 2015; Luppino et al., 2010). Economic consequences include increased health care costs and productivity losses (Goettler, Grosse, and Sonntag, 2017; Scharff, 2012).

Because the consequences of overweight are serious both for the individuals concerned and for society as a whole, measures must be taken to counteract the overweight and obesity "pandemic" (Meldrum, Morris, and Gambone, 2017). One sustainable, future-oriented approach is to start interventions at the point when consumers' relationships with food start: childhood. From an early age, children should be supported in developing the knowledge and skills and in perceiving the positive external stimuli they need to avoid becoming overweight in the first place and to develop and maintain a long-lasting high level of FWB (Baur and Garnett, 2019; Lumeng et al., 2015; Ravanbakht, Skinner, and Perrin, 2017), i.e., a positive subjective and objective evaluation of their physical, emotional, social, intellectual, spiritual, and self-determined relationship with food (see Chapter 2 and 3 for a more detailed explanation of the definition of FWB).

Therefore, our research goal is to investigate how family grocery purchases influence children's FWB and which measures can be taken by different stakeholders to shape food purchasing in such a way that it is most beneficial for children's FWB. The food purchasing context was chosen because, on the one hand, grocery stores are as inevitable as they are indispensable for the food supply and are therefore visited on an often-daily basis by caregivers and their children. On the other hand, grocery stores are viewed as an essential part of the "obesogenic environment" (e.g., Cobb et al., 2015; Cohen et al., 2015). Many researchers have accused grocery stores of fostering weight gain and obesity because they make ultra-processed and unhealthy foods easily available and accessible and even promote them (e.g., Charlton et al., 2015; Monteiro et al., 2013; Virtanen et al., 2015). In addition, grocery stores are now also targeting children and encouraging them to make unhealthy purchases, for instance, through the specific placement of products on shelves (Ebster, Wagner, and Neumueller, 2009), the placement of sweets and candies in the checkout area (Horsley et al., 2014; Wingert et al., 2014; Campbell et al., 2012), or advertising campaigns aimed specifically at children (Mehta et al., 2012; Harris, Schwartz, and Brownell, 2009; Berry and McMullen, 2008).

However, recent research suggests that grocery shopping with children can also be a valuable learning experience for children if used appropriately (e.g., Hémar-Nicolas and Ezan, 2018; Marshall, 2014; Wingert et al., 2014). "Food shopping is another way parents teach consumption and marketplace knowledge to children, training them to evaluate and compare prices, examine and interpret food labels, and make informed food choices, as well as imparting a broader array of planning and budgeting skills" (Bublitz et al., 2019, p. 144). Furthermore, the grocery shopping context offers opportunities for children to develop emotional coping strategies, for example, by enabling them to learn how to exercise impulse control and especially how to regulate in-store impulses while shopping (Mau et al., 2019). However, many caregivers do not seem to realize these potential benefits of grocery shopping for the development of their children's FWB. Instead, they often find grocery shopping with their children stressful and onerous and, as such, sometimes even avoid taking their children shopping with them (Haselhoff, Faupel, and Holzmüller, 2014; Schuhen et al., 2017).

Since both positive and negative influences seem to be possible, it is necessary to explore exactly which influences exist and which factors promote their effects. Insights into the influences of grocery shopping on children's FWB and, based on them, the creation of intervention measures to improve children's FWB are relevant not only for the well-being of children and, consequently, for the well-being of society as a whole but also for the success of food retailers and marketers. International organizations, public policy makers and researchers have already called on grocery retailers and marketers to acknowledge their social and moral responsibility by helping consumers reach a higher level of well-being (e.g., Hawkes, 2013; Hutter, Hoffmann, and Mai, 2016; Schrempf, 2014; Swinburn, Egger, and Raza, 1999). Such expectations are in line with current trends and customer wishes (Havas Group, 2017) and, according to the quality-of-life marketing concept and the positive marketing concept, are a promising approach to strengthening relationships with customers and supporting the achievement of long-term success (Mittelstaedt, Killbourne, and Shultz II, 2015; Sirgy and Lee, 1996). Thus, "under the pressure of regulators and a part of the public opinion, food retailers are therefore urged to endorse their social responsibility and, pragmatically, need to consider childhood well-being as a level of competitiveness and positive reputation" (Hémar-Nicolas and Ezan, 2018). Furthermore, policy makers and consumer protectors are relevant stakeholders because they need to understand how children are influenced during grocery shopping so that they can intervene early to limit negative consequences and promote positive consequences. The same observation applies to caregivers. Caregivers are able to promote their children's FWB during food shopping only if they are sufficiently informed about the underlying mechanisms and interrelationships that shape the influence of food shopping on children's FWB.

Studies have already been conducted that focused on the role and behavior of children during grocery shopping. These studies have investigated, for instance, the interaction between caregivers and children (Calderon et al., 2017), the influence of children on purchase decisions (Page et al., 2018), the influence of external factors such as marketing campaigns on children's product choices (Wingert et al., 2014), and what caregivers teach their children about social rules and norms in the grocery shopping context (Kharuhayothin and Kerrane, 2018). Although there is one study in which children's idea of FWB in a grocery retail context was examined (Hémar-Nicolas and Ezan, 2018), no study so far comprehensively investigated the influence of grocery shopping on all FWB dimensions that are presented in recent FWB literature (Ares et al., 2016; King et al., 2015).

Therefore, this paper presents the results of an ethnographic, observational study in which 116 children were observed during shopping trips with their caregivers. The study was conducted in two different store types, an organic grocery store and a supermarket, because it was assumed that the influence of a shopping trip on children's FWB can differ depending on the store's setup, product assortment and marketing measures. The study results, which were analyzed by means of a content analysis in the qualitative data analysis software MAXQDA, show that a combination of the store format characteristics (store layout, product assortment, marketing activities, playing options, and learning opportunities); caregivers' knowledge, abilities and motivation to involve and educate children; and children's current developmental stage determine the type and degree of influence of a grocery shopping trip on children's FWB. Thus, the study provides valuable insights into the effects of family shopping trips on children's FWB and informs recommendations for grocery stores, food marketers, policy makers, and caregivers. The results show that an integrated, collaborative approach is required, which is why all stakeholders are urged to play their parts in the endeavor to improve children's FWB in the long term. The study also points to areas for further research.

5.2 The Concept of Food Well-Being

The concept of FWB is based on a holistic understanding of the role of food in consumers' overall well-being and life quality. It incorporates a recognition that day-to-day food-related activities continuously influence consumers' relationships with food and their overall FWB (Block et al., 2011). One of these day-to-day activities is grocery shopping, which is a noticeably important and influential experience, as it generally occurs on a regular, sometimes even daily, basis. The experiences that consumers have flow into their overall FWB by influencing several subordinate dimensions. Previous research on well-being and FWB has suggested that FWB is primarily subdivided into five dimensions: the physical, emotional, social, intellectual and spiritual dimensions (Ares et al., 2016; King et al., 2015; Roscoe, 2009).

The physical dimension refers to bodily well-being resulting from food-related activities, such as dietary choices and eating habits (Ares et al., 2016; Roscoe, 2009). In our definition, we also include children's physical (in)activity that occurs due to food-related activities, such as walking to a grocery store or carrying grocery purchases or, as a negative example, sitting in the shopping cart while shopping despite the possibility of walking. Emotional well-being refers to the experience and processing of emotions that arise around food-related activities, including the perception, management and expression of emotions as well as coping styles and patterns that are applied in emotionally challenging situations (Adams, Bezner, and Steinhardt, 2016; Hettler, 1980; Roscoe, 2009). The social dimension includes consumers' relationships with others and the environment and the extent to which these are considered and reflected in their food-related purchase and consumption decisions (Hettler, 1980; Roscoe, 2009). Intellectual well-being refers to the degree to which an individual is committed to learning, uses resources to improve his or her own knowledge and competences, and engages in creative and inspiring activities to achieve a satisfying food-related life (Hettler, 1980). The spiritual dimension focuses on the part of one's food-related life that is associated with religious beliefs and convictions (Hawks, 1994). Although children might relate some parts of their food-related life to religious (or perhaps societal) rituals such as Christmas or Hanukkah, based on previous research findings, it can be assumed that the spiritual dimension does not play an important role in usual family grocery shopping in most Western families (Ares et al., 2014; Ares et al., 2013; Hémar-Nicolas and Ezan, 2018). For instance, Ares et al. (2013, 2014) investigated consumers' perception of well-being in a food-related context and repeatedly found that the spiritual dimension was not salient. Therefore, this dimension is not taken into account in the current study. Instead, another dimension is included in this research, which we refer to as the self-determined dimension. A person who scores high at the self-determined dimension is an independent, autonomous individual who is able and willing to make his or her own choices and to be responsible for them, independently of others and external factors (Mugel, Gurviez, and Decrop, 2019; Murphey et al., 1963). For children, the development of self-determination is crucial because in the course of their childhood, they are supposed to evolve into autonomous, self-determined individuals through socialization processes to develop a high level of eudaimonic (a sense of fulfillment and meaningfulness) and hedonic (high levels of positive affect and low levels of negative affect) well-being (Berk, 2011; Deci and Ryan, 2008; McNeal, 2007). This principle also applies to children's food-related lives (Hémar-Nicolas and Ezan, 2018). Therefore, we decided to include the self-determined dimension as a separate dimension in our analysis.

The five dimensions of FWB do not exist independently of each other but rather influence each other and partly even merge into one another (Grunert et al., 2007). Therefore, it is not sufficient to investigate the dimensions separately. To obtain a complete picture of the influence of grocery shopping on FWB and to be able to identify underlying relationships, the influence of grocery shopping on the dimensions must be considered as a whole.

5.3 Evolution of the Food Well-Being Dimensions in Children's Development Stages

The FWB of children in particular has been investigated as a holistic concept only once (Hémar-Nicolas and Ezan, 2018). In this study, the authors examined what well-being means to children in a food context. However, because the data obtained reflected only the subjective views of children, the findings were limited. Furthermore, because children are not just small adults but differ, for example, in terms of their needs, decision-making processes and consumption patterns, it is also not possible to simply transfer the findings of previous FWB-related research on adult consumers to children. Thus, a conceptualization of children's FWB is still lacking and urgently needed.

To be able to investigate the influence of grocery shopping on children's FWB, we first have to understand the development stages that children go through so that we can assess whether children behave according to their ages and are encouraged and challenged adequately. The development process of children can be roughly divided into four overarching development stages: the infant and crawling stage, early childhood, later childhood, and adolescence (Berk, 2011). In the following, we briefly summarize these overarching development stages and the role of grocery shopping in each stage (see Table 9 for an extensive overview).

Infant and crawling stage (0-23 months): Children learn to perceive and discover the world, including grocery stores, with all their senses (Berk, 2011; McNeal, 2007). They show increasingly conditioned and habitualized behavior. Emotional development progresses at a rapid pace (Berk, 2011). Through repeated contact with the supermarket, children can build a relationship with it. They learn to develop and express preferences for products (Malik and Marwaha, 2018; McNeal, 2007) and start to show behavioral self-regulation (Berk, 2011). The social influence of caregivers is essential in this phase because their buying and consumption behavior determines what children will later regard as the norm. Through caregivers, children also become familiar with the supermarket, have their first food shopping experiences and learn to express their wishes (McNeal, 2007; McNeal and Yeh, 1993). Furthermore, children start to identify products and brands and to categorize them according to their functions and properties, develop an evoked set of favorite products, and show target-oriented behavior. They also begin to explore the environment more independently (Berk, 2011; McNeal, 2007).

Early childhood (2-5 years): Children move more independently through the store. They strive for independence and want to make autonomous decisions (Malik and Marwaha, 2018; McNeal, 2007). As this independence is possible only to a limited extent, especially at the beginning, they often react irritably. It is difficult for them to resist temptations, but they slowly begin to develop coping strategies (Berk, 2011; McNeal, 2007). They also start to develop the ability to negotiate and compromise with others (Valkenburg and Cantor, 2001). Generally, their intellectual competences and abilities make a very large developmental leap, enabling them to count, develop a mental map of a store, and internalize the purchasing process (Berk, 2011; McNeal, 2007). Moreover, children's peers start to influence their purchase and consumption decisions (McNeal, 2007).

Later childhood (6-10 years): Children are becoming better at visualizing a grocery store as well as planning, organizing and conducting a purchase (Berk, 2011; McNeal, 2007). Consequently, they start to shop alone and to make their own purchase and consumption decisions based on their personal opinions (Berk, 2011; McNeal and Yeh, 1993). While doing so, they improve their ability to alternate between problem-oriented and emotion-oriented strategies (Berk, 2011). Furthermore, their improved communication and negotiation strategies strengthen their influence on household decisions (Valkenburg and Cantor, 2001). Generally, they are more susceptible to social influences and make purchase and consumption decisions based on comparisons with peers (Berk, 2011).

Adolescence (11-18 years): Children become more independent, self-centered, idealistic and critical (Berk, 2011), leading to more self-determined purchase and consumption experiences. Their personal and moral principles are strengthened, which can partly guide their decision making, for instance, by encouraging the purchase of animal and environmentally friendly products. At the same time, their concerns about the opinions of others and their own image increases, which influences their shopping behavior more strongly than before. Communication and problem-solving skills as well as decision-making processes continue to improve (Berk, 2011).

The prerequisite for these learning and development processes, however, is that children are given the opportunity to develop and flourish. Therefore, in our study, we investigate to what degree children are currently enabled to develop and improve their FWB according to their current developmental stage in different grocery store formats and what food retailers, marketers, policy makers and caregivers can do to positively influence children's FWB during the shopping process.

Table 9: Development processes of children that are relevant to food well-being

Development stage		FWB Dimensions				
Stage	**Age**	**Physical**	**Emotional**	**Social**	**Intellectual**	**Self-determined**
Infant and crawling stage	0-6 months	Children ... - ... start to distinguish between flavors and odours[1,5] - ... are able to use two or more senses at the same time, thus notice products in their sight line[5] - ... grab objects and turn their heads to look around[1] - ... make sensory contact with the marketplace[2]; initially by random (reflexes) and later through voluntary (motor memory) observation[5] and the recognition of objects[1] - ... show classically and operantly conditioned reactions[1] - ... show habitualized reactions[1]	Children ... - ... regulate emotions by shifting attention and self-calming[1]	Children ... - ... start to indicate preferences towards caregivers[3] - ... are directly influenced by the caregivers' knowledge and behavior in the marketplace: the caregivers' product choices determine what the children later consider to be the standard[5] - ... go through food-related experiences at the marketplace by accompanying their caregivers that initiate an association process in their mind that the marketplace is an important source for food as are the caregivers[5]	Children ... - ... show increasing recognition of visual stimuli[1] - ... show more efficient and flexible attentiveness[1] - ... form perception categories based on similar properties of objects[1] - ... begin to show joint attention with caregivers who name objects and events[1] - ... construct the first mental images of marketplace objects and symbols[2]	
	7-12 months	Children ... - ... sit on their own, crawl and walk[1] - ... can sit in the child seat of the shopping cart and can in this way see the products and the supermarket[5] - ... show more flexible and accurate reaching and grasping[1] - ... construct first mental images of marketplace objects and symbols[2]	Children ... - ... build a relationship with the supermarket as the number of shopping trips increases[5] - ... express positive emotions with motor language (shaking, kicking, smiling) triggered by products[5]	Children ... - ... use pre-verbal gestures to communicate[1] - ... articulate the first words[1] - ... use caregivers as safe reference points for enquiries[1] - ... show imitations of adult actions with objects[1] - ... verbalize first words that fascinate the caregivers so that they often meet their requests[5]	Children ... - ... show intentional and target-oriented behaviour[1] - ... start to categorize objects conceptually according to similar functions and properties[1] - ... understand the meaning of some words[1] - ... are able to identify their favorite supermarket, e.g., by the shopping carts' color[5] - ... realize that physical and social objects exist apart from any of their actions (object permanence)[5]	

Development stage		FWB Dimensions				
Stage	Age	Physical	Emotional	Social	Intellectual	Self-determined
	13-18 months	Children ... - ... show an improved ability to walk[1] - ... use small objects coordinated[1]		Children ... - ... ask their caregivers to go shopping[5] - ... make first requests through pointing and gesturing[2,3] cued by external stimuli in the supermarket[5] - ... use their acquired motor skills to guide the caregivers to desired products[5] - ... imitate other's behavior[3,5] - ... help with simple household tasks[3]	Children ... - ... explore the properties of items by treating them in new ways[1,5] - ... show context-independent imitation of adult actions with objects[1] - ... show improved recognition of people, objects and places[1] - ... improve continuously their vocabulary[1] - ... have an increased curiosity regarding products as a result of object permanence[5] - ... recall representations of products in their mind[2,5] - ... start to construct a product network in their mind[5] - ... repeat and memorize product names/labels named by the caregivers[5]	Children ... - ... follow simple instructions[1] - ... are able to take products from the supermarket shelves[5] - ... explore the environment more independently[3,5]
	19-24 months	Children ... - ... jump, walk on tiptoes and climb[1] - ... use small objects very coordinated[1]	Children ... - ... use language to express and regulate emotions[1] - ... start to show self-regulation, e.g., by delaying rewards[1] - ... establish an indirect relationship with the marketplace through transitional characters such as cartoon animals[5] - ... show a stronger relationship with the marketplace due to more contact points (via	Children ... - ... start to tolerate the absence of a caregiver[1] - ... express verbal requests for products[2,5] encouraged by the caregivers[5] - ... use an evoked set of products to give purchase directions to the caregivers[5] - ... learn that asking for products equals receiving them[5] - ... internalize the healthy and unhealthy behavior of the caregivers as standard[5]	Children ... - ... combine words[1] - ... develop ranking skills and establish an evoked set of favorite products[5] - ... realize in which store a certain product can be purchased[5]	

Development stage		FWB Dimensions				
Stage	Age	Physical	Emotional	Social	Intellectual	Self-determined
			advertisements, jingles and packaging)[5]			
Early childhood	2 years	Children ... - ... show an improved sense of balance; walking becomes more coordinated, hasty walking turns into running[1] - ... can successfully eat with a spoon[1] - ... become too heavy to be carried by the caregivers[5]	Children ... - ... understand the causes and consequences of basic emotions and how they manifest in behavior[1] - ... show proactive (instrumental) aggressions to satisfy a need or desire[1] - ... start to show moody behavior, as the lack of skills (dependence on the caregiver) interferes with the urge for independence[5]	Children ... - ... speak in simple phrases[1] - ... start developing a sense of morality[1] - ... eagerly observe at the fresh counter what the sales person gives to the caregiver to ensure that their requests are fulfilled[5] - ... show egocentric behavior: children consider every product in reach as their own[5]	Children ... - ... show a well-developed memory of recognition[1] - ... start to count[1] - ... use a large number of perceived and often social and linguistic references to understand the meaning of words[1] - ... show a rapid improvement of their vocabulary[1]	Children ... - ... start to develop a self-concept and feeling of self-worth[1], i.e., autonomy emerges[3,5] - ... seek independent walking[5]
	3-4 years	Children ... - ... show constantly improving physical and motor abilities[1] - ... successfully eat with a fork[1]	Children ... - ... demonstrate improved emotional self-regulation[1], however, they still have great difficulties to resist attractive stimuli[4,6] - ... show decreased proactive aggressions, while reactive aggressions (verbal and social) increase in frequency[1] - ... are unwilling to make a purchases on their own because of the overwhelming interior at the supermarket or the fear of getting lost (separation anxiety)[5]	Children ... - ... feel a higher level of self-worth through harmonic interactions with caregivers[1] - ... distinguish moral imperatives from social norms and personal choices[1] - ... learn cooperation and sharing skills[3,5] - ... are able to interpret vocal tones and face expressions, thus know when to negotiate with the caregivers[5] - ... are able to offer alternatives or compromises to persuade the caregiver to respond to a wish[4,7] - ... notice which items other children own and requests them too[5]	Children ... - ... understand the symbolic meaning of signs[1,5] - ... understand the relationship between cause and effect[1] - ... assign familiar items to hierarchically organized categories[1] - ... use inner speech to guide their behaviour[1] - ... show improved attention and ability to plan[1] - ... use scripts to remember familiar processes[1] - ... know the numbers one to ten and counts correctly[1] - ... start to understand the meaning of written words[1] - ... characterize new words on the basis of familiar words and expand the	Children ... - ... show an increased desire for autonomous decisions and actions due to improved motor skills and a well-developed memory[5] - ... select products while shopping with caregivers[2] - ... test limits on what behaviors are acceptable and how much autonomy they can exert[3] - ... request products that support their own self-concept[5] - ... take products and load the shopping cart independently if negotiations did not result in their favor[5]

Development stage		FWB Dimensions				
Stage	Age	Physical	Emotional	Social	Intellectual	Self-determined
				- ... demonstrates knowledge of brand names and supermarkets[5] - ... use motor and language skills to imitate older children or caregivers[5]	meaning of words through synonyms[1] - ... judge products by focusing on one striking characteristic[5], thus is not able yet to assess quality[4]	
	5-6 years	Children ... - ... lose their milk teeth[1] - ... start to use a knife to slice soft food[1]	Children ... - ... show improved abilities to interpret, predict and influence emotional reactions of others[1,5] - ... use coping strategies such as covering the eyes to resist a desirable product[4,8] - ... have first unpleasant experiences in the marketplace: employees and other customers may be annoyed by the first independent and rather slow purchasing attempts[5] - ... notice that marketers increasingly want to address them through advertising and enjoy having their focus on their pleasure[5]	Children ... - ... acquire a wide range of morally relevant rules and behaviours[1] - ... show empathic reactions more frequently[1] - have less conflicts with their caregivers due to their increasing ability to negotiate[4] - ... realize that products can be obtained either through the caregivers' or their own money[5] - ... realize that people have certain positions in the society such as the checkout employee who takes money in exchange for products[5] - ... intensely observe the selection and purchase behavior of other customers or children in the supermarket[5] - ... may be allowed to pay for the purchases as a form of cooperation in the caregiver-child relationship[5]	Children ... - ... have a better ability to concentrate and to plan[1] - ... show improved recognition and reproductive memory and scripts and autobiographical memory[1] - ... demonstrate an improved vocabulary[1] - ... construct a map of the supermarket: they know the position of products and are ready to make requests at the right moment[5] - ... show reversibility of thinking: they are able to trace their thinking through a mentally constructed network[5] - ... understand the purpose of money[5] - ... understand the concept of social objects: learn from the caregivers that products belong to someone, thus have to be purchased and cannot simply be taken off the shelf[5] - ... internalize the purchasing process[5]	Children ... - ... request, select and pay for a product for the first time as the caregivers watch[2]
Later childhood	6-8 years	Children ...	Children ...	Children ... - ... gradually include personality traits and social	Children ...	- feeling of self-worth is more differentiated,

Development stage		FWB Dimensions				
Stage	Age	Physical	Emotional	Social	Intellectual	Self-determined
		- ... lose their milk teeth and they get more and more permanent teeth. [1]	- ... understand that an individual can feel multiple feelings simultaneously[1] - ... show decreased physical aggressions; verbal and social aggressions may still occur[1] - ... sense and understand the feelings and viewpoints of others and respond to them[5] - ... feel insignificant in the marketplace since employees usually give little importance to their autonomous operations[5]	comparisons in their self-concept [1] - ... feel pride and guilt based on a personal feeling of responsibility[1] - ... understand that various people may have different perspectives due to different background knowledge[1] - ... develop a flexible view of moral rules and take prosocial and antisocial intentions into account[1] - ... resolve conflicts more effectively[1] - ... fully understand rules and regulations[3]	- ... display improved logical thinking leading to improved problem solving skills[1] - ... have an improved spatial understanding: clear, well-organized orientation and coherent cognitive maps (including the ways to and within grocery stores)[1,5] - ... have a more selective, adaptable and targeted attention[1] - ... show an improved ability to perform complex arithmetic tasks[1] - ... have an improved vocabulary and linguistic awareness[1] - ... tell narratives more structured, detailed and vivid[1] - ... read more fluently[1] - ... use their mind not only to store images of objects but also to operate with them[5] - ... have a good understanding of volume and weight[5] - ... transfer their store-specific knowledge to other types of stores[5]	hierarchically organized and decreases to a realistic level[1] - acquires a greater autonomy and reliability[1] - purchases products independently of parents[2] - takes charge of simple chores[3]
	9-11 years	Children ... - ... show improved reaction time; thus the performance of gross motor skills such as running and jumping is faster and more coordinated[1]	Children ... - ... adaptively alternate between problem-oriented and emotion-oriented strategies for emotional control[1] - ... show increased loyalty to brands[4]	Children ... - ... increasingly express negative emotions in a socially accepted way[1] - ... becomes aware of how one has to behave to be accepted in a group[4]	- spatial imagination develops further[1] - selective attention and ability to plan improve continuously[1] - multiple memorization strategies are used	- feeling of self-worth improves among the vast majority of children[1] - convictions regarding personal decision-making are strengthened[1] - increasing independent decision-making[3]

Development stage		FWB Dimensions				
Stage	Age	Physical	Emotional	Social	Intellectual	Self-determined
				- ... connects moral attitudes with social conventions[1] - ... show increased sibling rivalry[1] - ... show improved negotiation strategies which lead to a stronger influence on household purchases[4] - ... can see themselves with the eyes of another person[1] - ... are influenced in their gender identity by conformity pressure[1]	simultaneously, and elaborations are applied[1] - long-term knowledge grows and becomes more organized[1] - reflection on task performance and subsequent improvement of action strategies to achieve a goal (cognitive self-control)[1]	- growing need for independence from family[3]
Adolescence	11-14 years	Children ... - ... show strong gender-specific behavior: girls enter puberty generally two years earlier than boys; especially girls who are unhappy with their body image are at high risk of developing severe eating disorders[1] - ... show stronger stress reactions[1]	Children ... - have an increased interest in novelties[1] - ... have mood swings that correlate with situational changes: emotional lows tend to occur in adult-structured situations[1,9] - ... tend to determine their self-worth based on their body image[1,11]	Children ... - ... long for conformity due to group pressure[1] - ... have more conflicts with their caregivers due to their need for autonomy[1,10] - ... have a negative self-image and are perceived as less attractive by peers when they come into puberty unusually early (esp. girls) or late (esp. boys)[1]	Children ... - ... have an improved hypothetical-deductive and propositional thinking[1] - ... display improved cognitive self-control[1]	Children ... - ... become more timorous, self-centered, idealistic and critical[1] - ... incorporate in their self-concept separate and often contradictory personality traits[1] - ... spend less time with parents and siblings due to their striving for autonomy[1]
	14-16 years	Children ... - ... show improved motor skills (girls earlier, boys later)[1] - ... need an higher calorie intake due to their rapid growth (especially boys)[1]; unfortunately the increase in food demand comes at a time when the nutritional behavior of many adolescents is at its worst[1]	Children ... - ... show an increased and more differentiated feeling of self-worth[1]	Children ... - ... are more concerned about the opinions of others[1] - ... assesses problems from a societal perspective[1] - ... put increasing emphasis on social rules as basis for solving moral dilemmas[1] - ... argue in a more differentiated way in situations that cause conflicts between moral reasons, social conventions	Children ... - ... improve their hypothetical-deductive and propositional thinking even further[1]	Children ... - ... integrate their attributes into an organized self-concept[1] - ... show improved autonomous everyday decision-making processes[1]

Development stage		FWB Dimensions				
Stage	Age	Physical	Emotional	Social	Intellectual	Self-determined
				and personal freedom of choice[1] - … eat less often with their families which leads to an unhealthy diet[1]		
	16-18 years	Children … - … show improved motor skills (esp. boys)[1]		Children … - … have a self-concept that is more based on personal and moral principles[1] - … continue to improve moral judgement[1]	Children … - … show improved decision-making processes[1]	

[1]Berk, 2011; [2]McNeal and Yeh, 1993; [3]Malik and Marwaha, 2018; [4]Valkenburg and Cantor, 2001; [5]McNeal, 2007; [6]Mischel and Ebbeson, 1970; [7]Kuczynski and Kochanska, 1990; [8]Metcalfe and Mischel, 1999; [9]Larson and Richards, 1998; [10]Allison and Schultz, 2004; [11]Harter, 2006.

5.4 State of Research: Grocery Shopping and Children's Food Well-Being

Several studies have provided preliminary indications about how grocery shopping influences one or more FWB dimensions of children. Table 10 gives an overview of studies that were published within the last 10 years and that gave insights into the relationship between grocery shopping and children's FWB. This table shows the age of the children who took part in the studies, indicating their developmental stage, and classifies the findings into the individual FWB dimensions. In the following, the current state of knowledge regarding the influence of children's grocery shopping experiences on each FWB dimension is briefly summarized.

Grocery shopping seems to be able to influence physical well-being through both physical activity and nutrition. However, little is known about the exact influences of grocery shopping on the physical well-being of children that is induced by physical (in)activity. Generally, grocery shopping seems to be an opportunity for children to be physically active, for instance by pushing the shopping cart or carrying shopping bags (Haselhoff, Faupel, and Holzmüller, 2014). However, there also seems to be a certain risk involved, leading, for instance, to head and face injuries due to falls from the shopping cart (Clayton, Boron, and Mattila, 2014). More is known about the influence of grocery shopping on nutrition. Because of the high number of temptations in the shopping environment, children often tend to require unhealthy snacks during the shopping process, which could negatively influence their nutrition and, in the long run, their physical well-being (Berry and McMullen, 2008). Whether temptations are indeed able to negatively influence children's nutrition heavily depends on caregivers' reactions to children's requests (Wingert et al., 2014); however, which reaction is best does not seem to be entirely clear yet. While some researchers recommend limiting exposure to negative external influences (Huang et al., 2016), others suggest more intense involvement of children (Allirot, Maiz, and Urdaneta, 2017; Wingert et al., 2014). Nevertheless, accompanying their caregivers during grocery shopping generally seems to help children become accustomed to a high variety of foods and decreases their chances of developing neophobia, i.e., the unwillingness to try new foods (Allirot, Maiz, and Urdaneta, 2017).

In general, grocery shopping seems to be an emotional experience for children (Hémar-Nicolas and Ezan, 2018). In particular, younger children are emotion-driven shoppers who often act impulsively (Schuhen et al., 2017). For example, beautifully decorated surroundings and colorful packaging evoke emotions in children (Balcarová, Pokorná and Pilar, 2014; Berry and McMullen, 2008; Mau et al., 2016), which often lead to desires for products (Gram, 2015;

Wingert et al., 2014). Accordingly, it is the caregiver's task to set boundaries; however, not all caregivers are able to do so (Huang et al., 2016). Purchasing healthy food is often perceived as tedious (O'Brien et al., 2014). If caregivers are able to deny children's requests, children's subsequent reactions will depend on their age. Younger children are generally more disappointed and disappointed for a longer period of time than older children (Buijzen and Valkenburg, 2008; Lawlor and Prothero, 2011), indicating a gradual development process of emotional self-control. Overall, however, children enjoy family coshopping (Lawlor and Prothero, 2011), especially when they are actively involved and able to take part in decision-making processes (Marshall, 2014).

The shopping experience can also strengthen children's emotional bonds with their caregivers (Gram, 2015) and thus the social well-being of children. During family coshopping, caregivers function as socialization agents through whom children can learn how to make decisions and how to behave in a grocery store, including interactions with other customers or salespeople (Marshall, 2014; Mau et al., 2016). Furthermore, through repeated discussions and negotiations with their caregivers during the shopping process, children improve their negotiation skills, and over time, they increasingly apply a variety of strategies to convince their caregivers to purchase their preferred products (Ebster, Wagner, and Neumueller, 2009; Gaumer, Arnone, and Ashley-Cotleur, 2013). While some sources suggest that children sometimes try to achieve their goals through negative pester power (e.g., screaming, tantrums; Mayo and Nairn, 2009), others argue that pester power does not exist in this form and that it is more comparable to a constructive negotiation (Lawlor and Prothero, 2011); however, the nature of children's attempts to convince their parents to purchase preferred products also depends on children's age (Berry and McMullen, 2008). It seems that, at least over time, children and adults alike strive for pleasant, respectful interactions during the shopping process (Gram, 2015); several studies have shown that children are able and willing to act according to social norms and rules and do not want to be seen not adhering to these norms in a grocery shopping context (e.g., Gram and Grønhøj, 2016).

Considering the importance and the dominant role of food shopping in children's lives, surprisingly little is known about the concrete influences of grocery shopping on children's intellectual well-being. Research has shown that, over time, children internalize the purchasing process and develop the associated skills and abilities (Gram and Grønhøj, 2016). Through the shopping process, children experience food products sensorially (Gram, 2015), learn to evaluate and choose products based on specific selection criteria and their health-related influences (Mau et al., 2016; Schuhen et al., 2017), and develop an understanding of health- and nutrition-related terminology (Gram, 2015). While doing so, they tend to imitate their caregivers' behavior and to rely on the information that they have received from them (DeJesus, Shutts, and Kinzler, 2018; Fan and Li, 2010), highlighting the important role of caregivers.

Children's self-determination gained by grocery shopping experiences has changed over time. As a result of children's generally increasing participation in the shopping process, children today have more opportunities to strengthen their self-confidence and self-determination than, for example, forty years ago (Atkin, 1978; Gaumer and Arnone, 2010). Children start to develop their self-determination by independently exploring the grocery store (Ebster, Wagner, and Neumueller, 2009), expressing their preferences, and participating in food decision-making (Hémar-Nicolas and Ezan, 2018), through which their self-esteem can be strengthened as their requests are repeatedly fulfilled (Calderon et al., 2017). In particular, younger children want to feel that they have an important, decisive role in purchase decisions (Gaumer, Arnone, and Ashley-Cotleur, 2013). Children are strengthened in their independence when they are encouraged to actively participate in the shopping process and take on tasks such as carrying bags or checking a product's quality (Haselhoff, Faupel, and Holzmüller, 2014). Through grocery purchasing, they can also learn how to manage money (Lawlor and Prothero, 2011).

To summarize, the current state of research already provides valuable insights into the influence of food shopping on children's FWB. However, the studies that have been conducted so far also have several limitations that pave the way for further research. No study has investigated the influence of grocery shopping on FWB as a whole. Furthermore, often, the findings have not been attributed to children's specific development stage, making it difficult to understand the implications for research and practice. In addition, the previous studies have been conducted in different cultures, which makes it difficult to directly apply the results in another cultural context. Moreover, thus far, no attention has been paid to the influence of the store format, even though store formats can vary strongly in their family- and child-friendliness. In the following, we therefore provide a holistic investigation of the influence of grocery shopping on children's FWB in two different store types that vary notably.

Table 10: Literature research on the food well-being of children

	Age																	Food well-being dimensions				
Article	0	1	2	3	4	5	6	7	8	9	10	11	12	13	14	15	16	Physical	Emotional	Social	Intellectual	Self-determined
Berry et al., 2008																		x	x	x		x
Buijzen et al., 2008																			x			x
Ebster et al., 2009																			x	x		x
Fan et al., 2010																				x	x	
Gaumer et al., 2010																						x
Gram, 2011																		x	x	x		
Lawlor & Prothero, 2011																		x	x	x		x
Andresen et al., 2012																				x		x
Gaumer et al., 2013																			x	x		x
Sharma et al., 2013																						x
Balcarová et al., 2014																			x	x		
Clayton et al., 2014																		x				
Francis & Davis, 2014																		x		x	x	
Haselhoff et al., 2014																		x		x	x	x
Keller & Ruus, 2014																				x		
Marshall, 2014																			x	x	x	x
Pólya & Földi, 2014																		x				
Wingert et al., 2014																		x	x	x		
Gram, 2015																		x	x	x	x	
Calloway et al., 2016																			x	x		
Gram et al. 2016																			x	x	x	
Huang et al., 2016																		x	x			
Mau et al., 2016																			x	x	x	
Allirot et al., 2017																		x				
Bertol et al., 2017																				x		
Calderon et al., 2017																				x		x
Schuhen et al., 2017																			x	x	x	
DeJesus et al., 2018																				x	x	
Hémar-Nicolas et al, 2018																		x	x	x		x
Nekitsing et al., 2018																					x	
Page et al., 2018																				x		

5.5 Observational Study in Two Grocery Stores

To analyze the relationship between grocery shopping and children's FWB, an unobtrusive observational study combined with a short survey was conducted in two grocery store formats in a medium-sized city in Germany. We opted for an exploratory study because the effect of grocery shopping on children's FWB has not been previously investigated, necessitating an open and qualitative approach to first develop a basic understanding of the phenomenon (Silverman, 2006; Spiggle, 1994). Furthermore, previous studies have shown that observational studies are particularly suitable for the evaluation of the behavior of families and their children (e.g., Calderon et al., 2017; Haselhoff, Faupel, and Holzmüller, 2014; Rust, 1993). Especially in a grocery store setting, behavioral processes are often habitualized and carried out unconsciously (Buijzen and Valkenburg, 2008), which is why retrospective interviews and surveys are likely to not reflect the actual behavior of participants. In particular, smaller children are not able to retrospectively discuss their experiences without distorting them, due to their often still limited cognitive capacities (Borgers, De Leeuw, and Hox, 2000). The phenomenon under investigation might also have been considered sensitive by consumers and, therefore, could have led to distorted results or socially desired answering behavior if we would have used survey data alone (Silverman, 2006), which also justifies our study design.

5.5.1 Participants

A total of 100 observations were conducted (Table 11 gives an overview of the descriptive statistics of the sample). Each group observed consisted of one to two adults plus one to two children each. Of the 100 groups observed, 71 completed a short questionnaire about their demographic characteristics after completing their shopping trip. Since our research is based mainly on the observational data, we decided to also include those participants who did not complete the short survey, especially because they constituted only a minority of the participants. For children and caregivers whose demographic data we could not obtain, their ages were estimated. In total, 47% of the children and 66% of the accompanying caregivers were female. Most of the children were aged between two to five years old (49 children), followed by those aged six to ten years old (33 children). The smallest groups were adolescents (18 children) and infants (16 children). Thus, all age groups were included in the sample, allowing the analysis of the influence of grocery shopping on FWB in all developmental stages. In both store formats, most of the participating caregivers were married and employed. On average, the caregivers in the organic store were more educated and had a higher income than those in the supermarket.

Table 11: Descriptive statistics of the sample

	Total	Organic Store (OS)	Supermarket (SM)
Number of groups observed	100	50	50
Number of children observed	116	60	56
Number of accompanying caregivers	116	60	56
Gender of children	47% female	47% female	46% female
Gender of adults	66% female	65% female	68% female

Age categories	OS	SM
Children		
0-23 months	10	6
2-5 years	27	22
6-10 years	14	19
11-17 years	9	9

Age categories	OS	SM
Adults		
21-30	3	7
31-40	38	28
41-50	15	15
>50	4	6

Income (EUR)	OS	SM
Families		
< 1.250	0	1
1.251-2.500	5	5
2.501-3.500	12	6
3.501-4.500	4	8
> 4.501	15	6

Graduation	OS	SM
Adults		
No degree	0	1
CSE	2	2
O-levels	3	10
Specialized A-levels	5	3
A-levels	29	15

Marital status	OS	SM
Adults		
Single	4	4
Married	30	26
Divorced	3	2
Widowed	2	0

Education	OS	SM
Adults		
No degree	1	3
Apprenticeship	15	17
University degree	20	12
PhD	3	0

Occupation	OS	SM
Adults		
Employee	21	25
Management	2	0
Self-employed	11	2
Housewife	4	2

Occupation	OS	SM
Adults		
Retired	1	1
Other	2	0
Full time	22	15
Part-time	15	14

5.5.2 Procedure

Prior to data collection, three research assistants (one male and two female) were trained in the task of observing and interviewing consumers in a grocery store setting. At the beginning of their training, they received the theoretical background information needed to complete the observation, which included information about the children's FWB and the associated superordinate FWB dimensions as well as the developmental stages every child goes through and the knowledge and competences that a child should develop during each of these stages. Then they learned theoretically how to complete the observational form while observing the consumers' behavior. After that, the research assistants did a first observation in-store accompanied by the research project leader, followed by an extensive conversation about possible improvements. Then, another test and feedback phase took place. Since this new test round was successful, the study was started afterwards.

The observations took place in two German grocery stores, each representing a different store format: an organic store and a regular supermarket. The organic store differed from the supermarket in various aspects, such as fewer promotions (including those for children), comparably unobtrusive product packaging, a smaller and healthier assortment of products, broader aisles, an absence of background music and speaker announcements, and the presence of play areas for children. In every store, the study was conducted for one week (from Monday to Saturday) between 12 am and 8 pm on weekdays and between 8 am and 8 pm on Saturdays.

The procedure was the same in both stores. When a group of people entered the store that included one to two children between the ages of approximately six months and seventeen years old, they were followed by two observers through the store, and their verbal and nonverbal behavior as well as their shopping trip duration were documented until they passed through the checkout. Only groups with a maximum of two children were included in the study to enable a structured, complete observation. The two observers were disguised as employees carrying out an inventory and alternated during the observations so that consumers did not notice that they were being monitored. Since the observation was carried out in a public space and the collected data could not be traced back to specific individuals, this covert observation was ethically justifiable (Huber, 1993). After completing the shopping trip, the accompanying adult(s) were approached by the interviewer (who was not involved in the observation), and they were asked to participate in a short survey.

5.5.3 Observational Form and Questionnaire

The main focus of the observations was on the children's behavior. Since the relationship between grocery shopping and children's FWB had not yet been investigated, we decided to use an open approach (Weischer and Gehrau, 2017). The observers were instructed to document everything directly or indirectly related to FWB and its superordinate dimensions, including, for instance, physical activities; expressed emotions; interactions with accompanying adults, other customers, and sales people; verbally expressed food- and shopping-related knowledge and corresponding activities; as well as self-determined and autonomous behavior.

After finishing the shopping trip, participants were interviewed based on a short questionnaire. The information gathered about the caregivers included their age, gender, education level, profession, family status, income, and type of relationship with the observed child(ren). Furthermore, the age and gender of the observed children were documented.

5.5.4 Analysis

The observational forms were typewritten and analyzed using the qualitative research analysis software MAXQDA 18. To analyze the data, both theory-confirming and hypothesis-generating content analyses were applied (Cho and Lee, 2014). First, we prepared a provisional list of codes based on previous research findings and the theoretical background. The superordinate themes corresponded to the five FWB dimensions and were subdivided into mutually exclusive subcategories. Different, more specific themes and categories inductively emerged from the data during the analysis process, which required an improvement of the coding list. To ensure the reliability and accuracy of the derived themes and codes, the coding list was created in a collaborative, iterative process during which three of the authors extensively discussed, reviewed and improved the coding scheme until a common understanding and usage of the codes was achieved and the codes reflected the investigated phenomenon in its entirety (see the Appendix for the full list of codes). A mixed methods approach was applied for the subsequent evaluation and interpretation of the coded data: the codes' frequencies were quantified and the findings with respect to each code were summarized and enriched with examples.

5.6 Findings and Discussion

In the following, the results are presented. The findings are assigned directly to the five overarching dimensions so that the influences on the individual FWB dimensions can be examined separately and in detail. In addition, the influences on children in the different developmental stages are compared with each other and across the two store formats.

5.6.1 Physical Dimension

The results show that grocery shopping has an impact on children's physical activity. In both store formats, the observed physical behavior was mainly positive, which is in line with the findings of Haselhoff, Faupel and Holzmüller (2014). For instance, children ran and danced through the store, carried bags and pushed shopping carts. In the organic store, the children generally had more opportunities to move, for instance, due to the presence of a rocking horse and the wider aisles. Ten negative instances were observed across the two stores in which children were physically overburdened or physically inactive even though it would have been possible to be more active. For instance, one child, who was eight months old and who was obviously not able to sit alone yet, was placed in a shopping cart but repeatedly fell over, so he was constantly set upright or held by his mother. This observation was worrying because infants could be harmed when sitting prematurely (Dallinger, Oberndorfer, and Rupp, 2001). The main cause of avoidable physical inactivity in the supermarket was the presence of shopping carts with an integrated car in which children could sit during the grocery shopping trip.

Regarding nutrition, more health-oriented behavior was observed in the organic store compared to the supermarket. In particular, while 43%[6] of the children in the supermarket asked for unhealthy products, such as chocolate and lemonade, only 28% of the children in the organic store asked for such products. However, the children in the organic store asked slightly more often for healthy products (25%), such as fruits, compared to the children in the supermarket (20%). In the organic store, children sometimes even turned down unhealthy products suggested by their caregivers. In general, the number of caregivers who made healthy suggestions was the same in both stores; however, caregivers made fewer unhealthy suggestions in the organic store (17%) than in the supermarket (27%).

6 The percentages always indicate the share of the total number of children in each store format.

Furthermore, it was observed that children reacted to marketing measures and that these measures promoted both healthy (a tea-tasting stand) and unhealthy (sweets at the checkout) product choices, which has also been indicated by previous research results (Berry and McMullen, 2008). More children responded to marketing measures for unhealthy products in the supermarket (38%) than in the organic store (18%), which could have been because there were comparably fewer marketing campaigns and striking packaging as well as a smaller range of unhealthy products in the organic store.

5.6.2 Emotional Dimension

Our results confirm that grocery shopping affects children's emotional well-being. Across the two store formats, activities that were directly related to the purchasing process seemed to cause more negative than positive emotions. The through the shopping activities induced positive emotions were especially prevalent in the supermarket (34%) compared to the organic store (23%). Notably, the influence of grocery shopping on children's emotional state varied across their developmental stages. Children aged five and younger seemed to enjoy participation and involvement in the shopping process more and showed more positive emotional reactions than the other age groups. They often had fun while engaging in ordinary shopping activities, such as taking products off the shelves or putting them on the belt at the checkout, and had more distinct sensory-emotional experiences compared to the older children. This finding is consistent with previous research that indicated that children enjoy grocery shopping more when they are able to actively participate (Lawlor and Prothero, 2011; Marshall, 2014).

However, the current findings also show that children's inability to successfully complete a task, such as fetching a product, also leads to frustration, as was also indicated by McNeal (2007). Furthermore, in each store, nine children displayed negative pester power, which contradicts the conclusion that pester power plays only a minor role (Gram, 2015; Lawlor and Prothero, 2011). Most of these children were between two and five years old, which corresponds to the results of Berry and McMullen (2008). As the proportions of children who exhibited pester power were almost evenly distributed between the stores, it can be assumed that pester power is in large parts not triggered by particular marketing strategies or products but rather relates to children's developmental stage. Very young children are not yet in control of their emotions and tend to test their limits, resulting in an abundance of requests for random products (Malik and Marwaha, 2018; McNeal, 2007).

Children above the age of five often seemed to be bored or annoyed. These children were also often not involved in the shopping process. It can be assumed that they felt unchallenged or uninspired and were therefore bored by the shopping process. Other aspects that could have contributed to their lower level of participation were the caregivers' lack of involvement of the children and the children's desire to act independently of the caregivers (Berk, 2011; Malik and Marwaha, 2018). Moreover, emotional lows resulting from puberty often occur in adult-structured situations such as grocery shopping, which could have contributed to the older children's state of mind (Berk, 2011; Larson and Richards, 1998).

Interestingly, it was often secondary activities, i.e., activities not directly related to the purchasing process, that enhanced the children's emotional shopping experiences, for example rocking on a rocking horse, having fun with siblings, or dancing to the background music. Contrary to our expectation that children would spend substantial time on play opportunities, these opportunities were effectively used as short diversions in between other shopping activities. In the organic store, for instance, children spent some time on the rocking horse or in the play corner but also willingly stopped when their caregivers asked them to, allowing caregivers to continue grocery shopping without any major conflicts. Unfortunately, there were no age-appropriate opportunities for older children to distract themselves or to playfully engage in the shopping process.

The extent to which children had to exercise self-control or were guided to do so was also monitored. In general, in both store formats, with the increasing developmental stage of their children, caregivers tended to give their children more freedom of choice (Buijzen and Valkenburg, 2008), including unhealthy product choices and, in some cases, even the consumption of a product during the shopping process. Caregivers intervened more frequently in the supermarket than in the organic store, perhaps because the children in the supermarket had more demands. However, caregivers in the organic store also had higher income and therefore might have been more open to their children's wishes. This finding is consistent with the results of Ebster, Wagner and Neumueller (2009), who found a connection between caregivers' income and their compliance.

5.6.3 Social Dimension

In general, in both store formats, the communication between children and their caregivers was mainly harmonious and loving (80%), which confirms the results of Gram (2015). In one-third of the cases, comparably little or no communication was observed, and in only 20% of the cases, negative communication was documented; for example, one child was yelled at because he misnamed a product. Positive physical contact between caregivers and children was more frequent in the organic market (42%) than in the supermarket (27%). Such positive contact was expressed, for example, by a caregiver carrying a child, kissing a child on the cheek, or cuddling a child. In addition, the children in the organic market (70%) were more actively involved in the shopping trip than those in the supermarket (55%). In the organic store, young children in particular were encouraged to actively participate through the provision of shopping carts for small children. In contrast, in the supermarket, the integrated plastic car under the standard shopping cart, which small children could use to sit in during the shopping trip, discouraged small children from actively taking part in the shopping process. Because the car was positioned very low on the cart and was covered by the purchases, the children could also hardly communicate with the accompanying caregiver as soon as they sat in it.

Although the number of children who actively helped and worked together with their caregivers during the shopping process did not noticeably differ between the two store formats (77%), the types of cooperation and the frequency of the occurrence of these types varied considerably across the developmental stages and store formats. Notably, cooperation in the organic store was very prevalent among young children (up to five years) and their caregivers but declined in later childhood and adolescence, while the opposite was observed in the supermarket. In the organic store, the cooperation consisted mainly of jointly discovering and learning about grocery shopping and food products. In contrast, the caregivers in the supermarket seemed to attach more importance to the assistance provided by their children, making older children more likely to cooperate with their caregivers. These findings were also confirmed by the observations regarding the quality and quantity of communication as well as participation. While in the organic store, more and better communication was observed among younger children (up to five years) and their caregivers, in the supermarket, more extensive and gratifying communication was observed among older children and their caregivers. This finding could be because the caregivers had a different focus in the two store formats: the caregivers in the organic store could have been more interested in giving their children a nice (educating) shopping experience, while the caregivers in the supermarket might have been more goal-oriented and more interested in shopping effectively and efficiently. These divergent objectives could stem from differences in the education and income levels of the caregivers and the lifestyles that correspond with them. Another explanation could be that the caregivers in the supermarket also had fewer opportunities and/or motivation to teach their young children because of the more hectic environment and the often larger number of purchases. Additionally, children might have been more familiar with the supermarket, as people usually shop more frequently at supermarkets than organic stores, and therefore might have been better able to support their caregivers in this store.

Furthermore, slightly more discussions about purchase decisions between the children and their caregivers were observed in the supermarket (34%) than in the organic store (28%). This finding could be because children were less often tempted and had fewer requests in the organic store. However, in general, the discussions were very short, and extensive negotiations hardly occurred between the children and their caregivers. Among other reasons, this finding could be due to the caregivers' desires not to attract negative public attention. However, the children also learned about interpersonal communication by observing their caregivers in conversations with third parties and other people's interactions.

In general, communication with other people was more varied (with different people) in the supermarket than in the organic store. Due to the higher number of other customers, salespeople and fresh food counters, there were more possibilities to talk with other people and to learn about social behavior and norms in the supermarket than in the organic store. In addition, slightly more negative socialization was observed in the organic store (10%) than in the supermarket (7%). Negative socialization included, for instance, the caregiver speaking in an unfriendly manner with another person, food being consumed during the shopping process or a shopping cart being left behind in the middle of the store. The higher prevalence of negative socialization was a result of the caregivers' inconsistent and unrestrictive behavior, among other reasons. In both grocery stores, socially responsible behavior, such as using paper bags instead of plastic bags, was displayed only to a very limited extent. Nevertheless, it should be kept in mind that purchasing groceries in an organic store is already more socially responsible than purchasing groceries in a standard supermarket and that caregivers are setting an example of socially responsible behavior by shopping in such a store.

Furthermore, with respect to socialization it was relatively rare for the caregivers to actively teach their children norms and rules, such as not to run around loudly or to be considerate of other consumers, while in the store. In relation to the frequency of situations that required such behavior from caregivers, it was observed that the caregivers in the supermarket tended to make their children aware of social norms and rules more often than the caregivers in the organic store. Notably, in this context, sensory learning was often prevented by the caregivers in the supermarket, presumably because it did not comply with social rules of conduct.

5.6.4 Intellectual Dimension

Grocery shopping was shown to be relevant for the food-related intellectual development of the children. Particularly in the organic store, children discovered the environment and the food products sensorially, for example, by touching and tasting the products (45%). This type of discovery was much rarer in the supermarket (29%). As could be expected (Berk, 2011; McNeal, 2007), most of the children who had conspicuous sensory experiences were younger than six years old. The caregivers in the organic store motivated their children to discover foods sensorially more than the caregivers in the supermarket. However, sometimes sensory learning was also inhibited by the caregivers, especially in the case of very young children. Contrary to previous research findings that suggest that caregivers are the primary initiators of sensory learning (Gram, 2015), the children themselves also often showed interest in the sensory exploration of food, which is consistent with the children's statements gathered in the study of Hémar-Nicolas and Ezan (2018). Nevertheless, caregivers mostly have a significant influence on what kind of products children experience sensorially.

The children in the supermarket tended to sensorially examine more packaged products, whereas the children in the organic store tended to explore more fresh products. Because previous research has shown that children are more likely to accept vegetables when they have experienced them sensorially (Nekitsing, Hetherington, and Blundell-Birtill, 2018), it is important to understand what makes children willingly examine fresh products. The fact that sensory learning regarding fruits and vegetables was especially prevalent in the organic store might be due to the store's set up; to access the other areas of the store, customers have to go through the vegetable and fruit department. In the supermarket, on the other hand, the fruit and vegetable department is slightly removed from the main shopping area and therefore has to be deliberately targeted. A further explanation could be that the caregivers also paid more attention to the vegetables and fruits in the organic store.

While more children in the organic store (23%) than in the supermarket (18%) demonstrated declarative knowledge (learning and preserving of factual knowledge; Vidgen and Gallegos, 2014), the children in the supermarket showed more competence when it came to selecting and purchasing the products, i.e., they displayed more procedural knowledge (34%) (Vidgen and Gallegos, 2014). For example, some of them were able to independently order products at the fresh food corner. Much fewer children showed shopping competence in the organic store (23%); they tended to be passive in this regard. Notably, in general, children did not show their knowledge as often as was expected based on previous research findings (Gram, 2015; Haselhoff, Faupel, and Holzmüller, 2014). This finding might be due to the low number of situations that demanded that the children demonstrate their knowledge.

Furthermore, the caregivers in the organic store were observed to actively teach their children (35%) more often than the caregivers in the supermarket (27%). The children in the organic store (27%) were also provided with knowledge by third parties more often than the children in the supermarket (18%). On the other hand, the children in the supermarket consciously observed their caregivers while they conducted shopping tasks more often than children in the organic store (25% vs. 15%, respectively). In the organic store, some children did not experience important learning moments, such as paying at the checkout or ordering at the fresh food counter, because they were busy with the rocking horse that stood nearby. Thus, it can be concluded that different types of learning are dominant in the two store formats (instrumental vs. vicarious learning/modeling; Francis and Davis, 2014).

Finally, the transfer of nutrition- or health-related knowledge did not play an important role, confirming the results of O'Dougherty, Story and Stang (2006). Only one case was observed in which the health consequences of consuming a food product were discussed.

5.6.5 Self-Determined Dimension

Differences between the two store formats could also be observed regarding the children's self-determination. Although it was observed in both store formats that children were allowed to move freely, which has been shown to positively influence self-determination (Ebster, Wagner, and Neumueller, 2009), in the organic store, children moved more independently through the store. This trend was especially notable for children under the age of six, which corresponds to the assumption that children in early childhood strive for more autonomy and therefore want to move more and more independently through the grocery store (McNeal, 2007). The fact that children were allowed to move more freely in the organic store could be due to the wider aisles, the more spacious placement of items and the low height of the shelves, giving caregivers more opportunities to keep an eye on their children, even when they ran away. Although the children moved more freely in the organic store, they did not ask for products more often; therefore, the findings of Ebster, Wagner and Neumueller (2009) that a higher degree of free movement goes hand in hand with more demands cannot be confirmed.

Children in the organic store generally acted in a more self-determined manner (83%) compared to the children in the supermarket (68%), for example, by taking products from the shelves or putting them on the belt at the cash register. While in the organic store, younger children especially showed self-determined behavior, in the supermarket, older children more commonly exhibited such behavior. In the organic store, the self-determination of younger children was supported by the shopping carts that were made specifically for smaller children, among other factors. For the supermarket context, it can be assumed that the strong involvement of the older children in the shopping process significantly influenced their self-determination, as has been suggested by previous research (Haselhoff, Faupel, and Holzmüller, 2014).

In contrast to the predominant image of the pestering child, the caregivers often asked for their children's opinions, including caregivers encouraging their children to communicate their preferences or asking them to give an opinion when choosing between two alternatives. This behavior was a bit more common in the supermarket (38%) than in the organic store (30%). In the organic store, smaller children especially were asked for their opinions. Although the caregivers' intentions to involve their children seemed to strengthen the children's self-determination and enabled them to participate more in the shopping process, it is questionable whether children aged five and younger are able to make reasonable and health-oriented decisions. On the other hand, the children's active involvement improves their negotiation skills, which are mainly developed between the ages of two to five (Valkenburg and Cantor, 2001).

Furthermore, it seemed that some children learned through their involvement how to handle money in a grocery shopping context, which in the long run also promotes their self-determination. For example, one mother told her children that they were allowed to buy chocolate but only with their own pocket money. However, overall, only a few instances were observed in which children indeed actively learned how to handle money, contradicting the findings of previous research, which has suggested that grocery shopping often serves as an opportunity to learn the handling of money (Lawlor and Prothero, 2011).

5.7 Implications for Theory

This study shows that grocery shopping plays a significant role in children's different developmental phases and that it influences children's FWB in the short and long run. Figure 11 shows the overarching relationships involved in this influence. In a nutshell, the influence of grocery shopping on the five FWB dimensions arises from a combination of the characteristics of the store format; caregivers' knowledge, abilities and motivation to involve and educate children (Bublitz et al., 2011); and children's current developmental stage.

The findings show that different store formats can have varying influences on children's FWB and are able to promote and strengthen different food-related competences and skills based on their specific characteristics. In particular, five characteristics emerge from our results that seem to be highly influential: store layout, product assortment, marketing activities, playing options and learning opportunities. The store layout refers to the spatial design of the store, including, for instance, the number and width of aisles, shelf heights and the arrangement of food categories. The open structure of the organic store, for instance, allowed children to move more freely than the narrower structure in the supermarket,

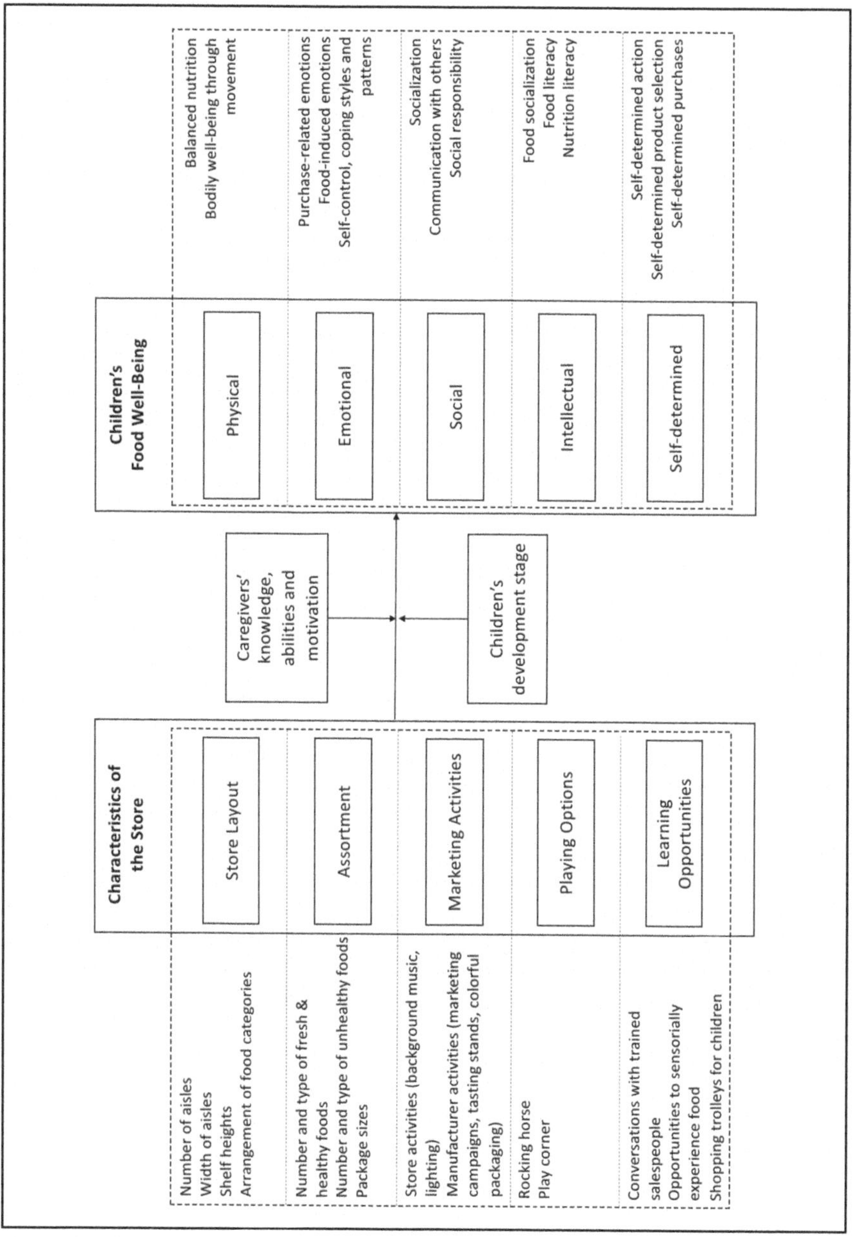

Figure 11: The relationship between grocery shopping and children's food well-being

influencing their physical and emotional well-being positively. The product assortment encompasses, among other aspects, the proportion and types of healthy and unhealthy foods and package sizes. For example, more sweets were available in the checkout area of the supermarket than in that of the organic store, which challenged the children's self-control. Furthermore, there were also significant differences in the amount and types of marketing activities in the two store formats that influenced both the children and their caregivers. These marketing activities can be divided into store activities, such as the background music and lighting, and manufacturer activities, such as marketing campaigns and colorful packaging. At the supermarket, for example, children were confronted with colorful packaging more often than in the organic store. Furthermore, the playing options had a significant influence on the children's behavior. In the organic store, where several playing options were present, children were observed to gladly use the rocking horse and the play corner, leading them to have more positive, relaxed experiences during the shopping trip.

Another difference between the store formats are the learning opportunities. For instance, the presence of shopping carts for children in the organic store promoted their participation and thus positively influenced their self-determination. Furthermore, some salespeople in the supermarket spoke in a friendly manner to some of the children, which might have led to the activation of learning processes regarding social and intellectual well-being. However, very few elements in the stores actively promoted learning.

Whether children are able to exploit the characteristics of a store format in the best possible way depends to a large extent on their caregivers. The caregivers need to have the knowledge, the abilities and the motivation to involve their children in the shopping process to encourage them to discover the store and to actively impart their knowledge and skills to them. Knowledge comprises declarative (factual) and procedural (action-related) knowledge about children's food- and nutrition-related needs as well as general nutrition and food literacy (Block et al., 2011; Vidgen and Gallegos, 2014). The abilities to involve children refers to factors such as the available time, financial resources or the state of mind during shopping. Motivation comprises the degree of willingness to involve children in the shopping process and support them in the development of their FWB.

Finally, the influence of family grocery shopping on children's FWB strongly depends on the developmental stage of the children. The results show that children need to be involved according to their level of development. To develop a high level of FWB it is important that children are neither over- nor underchallenged (Dodge et al., 2012), and that they are encouraged in a way that corresponds to their playful but constantly changing nature.

5.8 Recommendations for Food Retailers and Marketers

The study findings provide valuable insights into the external influences that affect children's FWB in the grocery shopping context and therefore inform recommendations for food retailers, especially for the management of organic food stores and supermarkets, and marketers that are aimed at the improvement of children's FWB (see Table 12 for an overview). The consideration of children's FWB and thus a family-friendly orientation could translate to an extraordinary competitive advantage for grocery stores because families are a consumer group with great purchasing power. Furthermore, the early establishment of relationships with young consumers can lead to strong long-lasting relationships.

5.8.1 General Recommendations

In general, the aim of food retailers and marketers should be to create a shopping experience that is both educational as well as aligned with children's playful and hedonic nature. Thus, on the one hand, grocery shopping should support the achievement of learning goals, which is why children should be encouraged and enabled to actively participate in the shopping process and to take part in shopping-related family decision making. On the other hand, grocery shopping should provide a hedonic experience so that a positive relationship with food can arise. The provision of a hedonic experience involves giving children the freedom to discover the grocery store in a playful way and to become familiar with the shopping context slowly and easily by means of the integration of hedonic elements according to their stage of development.

Various instruments are available to grocery retailers to achieve these desirable effects. With more aisles, lower shelf rows and less cluttered walkways, retailers can create an open atmosphere where children can move freely. Moreover, slight changes in the store design can foster children's participation in the shopping process, such as a children's staircase at the fresh food counter so that even smaller children can reach the counter, view the assortment of items, and talk to the shop assistants. The product assortment should be more adapted to the nutritional needs of children and by means of a well thought-out choice architecture children's attention should be drawn to healthy products, not to unhealthy products (Bucher et al., 2016). Retailers could work together with manufacturers of healthy products to create marketing campaigns that promote healthy food choices by placing healthy products within children's reach and line of sight and by playfully showing them that healthy products are palatable too. One example of successful marketing for healthy products that is partly also aimed at children is the "Eat 'Em Like Junk Food" campaign for baby carrots (Chazin, 2013).

In general, grocery stores offer very few possibilities for children to actively improve their food-related knowledge and competences in a child-friendly manner. Therefore, food retailers could provide child-friendly, easy-to-understand information on nutrition and food, for instance, through in-store learning stations, stickers for collecting, and educational videos in the online store. Because of its topicality, special attention could be paid to responsible und sustainable purchase and consumption behavior. Given children's digital fluency even at a young age, digital devices should be integrated as communication and experiential tools (Muzellec et al., 2016). In particular, edutainment and gamification of the shopping process should be considered. For example, previous research has shown that when children regard healthy nutrition as part of a playful competition with others, a positive change in their nutrition can be achieved (Raju, Rajagopal, and Gilbride, 2010). Generally, care must be taken to create measures that appeal to different age groups so that children at different stages of development feel encouraged. Furthermore, to involve the entire family, reward programs for families could be introduced, for instance, a bonus program that rewards the purchase of healthy food. For all these FWB-enhancing activities, retailers could also work together with governmental organizations (e.g., Federal Ministry of Food and Health).

Table 12: Implications for retailers, public policy and caregivers

	Retailers/Marketers	Public Policy	Caregivers
Physical	No shopping carts with an integrated plastic car below or other elements that could prevent children from moving freely. Instructions on shopping carts about how and at what age children should be placed inside. Enough room in store for children to run around. Promotion of healthy products in cooperation with manufacturers.	Education of caregivers on the physical capacity of children according to their developmental stage. Education of and guidelines for retailers on the physical demands of children. Education of caregivers on the nutritional needs of children.	Caregivers should allow children to physically discover the grocery store and its assortment to an appropriate extent. Caregivers should suggest healthy rather than unhealthy products to children. Unhealthy food should not be used as a reward or appeasement.

	Retailers/Marketers	**Public Policy**	**Caregivers**
Emotional	Offering of a variety of activities to facilitate play and engagement opportunities (esp. edutainment elements) as well as food-related hedonic experiences (e.g., tasting stands, emotional promotion of healthy foods) for children of different age groups.	Education of caregivers, retailers and marketers about the importance of the emotional dimension of food for children which forms the basis for a long-lasting positive relationship with food. Development of recommendations for the different parties involved on how to strengthen the emotional well-being of children during shopping.	Caregivers should support an emotionally positive shopping experience by involving children and creating a positive shopping atmosphere. Initially, children will want to test their limits or try to use pester power. However, caregivers must remain consistent. A balance must be created between functional and emotional shopping.
Social	Creation of an open and friendly atmosphere. Training of salespeople on how to communicate with children.	Education of caregivers, retailers and marketers about grocery shopping experiences as opportunities to teach children about food-related	Caregivers should use grocery shopping as opportunity to teach their children about social interactions as well as social rules and norms.
Social	Creation of a relaxed shopping atmosphere (e.g. through quiet music) that facilitates harmonious interactions.	social interactions as well as social rules and norms.	Caregivers should view grocery shopping as family activity and as an opportunity to bond with their children.
Intellectual	Implementation of edutainment experiences tailored to children in different development stages. Spatial positioning of play opportunities in such a way that they do not distract from learning moments.	Education of caregivers, retailers, and marketers about the food-related intellectual needs (conceptual and procedural knowledge) of children according to their developmental stage.	Caregivers have to be a positive example and have to actively teach their children conceptual and procedural knowledge on food and the grocery shopping process.

	Retailers/Marketers	Public Policy	Caregivers
Self-determined	Training for salespeople on how to involve and talk to children. Creation of opportunities for children to express themselves and actively participate in the shopping process. Implementation of measures that support autonomous and self-determined behavior, e.g., a staircase for children at the fresh food counter.	Encouragement of caregivers, retailers and marketers to help children to develop self-determination. However, it must be kept in mind that it is not appropriate to leave the child in charge in every situation. Children also need protection and guidance.	Children should be given the opportunity to act and decide for themselves to an appropriate extent and to grow with grocery shopping-related challenges. However, both younger and older children must also be shown boundaries and be pointed in the right (healthier) direction.
General	Attention should be paid to children's FWB in the creation of a store's layout and its marketing measures because children often (co-)determine purchase decisions and are the consumers of tomorrow, necessitating the establishment of a positive, long-lasting consumer-provider relationship.	Establishment of a seal of approval for family friendliness and the support of FWB. Information campaigns for caregivers, retailers and marketers on the importance of children's FWB and how it can be positively influenced during grocery shopping trips (list of recommendations).	Caregivers need to be aware that shopping with their children is an important family activity that can influence the development of their children's FWB when used properly.

5.8.2 Recommendations for Organic Stores

The simple and open structure of organic stores allows children, especially smaller children, to move freely and develop playfully. Distractions such as conspicuous marketing campaigns, music or crowds are hardly present, giving caregivers enough opportunities to spend time with their children and to teach them about the grocery shopping process. However, freedom sometimes leads caregivers to be less restrictive. Furthermore, the health-oriented product assortment of organic stores supports a healthy product selection, and their child-friendliness (e.g., through the presence of a play corner) influences children's emotional well-being.

Organic grocery stores especially offer opportunities for younger children, aged younger than six years, to discover the grocery store freely. This discovery journey could be improved by implementing more elements in the store through which children can learn about food and the grocery shopping process. For example, instead of an ordinary play corner, a miniature grocery store could be built. However, it must be ensured that these play possibilities do not distract the children from important learning moments such as paying at the cash desk due to their spatial proximity. Furthermore, to encourage children in their learning process, learning stations could be implemented. Since caregivers were observed to have more time and patience in the organic store to teach their children, learning stations could support interactive learning and discussions between the children and their caregivers. Furthermore, special attention should be paid to older children, as they were often not or only to a limited extent involved in the shopping process. For them, grocery store visits could, for instance, become more interesting through a gamification of the shopping process (e.g., whoever finds the answer to a food product-related question wins a smoothie) or by using gamified in-store mobile applications.

5.8.3 Recommendations for Supermarkets

Shopping in supermarkets often seems to be strongly guided by utilitarian motives (efficiency and effectiveness) and is therefore very goal-oriented. To make shopping effective and efficient, especially older children often take on an assistive function and actively support their caregivers during shopping. The hectic environment in supermarkets, characterized by small aisles, many customers, a large assortment of products, and speaker announcements, makes it difficult for caregivers to properly deal with children and their needs. This is particularly unfortunate due to the often large number of temptations in the supermarket that require substantial self-control on the part of children, which they can often only acquire by their parents teaching them.

Because the hustle and bustle of the supermarket often does not allow caregivers to take the time and teach their children, measures should be implemented to destress shopping trips, such as playing calm, relaxing background music and creating a more spacious store layout. Furthermore, young children in particular should be more integrated into the purchase process, for example, by means of providing shopping carts for children. At the same time, elements that restrict children's participation, such as plastic cars under shopping carts, should be avoided. Moreover, elements should be implemented through which children can engage themselves, for example, in the form of self-explanatory learning stations, so that children, especially those who are not yet able to help with shopping, are meaningfully engaged and their caregivers can shop in peace. Additionally, more children-friendly elements, such as a thematically aligned play corner for younger children or in-store mobile applications for older children, could be integrated.

5.9 Implications for Public Policy

Caregivers primarily determine the extent to which food shopping influences children's FWB. They determine where shopping trips take place and to what extent children actively participate in the shopping process. Additionally, they are responsible for teaching and instructing children during the process (e.g., Pólya and Földi, 2014). Nevertheless, research shows that caregivers avoid taking their children grocery shopping, as they perceive it to be a stressful and time-consuming activity (e.g., Schuhen et al., 2017). Thus, there must be a paradigm shift. Food shopping with children should no longer be seen as a necessary and stressful evil but as an opportunity for caregivers to spend time with their children and take them one step further in their development. It is therefore essential to inform caregivers, for example through public health campaigns, about how and to what extent children can benefit from food shopping and how caregivers themselves can support children in their food-related learning and development during grocery shopping (Table 12 provides examples on how caregivers can positively shape the grocery shopping trip to help their children develop a high level of FWB).

In addition, public policy and consumer protection organizations should inspire and motivate retailers to pursue a family-friendly strategy that also takes children's FWB into account. To foster FWB-oriented store formats, policy makers or consumer protection organizations could publicly endorse retailers that voluntarily work on contributing to consumers' FWB, for instance through government subsidies or acknowledgment in the form of public press releases. A possible motivator for retailers could also be the establishment of a seal of approval which indicates a store's level of FWB-friendliness. This strategy would allow retailers to differentiate themselves from the competition and gain a competitive advantage, while for families, it would be an easy-to-understand guide. To establish a seal, however, a tool must first be developed to measure the FWB-friendliness of grocery stores. The key characteristics of store formats identified in this paper (store layout, product assortment, marketing activities, playing options and learning opportunities) could serve as overarching categories for the quality criteria that need to be included in this tool. Furthermore, elements that have already been identified as particularly influential in the grocery retail context, such as the check-out area, should receive special attention in the stores' FWB-related evaluations. For example, it could be assessed to what extent healthy foods, that fulfill certain nutritional standards, or nonfood products instead of unhealthy foods are placed at the checkouts. Major food retailers such as Aldi have already partly implemented 'healthier' checkout areas and have received positive feedback from caregivers (Rivlin, 2016). Another measurable and effective improvement would be the reduction of marketing measures for foods and beverages with high sugar and fat content aimed at children and the redirection of attention towards healthy alternatives, for instance through the use of secondary placements (Rivlin, 2016). These and other measures could flow into the stores' FWB-related evaluation and the decision as to whether or not they deserve the seal of approval for a high level of FWB-friendliness.

5.10 Limitations and Future Research

This study has limitations that inform future research. First, it is an exploratory, mainly qualitative study, allowing a broad approach to build a holistic picture of the possible influences of grocery shopping on children's FWB. However, this approach also prevents individual influences from being investigated in detail, requiring future studies to examine the individual influences in depth. Second, since the qualitative data collection and analysis were comparably subjective and the sample size was comparably small, future (quantitative) research is needed to confirm the findings. Third, the current study presents only the short-term influences of grocery shopping on FWB and therefore does not allow conclusions for medium- or long-term effects. Accordingly, it is necessary to conduct longitudinal studies to enrich the findings. Fourth, the study was carried out in only two specific grocery store formats, necessitating observational studies in additional store formats to generate a more complete picture. Within these studies, special attention should be paid to the consumer groups who visit specific store formats and their group-specific characteristics because it can be assumed that the target groups of the different store formats differ considerably in their backgrounds and lifestyles and therewith also with respect to their motives regarding their children's food-related education and well-being. Organic store shoppers, for instance, are likely to be, on average, more concerned about healthy choices and options, and they are likely to have raised their children with similar values. This is also one reason why it was difficult to compare the families in the two stores in the current study. It would also be particularly interesting to examine the behavior of vulnerable families, such as low-income families or overweight families, and how this can be positively influenced. Fifth, the study was conducted in Germany, which makes it difficult to generalize the findings to other countries, especially as food shopping is strongly influenced by social customs and cultural influences, requiring the collection of data in other regions and countries. Generally, future research should identify and test the types of interventions that the different retailers could use to enhance children's FWB so that tangible and evidence-based measures can be derived.

5.11 Appendix: Coding List

Table 13 presents the list of codes that was made by means of a combination of bottom-up and top-down coding and that was used for the data analysis.

Table 13: List of codes

Dimension	Category	Meaning
Physical	Nutrition-related	Healthy/neutral/unhealthy product[7] suggestions and purchase decisions initiated by caregivers.
		Healthy/neutral/unhealthy product suggestions and purchase decisions initiated by children.
		Arousal of interest in healthy/neutral/unhealthy products through marketing activities.
	Body-related	Positive/neutral/negative physical activities in-store.
Emotional	Purchase-related emotions	Positive/negative emotions caused by activities and situations directly related to the purchasing process.
		Positive/negative emotions caused by activities and situations not directly related to the purchasing process.
	Sensorial emotional experiences	Positive/negative emotions evoked by the sensory experience of the products.
	Emotional control	Exertion of high/low self-control regarding emotionally driven purchasing behavior.
Social	Interaction	Positive/negative interaction with caregivers through verbal communication, physical contact, eye contact, or cooperative behavior.
		Positive/negative interaction with third parties through verbal communication, physical contact, eye contact, or cooperative behavior.
		Positive/negative interaction between caregivers and third parties which do not directly involve the child.
	Socialization	Positive/negative behavior of children or caregivers related to social norms, rules and values.
		Teaching of social norms, rules and values by caregivers and others.

7 The classification into unhealthy (e.g., salty snacks, chocolate), neutral (e.g., bread, cheese) and healthy products (e.g., vegetables, fruits) was based on categorizations of previous research (Huyghe et al., 2017; Khan and Dhar, 2007; Milkman, Rogers, and Bazerman, 2010).

Dimension	Category	Meaning
	Social responsibility	Positive/negative behavior related to purchase and consumption behavior in the interest of third parties.
Intellectual	Food literacy	Children's existing/missing background knowledge related to food (declarative knowledge).
		Children's existing/missing competences related to purchasing processes (procedural knowledge).
		Children's existing/missing competences related to recipes and food processing (procedural knowledge).
	Food socialization	Transfer of correct/incorrect background knowledge related to food by caregivers and others (declarative knowledge).
		Active or passive transfer of correct/incorrect knowledge on purchasing processes by caregivers and others (procedural knowledge).
		Transfer of correct/incorrect knowledge on recipes and food preparation by caregivers and others (procedural knowledge).
	Sensory learning	Encouragement/inhibition of experiencing and discovering products through sensory stimuli.
	Creative action	Encouragement/inhibition of inspiration related to experimenting with new recipes or food processing
Self-determined	Freedom of movement	Exploitation/no exploitation of the possibility to move freely in the store.
	Autonomous action	Occurrence/no occurrence of autonomous behavior as a result of self-initiative or encouragement from third parties.
	Expression of opinion	Expression of opinions related to purchasing decisions inquired by caregivers.
		Expression of opinions related to purchasing decisions initiated by children.
	Handling of money	Situations that encourage/inhibit the learning of handling money.

6 Impulsivity Makes More Susceptible to Overeating After Contextual Appetitive Conditioning[8]

6.1 Introduction

The prevalence of overweight and obesity has been rapidly increasing, adversely affecting quality of life and leading to increased health care costs (Flegal et al., 2010; Sturm, 2002). The obesogenic environment plays an important role in the current rise in obesity prevalence (Swinburn, Egger, and Raza, 1999), although it is not clear yet why some people are more vulnerable to overeat in a tempting environment than others. The abundant environment is characterized by many cues that signal high-calorie food availability (Burton, Smit, and Lightowler, 2007; Rodin and Slochower, 1976), and classical conditioning has been put forward as a mechanism that might explain why it is so difficult for some people to resist environmental temptations: in case of strong reinforcers, like tasty high-calorie foods, one easily learns to associate a predictor of intake with the actual eating. The learning of such an association facilitates cue-elicited eating: the cue prepares the person for intake, for instance by increasing salivation, elicits a desire to eat, and stimulates actual eating, frequently in the absence of physical hunger (Jansen, 1998; Jansen et al., 2010; Wardle, 1990). Virtually any cue has the ability to become associated with food intake and to elicit preparatory responses of the body. These preparatory responses, also termed cephalic phase responses, are thought to be experienced as a desire to eat (Jansen, 1998; Nederkoorn, Smulders, and Jansen, 2000; Powley, 1977). Both the physiological preparatory responses and eating desires are labeled cue reactivity (Jansen, 1998; Jansen et al., 2010). Classical conditioning studies with animals show that contexts might act as conditioned stimuli as well: sated rats showed an increased food intake in a cage previously associated with eating (Boggiano et al., 2009; Petrovich et al., 2007). The current obesogenic environment provides many opportunities to associate everyday contexts with food intake and therefore is able to elicit frequently recurring cue reactivity and overeating in conditioned contexts. Indeed, it has been found that among eating behavior characteristics the

8 Reference: Van den Akker, Karolien, Jansen, Anita, Frentz, Florentine, Havermans, Remco. (2013). Impulsivity Makes More Susceptible to Overeating After Contextual Appetitive Conditioning. Appetite, 70, 73-80.

F. Frentz, *The Pursuit of Food Well-Being*, Handel und Internationales Marketing Retailing and International Marketing,
https://doi.org/10.1007/978-3-658-30366-2_6

strongest correlate of future weight gain was habitual overeating, or the susceptibility to overeat in response to everyday cues within the environment (Hays and Roberts, 2007).

Very few experimental studies have been conducted investigating classical conditioning as causal mechanism for context-induced cravings and overeating in humans. In these studies, an initially neutral contextual stimulus is repeatedly paired with food intake (the unconditioned stimulus, US) so this context becomes a predictor (conditioned stimulus, CS) for consumption. A study in preschool children found evidence of contextual conditioning of meal initiation (Birch et al., 1989), and a conditioning procedure using chocolate shows differential acquisition of craving and automatic approach tendencies towards a specific contextual cue (a tray) (Van Gucht et al., 2013; Van Gucht et al., 2010; Van Gucht et al., 2008a; Van Gucht et al., 2008b).

Appetitive conditioning studies usually do not take personality characteristics into account. It is known however that obesity, overeating and impulsivity frequently go together; several studies have found that trait impulsivity is positively associated with obesity (Nederkoorn et al., 2006a; Nederkoorn et al., 2006b; Rydén et al., 2003). Furthermore, impulsivity has been associated with increased food cue reactivity (Tetley, Brunstrom, and Griffiths, 2010), increased attention for food cues (Hou et al., 2011), binge eating (de Zwaan et al., 1994; Nasser, Gluck, and Geliebter, 2004) and increased food intake (Guerrieri, Nederkoorn, and Jansen, 2008; Nederkoorn, et al., 2006b). It has even been reported that obese children receiving cognitive behaviour therapy lost significantly less weight with increasing impulsivity (Nederkoorn et al., 2007). A possible role of impulsivity in conditioning has been proposed as well. Gray's BIS-BAS theory postulated that trait impulsivity should be related to activation of a system sensitive to appetitive conditions (i.e., the behavioural activation system or BAS) (Corr, Pickering, and Gray, 1995). It can be argued that impulsives' stronger output of the BAS is related to changes in arousal and emotional states which in turn can strengthen CS–US associations currently undergoing processing (Corr, 2001). Other authors have proposed impulsivity to be related to an increased strength (and/or number) of appetitive associational resources, thereby rendering them predisposed to forming appetitive associations (Zinbarg and Revelle, 1989). However, evidence for the validity of these models is scarce (e.g., Corr, Pickering, and Gray, 1995; Gupta and Shukla, 1989; Paisey and Mangan, 1988; Zinbarg and Mohlman, 1998). Knowing that impulsivity is positively associated with overeating and obesity, it is of interest to study whether impulsivity predicts a facilitated acquisition of conditioned responding to a CS that signals a food reward and, in this way, stimulates overeating in especially the high impulsive people.

In the present study, a Virtual Reality (VR) laboratory is used to create different contexts that are either associated with milkshake intake or not. In VR, participants are immersed in a programmed three-dimensional world, while perceiving this virtual world as 'real' (Hoffman et al, 2003). These complex environments likely have a stronger connection to real-life situations than the usual distinct stimuli (e.g., pictures or objects). It is expected that after conditioning, the intake-associated environment (CS+) will elicit a stronger desire for milkshake, an increased expectancy to receive milkshake, more salivation and an increased intake during a bogus taste test, compared with a control environment (CS–). The CS+ is also expected to be liked more. Further, it is predicted that impulsivity facilitates conditioning.

6.2 Method and Materials

6.2.1 Participants

Seventy participants took part in the study. Female students were invited for participation if they were proficient in Dutch, aged between 18 and 25 years, had a normal BMI (19–25) and were in the 1st or 2nd year of their bachelor program. Furthermore, to be included in the study their score on the Restraint Scale had to be below 15, meaning that they are unrestrained eaters (Polivy, Herman, and Howard, 1988), and a requisite was that they liked at least one milkshake flavor (vanilla, chocolate, or strawberry). The questions were incorporated into a set of filler items. Participants were asked to have a small meal (e.g., a sandwich) two hours prior to the experiment, and to refrain from calorie intake thereafter. To reduce demand characteristics, participants were told that this study was about investigating 'the influence of environmental stimulation on taste perception'. They received either €10 or were given course credits for participation. The study's procedure was approved by the local ethical committee.

6.2.2 Measures

Questionnaires were administered in Dutch.

Desire and expectancy: 100mm-Visual Analogue Scales (VAS) were used to assess subjective desire for milkshake and expectancy to receive milkshake (Huskisson, 1974; Van Gucht et al., 2008a). The desire-VAS was accompanied by the question 'How strong is your desire for milkshake at this moment?', and the expectancy-VAS was accompanied by the question 'How strong do you expect to be allowed to taste milkshake at this moment?'. Ratings ranged from 0 (no desire for milk- shake at all / certainly expect not to taste milkshake) to 100 (very strong desire for milkshake / certainly expect to taste milkshake). The order of presentation of these two VASs was randomized.

Salivation: Salivation was measured using dental rolls (Hartmann, nr 2, 10×35 mm) which the participant was instructed to place and remove herself. Two dental rolls were placed between the cheek and lower gum on the left and right sides. A third, halved dental roll was placed under the tongue. They were removed after precisely 1 min. The dental rolls were kept in a sealed plastic bag and their weight was registered before and after the saliva was collected, using a weighing scale accurate to 0.01 g (Mettler Toledo, PB3002).

Intake during taste test: Ad libitum milkshake intake was measured during a 5-minute bogus taste test, during which participants answered questions about supposed differences between three identical milkshakes. The flavor of these milkshakes was identical to the flavor during conditioning (vanilla, chocolate, or strawberry). Liking of the milkshake was measured during the taste test. The milkshakes were weighed before and after the taste test to assess total food intake. Each cup contained approximately 250g of milkshake, equivalent to 300 ml and 450 kcal.

CS preference: CS liking was measured using two different questionnaires. Before and after conditioning, participants rated their liking for the CS+ and CS– environments on a VAS accompanied by the question 'How much do you like this environment?', ranging from 0 (not at all) to 100 (very much). Additionally, after conditioning, participants were asked to give a ranking on how much they liked the four different virtual environments they had been exposed to, from most liked to least liked. This was done to assess the preferred CS (CS+ or CS–).

Contingency awareness: Participants completed a contingency awareness check to find out whether they were aware of the association between the CS+ and milkshake intake.

Presence: Feelings of presence in the virtual environments were measured using a questionnaire, adapted from another study (Hoffman et al., 1998; experiment 2, items A, D, E G). An average score was calculated. This was assessed since low levels of presence can have a substantial impact on responding (Witmer and Singer, 1998).

Nausea: To check for nausea due to exposure to virtual environments, participants were asked to indicate whether they felt nauseated before and after AR exposure on a VAS ranging from 0 (not at all nauseated) to 100 (extremely nauseated).

Hunger: To control for hunger at the start of the experiment, participants filled in a VAS accompanied by the question 'How hungry are you at this moment?' ranging from 0 (not hungry at all) to 100 (extremely hungry).

Milkshake liking: To control for possible differences in liking of milkshake, participants filled in a VAS accompanied by the question 'How much did you like the milkshakes?' ranging from 0 (not at all) to 100 (extremely).

Barrett Impulsivity Scale-11 (BIS-11; Patton, Stanford, and Barratt, 1995): The BIS-11 was used to measure impulsivity. It is a self-report questionnaire and consists of 30 items. Each statement can be rated on a 4-point scale, ranging from rarely/ never to always/almost always. Total scores were calculated, a higher score indicating higher impulsiveness. The BIS-11 has good internal consistency and good construct validity (Patton, Stanford, and Barratt, 1995).

Revised Restraint Scale (RS; Polivy, Herman, and Howard, 1988): The 10-item RS was used to assess dietary restraint, i.e., the intention to restrict food intake. Scores range from 0–35, a higher score indicates increased intentions to restrain intake.

6.2.3 Stimuli

US: The intake of milkshake served as the US. During conditioning, small milkshake cups with lid and a translucent straw were used. Each cup was weighed before and after a conditioning trial. One cup contained approximately 10g (18 kcal) of freshly-prepared milkshake, of which on average 5.41g (±1.22) was ingested during a CS+ trial. The milkshakes were kept in a cooler that remained out of sight of the participants at all times. Milkshakes could not be smelled.

CS: Four different virtual environments were used. One environment served as practice and acclimation environment, which was a largely empty room. The other three environments were presented during conditioning: An Italian square served as the (neutral) environment that appeared during the inter-trial interval (ITI), and two rooms served as CS+ or CS–; one of these depicted (non-food related) paintings, a window and seats, another room depicted a dojo (Japanese room to practice martial arts). These environments were accompanied by two distinct musical pieces (Beethoven's Violin romance no. 2 F major and Mussorgsky's Pictures at an Exhibition), which have been found to be emotionally neutral (Mitterschiffthaler et al., 2007). Which room and musical piece combination (four combinations) served as CS+ or CS– was counterbalanced across participants.

Augmented Reality (AR): In AR, virtual environments are visible, but objects that are close to the participant in the real world can still be perceived (Botella et al., 2005). In this experiment, AR was used so the participant could see her own hands and the milkshakes, and she was able to fill out VAS questionnaires. To display the virtual environments, a Head-Mounted Display (HMD) was used (NVIS nVisor ST50), which was placed on the head of the participant. An HMD enables the display of virtual environments on screens inside the

HMD. A tracking system was used to precisely locate movements of participants' heads (PhaseSpace), and the images projected on the screens inside the HMD change according to the participants' movements. Thus, when a participant turns her head to the left, the virtual images change according to her head movement. The software used for programming is Vizard Virtual Reality Toolkit, WorldViz. A sound system was used to play pre-recorded instructions and musical pieces (Ambisonic Auralizer System, WorldViz).

6.2.4 Design and Procedure

See Figure 12 for an overview of the study's design. Participants were run individually between 11 AM and 6 PM. Upon arrival in the laboratory, the participant gave written consent. She was seated at a table during the whole experiment. The participant was instructed on how to fill in a VAS, and was then asked to rate her hunger and nausea. Also, a baseline measure of saliva production was conducted. When looking around in the virtual environment, she had to take care not to move her head too fast, which was done to minimize cybersickness. She was explicitly informed that one of the environments would be followed by being asked to drink something. After thirty participants had participated in the study, twelve still appeared unaware of an association between the rooms and being allowed to drink milkshake. Therefore, we changed the instructions regarding the CS–US contingency slightly by additionally showing participants colored, printed pictures of the environments during this introduction session (no milkshake was given yet).

A participant first received an acclimation and practice session in AR, after which the conditioning procedure started (duration approximately 30 minutes, see Figure 12). She then performed a taste test in either the CS+ or CS– environment, depending on which condition she had been assigned to. Assignment to a condition was random and counterbalanced. All instructions given during conditioning and the taste test were pre-recorded and played through the sound system.

Conditioning: In total, 6 CS+ and 6 CS– trials were presented to each participant. The order of the presentation of these trials was random, but with the restriction of no more than two consecutive trials of the same trial type. Further, the first two and last two trials always consisted of one CS+ and one CS–, counterbalanced across participants. A trial started when the CS+ or CS– environment became visible. The participant was told to look around slowly. After 30 seconds, she filled out the first desire and expectancy-VAS. Then, a milkshake cup was placed on the table in front of her, and she picked it up and placed the milkshake's straw into her mouth but was not allowed to drink. She still was

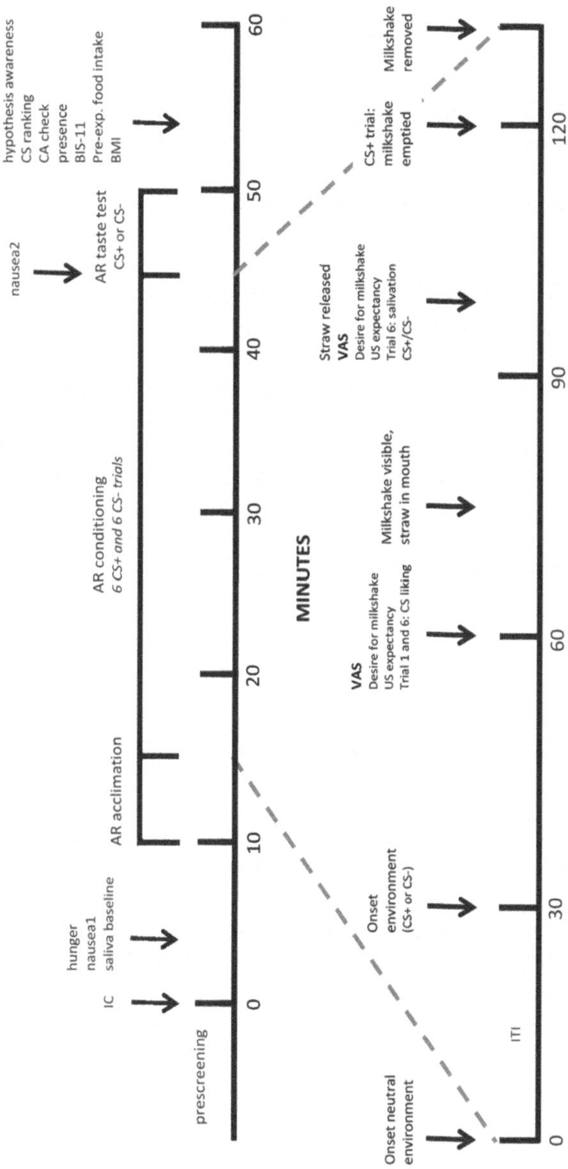

The upper time line depicts the chronological order (from left to right) of the entire experimental procedure. The lower time line specifies a single conditioning trial. The onset of an environment automatically causes the offset of the previous environment.

Figure 12: Overview of the study's design

exposed to the environment. After another 30 seconds, she placed the cup on the table and filled in the second desire and expectancy-VAS. In case of a CS– trial, the milkshake cup was now removed. In case of a CS+ trial, the participant picked up the milkshake cup again and emptied it. After this, the inter-trial interval (ITI) started, during which the neutral environment appeared for 30 seconds. During the 1st and 6th CS+ and CS– trials, CS liking was assessed. On both the 6th CS+ and the 6th CS– trial, salivation was measured. After all conditioning trials had been completed, the participant filled in a 2nd nausea VAS during the ITI, after which the taste test started.

Taste test: Depending on the participant's assigned environment, the CS+ or CS– environment was presented during the taste test. Three large milkshake cups with lids were placed in front of the participant. The participant received questions about the taste of the milkshakes, and was told that if she would finish early she was invited to drink as much as she liked to. After the taste test the HMD was removed.

Questionnaire: After the taste test, the participant filled out the following questionnaires: her ideas about the study's hypotheses, CS ranking, contingency awareness, presence, BIS-11, and time of pre-experimental food intake. Finally, the participant's weight and height were measured. She was thanked for participation and received her reward.

6.3 Results

6.3.1 Exclusion of Participants and Statistical Analysis

Three participants were excluded from analysis: one participant because she felt too nauseated to perform the taste test, another because she did not understand the instructions and a third was excluded because she scored > 3 SDs above the mean on the BIS-11.

Despite the explicit instructions regarding the US-environment association, a substantial part of the sample (23.9%; see Table 14) could not retrospectively indicate which room had been followed by being allowed to drink milkshake and/ or did not develop a differential expectancy. These participants were classified as not being aware of the contingency between an environment and the opportunity to drink (non-CA). Previous studies have shown that contingency awareness is likely necessary for the formation of associations (Hogarth et al., 2006; Lovibond and Shanks, 2002). Therefore, contingency awareness was included as a between-subjects variable in the ANOVAs.

Differential acquisition of expectancy and desire for milkshake were analyzed using 2 x 6 (CS–type x Trial) repeated-measures ANOVAs. Analyses were conducted on the 2nd expectancy and desire-VAS scores of each trial[9]. Saliva production was also analyzed using repeated-measures ANOVA, with measurement (baseline, CS+, CS–) as within-subjects variable, as was CS liking, with CS–type (CS+, CS–) and Trial (1st, 6th) as within-subjects variables. Preference for the CS+ over the CS– was tested using a binomial test. The total score of the BIS-11 was included as covariate in the ANOVAs to study effects of impulsivity on US- expectancy, desire for milkshake, salivation and CS liking. A student's t-test was used to test for differences in milkshake consumption across conditions (taste test environment: CS+ or CS–). A hierarchical linear regression model was used to analyze the effects of impulsivity and condition on milkshake consumption. Greenhouse-Geisser epsilon corrections are reported for repeated-measures analyses whenever sphericity was violated.

6.3.2 Participant Characteristics

No significant differences across conditions emerged for age, BMI, hunger, BIS-11 total, RS, presence and milkshake liking, however nausea differed significantly between conditions (see Table 14).

Table 14: Participant characterstics across conditions

	CS+ taste test M(SD)	**CS- taste test** M(SD)	***F*(1, 65)**	***p***
n	34	33		
Contingency aware	25	26		
Age	19.71 (1.53)	19.67 (1.83)	0.01	.92
BMI	22.06 (2.08)	21.49 (1.72)	1.51	.22
Baseline hunger	48.74 (21.33)	49.45 (24.10)	0.02	.90
BIS-11	60.59 (8.08)	58.18 (9.46)	1.26	.27
Restraint Scale	9.48 (2.98)	9.42 (3.26)	0.09	.77
*Presence**	57.06 (12.78)	55.88 (16.83)	0.10	.75
Baseline milkshake liking	65.88 (24.55)	73.85 (14.80)	2.57	.11
Nausea	26.35 (27.78)	13.67 (17.60)	4.95	.03

*Due to missing data, the degrees of freedom for this analysis were 1,64.

9 Each trial included two VAS measurements for each CS-type. Analyses including the first VAS scores of each trial revealed similar patterns.

6.3.3 US Expectancy and Desire for Milkshake

Overall, differential acquisition of expectancy was present, as indicated by a significant CS–type x Trial interaction, $F(3.12, 202.50) = 33.84$, $p < .001$ (see Figure 13). Including contingency awareness (CA) as between-subjects variable yielded a significant CS–type x Trial x CA interaction, $F(3.62, 231.62) = 14.93$, $p < .001$. Contingency non-aware participants failed to develop differential expectancy, $F(5,75) = 0.46$, $p = .81$ (see Figure 13c and 13e). Impulsivity had no significant effect on the differentiation, $F(3.18, 203.34) = 1.68$, $p = .17$.

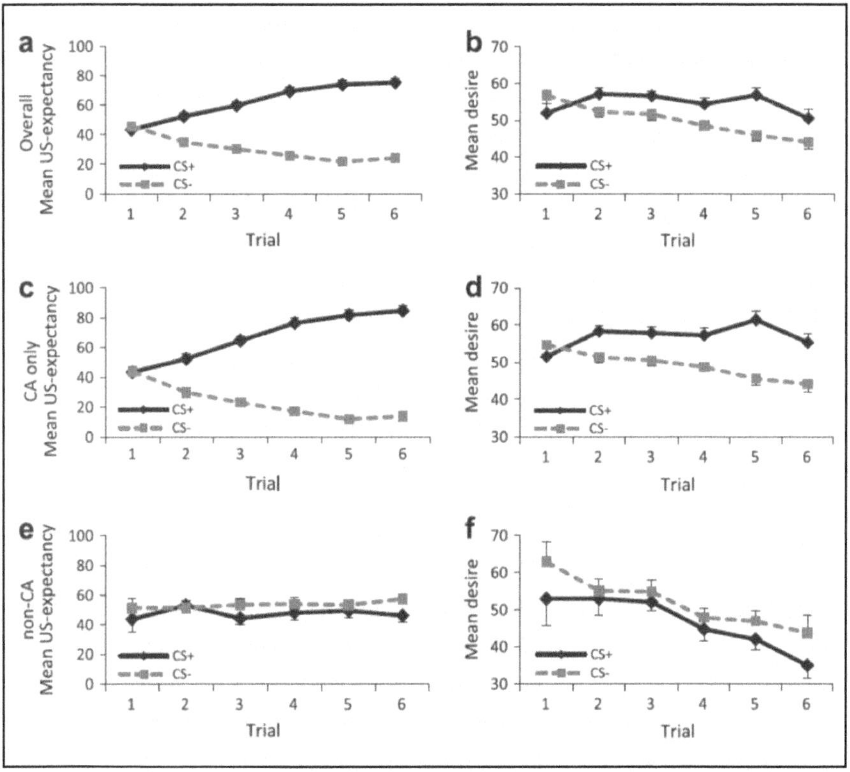

Figure 13: Mean US expectancy and desire for milkshake (+SEM) by CS-type and trial.

Participants also developed a differential acquisition of the desire for milkshake, as shown by a significant CS–type x Trial interaction, F(3.03, 200.51) = 5.81, p = .001 (see Figure 13b). This differentiation was characterized by a decrease in desire for milkshake in response to the CS–, F(2.98, 196.43) = 7.38, p < .001, while no change in desire for milkshake was found for the CS+, F(3.10, 204.50) = 1.90, p = .13.

No significant interaction between acquisition of differential desire for milk- shake and CA was found, F(3.04, 197.27) = 1.39, p = .25. However, the CA x trial interaction was significant, F(3.04, 197.27) = 2.67, p < .05, indicating an overall decrease in desire for milkshake in the non-CA group, F(2.69, 39.35) = 4.65, p = .001 but no overall change in the CA group, F(3.00, 150.20) = 1.09, p = .36 (see Figures 13d and 13f). Impulsivity did not influence differential desire over time, F(3.03, 197.07) = 0.68, p = .57).[10]

6.3.4 *Salivation*

Salivation differed significantly between the three measurements (see Figure 14), F(2, 128) = 4.97, p = .01, with Bonferroni-corrected pairwise comparisons indicating that salivation in the CS+ was significantly higher than baseline (p = .01) but not compared with salivation in the CS– (p = .49). Salivation in the CS– did not significantly differ from baseline (p = .32) (see Figure 15). No interaction with CA was found, F(2,126) = 0.06, p = .94, nor with impulsivity, F(2, 126) = 0.42, p = .66. As expected, the conditions did not differ in salivation pattern, F(2, 126) = 1.71, p = .19.

6.3.5 *Milkshake Consumption*

Overall: Taste test environment did not influence total milkshake consumption, t(65) = 0.28, p = .78 [mean consumed milkshake in the CS+: 137.23g (±97.39); CS–: 130.73 (±89.00)].

10 The differential acquisition of US expectancy and desire for milkshake did not differ between the conditions, and the CS-type x Trial x Condition interactions were not significant, F(3.10, 198.56)=0.85, p = .47; F(3.03, 196.77) = 1.13, p = .34. Thus, as expected, the conditions did not differ in acquisition of differential US expectancy and desire for milkshake.

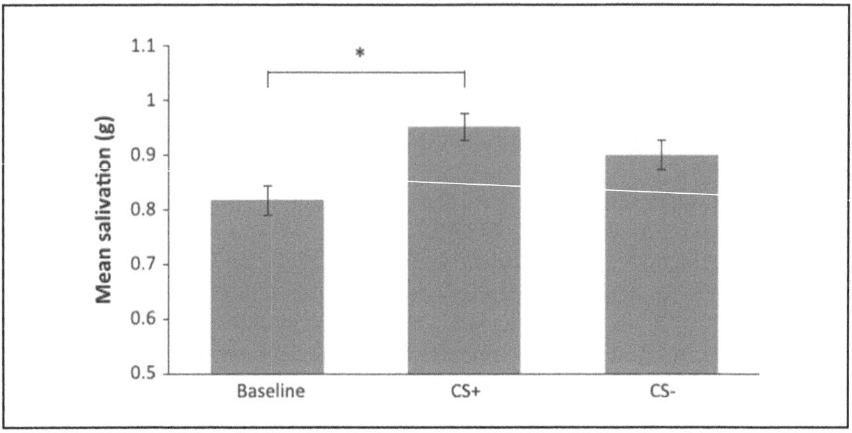

Figure 14: Mean salivation (+SEM) at baseline, CS+ and CS-

Impulsivity: To examine influences of impulsivity on milkshake consumption, a regression analysis was conducted (see Table 15 and Figure 15). Both nausea and milkshake liking correlated significantly with total milkshake consumption, $r(65) = -0.25$, $p = .04$, $r(65) = 0.25$, $p < .05$ and with each other, $r(65) = 0.42$, $p < .001$. Since the conditions significantly differed in nausea but not in liking (see Table 15: nausea in the CS+ condition was higher), nausea was included in the regression model[11]. All variables were centered before entering in the regression model. The analysis showed that condition and impulsivity interacted ($\Delta R^2 = 0.06$, $p = .04$). Follow-up analyses revealed that participants who were highly impulsive (1 SD above the mean of the BIS-11) consumed significantly more milkshake in the CS+ than in the CS– ($p = .04$). In contrast, within low-impulsive participants (1 SD below the mean of the BIS-11) no difference in milkshake consumption between the conditions was found ($p = .44$). Analyzing the slope of the CS– regression line revealed a trend ($p = .08$), suggesting a decreased food intake in the CS– in more impulsive relative to less impulsive participants. The slope of the CS+ regression line was not significant ($p = .24$).

11 When excluding participants who scored highest on nausea (scoring ≥ 50 on the 2nd nausea-VAS, n = 10) instead of entering nausea as covariate in regression analysis, the condition*impulsivity interaction remained significant ($\Delta R^2 = 0.09$, $p = .03$). Thus, both methods to control for nausea resulted in similar effects.

Table 15: Summary of the hierarchical regression analysis

Variable	B	B (s.e.)	β
Step 1			
Nausea	-0.98	0.47	-0.25*
Step 2			
Nausea	-1.11	0.49	-0.29*
Condition	-22.09	23.47	-0.12
Impulsivity	-0.65	1.30	-0.06
Step 3			
Nausea	-0.93	0.48	-0.24#
Condition	-18.97	22.92	-0.10
Impulsivity	2.43	1.95	0.23
Condition x Impulsivity	-5.35	2.59	-0.38*

R^2 = 0.06 for Step 1 (p = .04), Δ R^2 = 0.02 for Step 2 (ns), Δ R^2 = 0.06 for Step 3 (p = .05); *p < .05; #p < .06

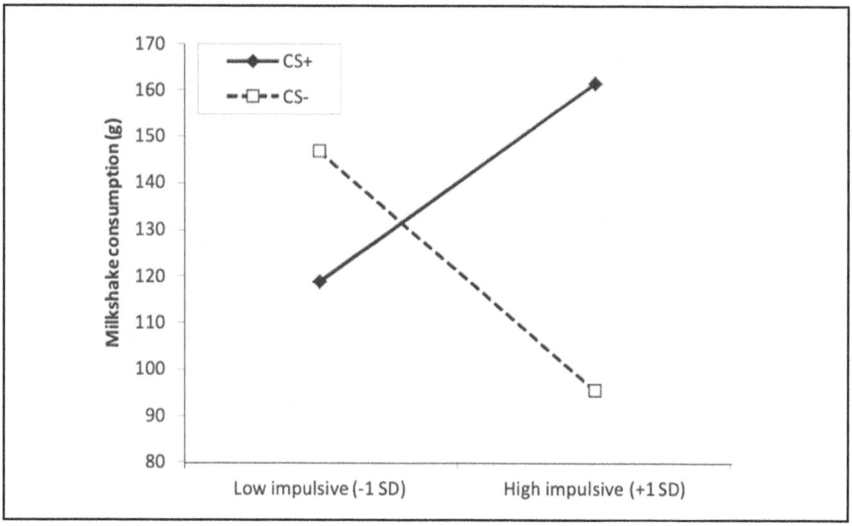

Figure 15: Milkshake consumption in low and high impulsive participants, for the CS+ or CS- taste test

CA: CA was added to the model (not shown in the model) and was not found to predict milkshake consumption overall, b = -.09, t(62) = -0.72, p = .47. Furthermore, no significant Condition x Impulsivity x CA interaction was found, b = -.002, t(60) = -0.02, p = .99, suggesting no differences in milkshake consumption patterns between CA and non-CA participants.

6.3.6 CS Liking

Conditioned CS liking was evident with repeated-measures analyses when including CA in the CS–Type*Trial interaction, F(1, 63) = 5.92, p = .02; CA participants developed a significant differentiation in CS liking, F(1, 49) = 6.67, p = .01 [mean change in CS+ liking: 0.80 (±14.84); CS–: -8.10 (±18.48)], whereas non-CA participants did not, F(1, 14) = 1.79, p = .20 [mean change in CS+ liking: -8.43 (±18.79); CS–: 0.13 (±13.37)]. Impulsivity did not have an effect on this interaction, F(1, 61) = 2.21, p = .14. In the ranking, the CS+ was not more preferred than the CS–; the CS+ was preferred by 56% of the participants, p = .46.

6.4 Discussion

This study provides evidence of contextual appetitive conditioning in females. After six conditioning trials, conditioned cue reactivity in response to the contextual CS+ was found: participants salivated significantly more in response to this context compared to baseline and this increase was non-significant for the CS–. Likewise, the contextual CS+ elicited a greater desire for milkshake and higher US expectations than the CS– after conditioning. Differential CS+ liking increased on the within-subjects assessment in contingency-aware participants, also indicating conditioned responding. In line with previous research, this conditioning appeared to depend largely on awareness of the contingency between the CSs and the US. Impulsivity did not moderate the acquired context cue reactivity (salivation and subjective responses). However, increased consumption after appetitive conditioning was found in impulsive participants: high impulsive participants consumed more milkshake when being present in the CS+ compared with the CS–, while low impulsive participants consumed similar amounts in the CS+ and CS–.

This study contributes to the existing literature by showing that not only isolated proximal food cues but also complex non-food related environmental stimuli are able to become triggers of conditioned appetitive responding in humans. Another new finding was that preparatory responses of the body (salivation) may be involved in human contextual appetitive conditioning: we found some evidence that initially neutral contexts are able to elicit an adaptive physiological change that is similar to physiological reactions to the sight or smell of food. The current obesogenic environment (context) offers many potential opportunities to associate different contexts (e.g., home, office, friends) with calorie intake, and in this way stimulates contextual appetitive conditioning. Contextual eating might be considered a form of habitual eating that occurs relatively automatic without people being aware of these conditioning processes and context-induced cue reactivity. Intriguingly, those participants in our sample who were unaware of the CS–US contingency also showed some evidence of conditioned responding on the behavioral measures, suggesting that they, too, prepared for food intake. Not intervening on these conditioning processes might make it more difficult to change overeating patterns. It was for instance found that conditioned food cue reactivity was absent in successful post-obese dieters - presumably extinguished - whereas it was present in unsuccessful obese dieters (Jansen, Havermans, and Nederkoorn, 2011; Jansen et al., 2010).

Another new and intriguing finding is that impulsivity was a significant predictor of milkshake consumption in the CS+. Although the milkshake US was available in both the CS+ and CS– during the taste test (in large amounts), only the more impulsive participants ingested significantly more milkshake in the food-associated environment (and not in the CS–). Since impulsivity did not appear to moderate the acquisition of other conditioned responses over trials, these data seem to suggest that impulsivity as measured by the BIS-11 is not related to a facilitated acquisition whereas it is to the behavioural expression of the (conditioned) motivational state (i.e., increased intake) (Corr, 2001). This is consistent with previous research reporting that increased food intake in impulsive participants only occurs when participants are hungry (Nederkoorn et al., 2009). Our findings are also in line with the idea that 'rash impulsiveness' is related to an inability to inhibit predominant approach responses, since our present measure of impulsivity (the BIS-11) is supposed to provide a measure of this form of impulsiveness (Dawe, Gullo, and Loxton, 2004). Thus, once an approach response was activated by the CS+, the high impulsives in our study might have been unable to inhibit approach behavior and subsequently increased their food intake. On the other hand, the present findings also suggest a trend towards higher impulsivity being related to a suppression of intake in the CS–, possibly pointing towards more effective response inhibition in a non-food associated context (see also Jansen et al., 1989). In the CS–, participants were exposed to milkshake cups but were not allowed to consume the milkshake. It is possible that the more impulsive participants had to put greater effort into inhibiting their approach response in the CS–, which could have led to effective inhibitory learning in impulsives in specifically this context. This suggests that high impulsives (e.g., binge eaters and people with obesity) could benefit from food cue exposure therapy, in which a food cue is repeatedly presented while the actual eating is prevented (i.e., inhibited) in order to decrease cue reactivity. However, the present experiment was not designed to test these ideas, and future studies should include truly neutral stimuli to see whether the increased intake in the CS+ compared with the CS– in higher impulsives is due to facilitatory or inhibitory mechanisms, or a combination of both.

It is possible that impulsivity is related to an increased speed of acquisition of conditioned responding to food cues under certain conditions. For instance, previous findings have suggested that both the size and type of the US may be important for an increased acquisition speed in impulsives: extraverts vs. introverts have been found to show stronger appetitive conditioning of electrodermal responses when stronger, but not when weaker, sexual stimuli were involved (Paisey and Mangan, 1988), and a positive relation between reward responsiveness and speed of acquisition of US expectancies has been reported when a monetary reward was involved but not when an ego-related reward was involved (Zinbarg and Mohlman, 1998). In contrast, in our study, participants received a food reward during conditioning which was relatively weak (i.e., a very small amount of milkshake). Additionally, the same reward may be perceived differently by different participants; for instance, impulsive individuals could have been disappointed by the small US in the present study (Corr, 2001). Moreover, different measures or forms of impulsivity might also be differentially related to appetitive conditioning (Corr, 2001; Papachristou et al., 2013).

Cue and context-elicited cravings are well-known in addiction research (Drummond, 2001). Cue exposure therapy has been used in the treatment of both addiction and eating disorders. A major problem with cue exposure treatment is renewal, in which a supposedly extinguished response re-emerges after treatment when a patient returns to the acquisition environment (Bouton, 2002; Havermans and Jansen, 2003). This is thought to occur because of differences between the contexts in which the behavior was learned, extinguished and tested, and stresses the need for exposures in the context that is associated with intake or use (Bouton, 2002; Havermans and Jansen, 2003; Jansen, 1998; Thewissen et al., 2005). VR and AR could therefore become useful tools for improving cue exposure therapy: it is possible to create contexts very similar to those in which one usually overeats or uses a drug. Researchers conducting experiments and/or therapies involving food in AR or VR should however be aware of the possibility of inducing additional nausea in participants by the incorporation of sensory exposure to foods ('cybersickness'). Nausea might in particular affect appetitive responding.

In sum, the present study adds to the existing literature that contextual appetitive conditioning induces conditioned responding (i.e., an increased desire for food and an increased liking of the CS) in healthy women, and it provides some evidence for the involvement of preparatory responses of the body (i.e., a conditioned salivary response). This study also uniquely associates impulsivity with increased food consumption in specifically a conditioned food-associated context. Future research should elucidate the complex role of impulsivity in the acquisition and expression of appetitive conditioning and ask the question why impulsivity is related to increased vulnerability to conditioned context-induced overeating. Also, research is needed on the implications for cue/context exposure therapy, and how AR and VR can be used to develop optimal exposure therapy for appetitive disorders and substance use disorders.

7 Understanding Planning for Unplanned Purchases: Antecedents and Exploitation of In-Store Slack[12]

7.1 Introduction and Motivation for Replication

Several studies support the idea that consumers use a form of mental budgeting where they allocate money to mental accounts and try to resist further purchases when the budget is depleted. These mental budgets are used at the shopping-trip level, even if implicitly, to enhance self-control, regulate purchase behavior, and support the attainment of shopping goals (Kahneman and Tversky, 1984; Thaler, 1985; Heath and Soll, 1996).

Although mental budgets have already been examined with respect to purchases (Heath and Soll, 1996), Stilley, Inman, and Wakefield (2010a) introduced an expansion of this approach by means of the idea of in-store slack. In particular, Stilley, Inman, and Wakefield (2010a) suggest that consumers tend to create mental budgets with two parts, an itemized portion and an in-store slack. While the itemized portion corresponds to the amount of money that a consumer allocates to spend on items whose purchase has been planned and therefore helps shoppers avoid unplanned purchases, in-store slack is the portion of the mental budget to be spent on unplanned purchases and thus helps limit unplanned purchases by preventing self-control depletion (Stilley, Inman, and Wakefield, 2010a). The main reason for the existence of in-store slack is that customers anticipate forgotten needs. Additionally, some customers may deliberately reserve some in-store slack to ensure they have sufficient financial flexibility to make impulsive decisions or to increase the hedonic value of their shopping trip (Babin, Darden, and Griffin, 1994; Stilley, Inman, and Wakefield, 2010b).

Although theoretically well conceptualized and empirically confirmed, the concept of in-store slack is worth revisiting due to the limitations of the initial studies by Stilley, Inman, and Wakefield (2010a, 2010b). First, Stilley, Inman and Wakefield restrict their studies to grocery purchases, making it necessary to investigate the role of in-store slack with respect to other product categories. Second, their studies are limited to the United States and consider only one store

12 Reference: Marx, Paul, Schramm-Klein, Hanna, Mau, Gunnar, Frentz, Florentine. Understanding Planning for Unplanned Purchases: Antecedents and Exploitation of In-Store Slack. Journal of Marketing Behavior, in print.

F. Frentz, *The Pursuit of Food Well-Being*, Handel und Internationales Marketing Retailing and International Marketing,
https://doi.org/10.1007/978-3-658-30366-2_7

format, requiring a replication of the study in other countries and in varying store formats. Third, the studies do not sufficiently consider the factors responsible for the emergence of in-store slack. Therefore, the current study strives to expand the knowledge about the in-store slack by replicating the study of Stilley, Inman and Wakefield (2010a) in different store formats in Germany and by including more factors that are likely to be responsible for the emergence of the in-store slack.

7.2 Study Procedure, Method, and Data

We conducted a field study that involved four different store formats: drug store, organic food store, supermarket, and grocery discounter. In essence, we followed the procedure of Stilley, Inman, and Wakefield (2010a) while extending it with additional queries in order to provide insights into customers' behavior regarding their budgeting, shopping trips and utilization of in-store slack.

The study took place for six weeks. Care was taken to ensure that for each store type on each day of the week at all times of the day, data were collected to reach a representative sample. Teams of interviewers intercepted shoppers before they entered a store. First, respondents specified the total amount of money they planned to spend on the current trip, i.e., the total trip budget. Next, they listed the items they planned to purchase and estimated the costs of each of these items which together made up the itemized portion of their mental budgets. This information allowed us to calculate their in-store slack by subtracting the itemized portion from the reported total. Furthermore, they indicated the number of people they were purchasing goods for and the reason for their shopping trip (browsing trip, stocking up, and/or urgent need). To be able to estimate the respondents' familiarity with the store, they were asked how often they usually visit the store by means of a rating scale ranging from 1 (once a year) to 7 (more than three times a week) and how familiar they are with the product arrangement of the store by means of a Likert scale ranging from 1 (not at all familiar) to 7 (very familiar) (Simonin and Ruth, 1998). Then, the respondents went shopping while being unobtrusively observed, during which it was recorded whether the respondents were accompanied during the shopping trip and whether they used a shopping list, a shopping cart and a basket. Furthermore, the time they spent shopping was documented.

After respondents checked out, the interviewer took a photo of their receipt. In this way, we were able to see how the respondents had paid for the purchases (card or cash payment) and how much the respondents had spent in total and on planned and unplanned purchases. Among others, this enabled us to calculate the utilization of in-store slack. Furthermore, the respondents evaluated the store.

They described how they found their way around the store by rating three items ("The store is well arranged", "You can easily remember where to find something", and "The product arrangement makes shopping easy"; Montoya-Weiss, Voss, and Grewal, 2003) and evaluated the store's atmosphere by rating two items ("This store is a pleasant place to shop" and "The store has a pleasant atmosphere"; Baker, Grewal, and Parasuraman, 1994; Wu and Petroshius, 1987) on 7-point Likert scales ranging from 1 (totally disagree) to 7 (totally agree). Furthermore, respondents answered questions about their usual shopping behavior. They indicated how impulsively the usually shop by means of three items ("I often by things spontaneously", "'Just do it' describes the way I buy things", and "I often buy things without thinking"; Rook and Fisher, 1995) on a 7-point Likert scale, ranging from 1 (totally disagree) to 7 (totally agree). Moreover, they indicated their monthly budget for purchases and their average trip spending. Finally, they answered questions regarding their demographic characteristics. At the end, the respondents were debriefed and given a pack of gummy bears as a thank-you gift.

We collected a sample of 597 responses from which 191 were discarded due to respondents' failure to indicate the itemized portion of their budgets or due to missing data. All remaining respondents were able to indicate their mental budget for the current shopping trip and bought at least one item. Ultimately, we had 406 responses, 73.2% of which were from female shoppers. In total, 84.5% of the respondents used no shopping list, 42.4% purchased products solely for themselves, 54.7% used a shopping basket or a shopping cart on the trip, and 100% allowed us to use their responses for the study.

7.3 Analysis and Results

To analyze the data and to test our hypotheses, we performed a series of analyses including analysis of variance (ANOVA) of some important measures and two regression analyses.

7.3.1 Existence and Size of In-Store Slack Across Different Store Formats

The ANOVA (Table 16) reveals the existence of in-store slack in all four store formats, supporting the assumption that in-store slack exists for product domains other than grocery. It can also be seen that in-store slack differs for the different store formats. Consumers had the proportionately smallest in-store slack in the drug store (18.84%), followed by the organic store (25.22%) and the supermarket (32.86%). By far, the biggest in-store slack was found at the discounter (54.94%). This difference is significant and deserves further investigation. In general, we can note that the drug store differed strongly from the other stores regarding the composition and utilization of the mental budget. Here, we found the lowest total trip budget, the smallest number of purchased goods, and the smallest in-store slack utilization. The only commonality of the drug store with the other shops was the number of people who had a shopping list, which was comparable to the organic store and the discounter. The other three store formats had many more similarities: total shopping trip budget, in-store slack utilization, and number of products purchased in the discounter did not differ significantly from what was observed in the organic food store and in the supermarket.

Based on the comparably large in-store slack found in the discounter, we conclude that people who patronize discounters plan their trips less precisely than do shoppers at other stores. This difference could be explained by the lower risk that people anticipate at a discounter due to its low prices. Hence, they can plan their purchases less precisely and more easily rely on their budget's "unplanned" portion because the low prices allow them to fill their shopping carts either way. Furthermore, because a part of a discounter's assortment changes on a regular basis, consumers might want to have the opportunity to explore and see what is available.

Table 16: Existence and size of in-store slack across store formats

Variables	Drug Store N=159	Organic Store N=109	Supermarket N=78	Discounter N=60
In-store slack, Euros (%)	2.41(18.84)[a]	5.71(25.22)[b]	5.84(32.86)[b]	10.12(54.94)[c]
Total trip budget (TTB), Euros	12.79[a]	22.64[b]	17.71[c]	18.42[bc]
Number of products	4.18[a]	7.15[b]	6.92[b]	6.65[b]
Shopping list (SL), 1/0 dummy	.11[a]	.15[a]	.32[b]	.07[a]
In-store slack utilization	.51[a]	.74[b]	.66[b]	.65[b]

[a, b, c, d] different indices indicate significant differences between groups in post-hoc tests ($p < .05$)

7.3.2 Antecedents of In-Store Slack

To determine the antecedents of in-store slack, we ran a regression with in-store slack as the dependent variable (see Table 17). We can see that higher in-store slack is associated with higher monthly budgets and higher shopping trip budgets. By contrast, a higher degree of planning, shown by a higher number of planned items and the existence of a shopping list, reduces in-store slack. Purchasing frequency and familiarity with the shop do not have any significant effect on in-store slack. Interestingly, the shopping motive does not play a significant role either.

Furthermore, the results indicate that the store format, which we included as dummy variables, determines, at least sometimes, in-store slack. Consumers tend to have greater in-store slack when shopping in a discounter compared to other store formats. Compared to the supermarket, we find that the number of planned products and the use of a shopping list have a particularly strong negative effect on in-store slack. Moreover, higher average trip spending leads to lower in-store slack in the drug store. Beyond that, the store format has little influence on in-store slack.

Table 17: Antecedents of in-store slack (regression)

	Non-standardized Coef. Beta	**Standardized Coef. Beta**	***t*-value**
Intercept	-.363		-.155
Total trip budget (TTB)	.388	.683	12.407***
Number of planned products (NPP)	-.548	-.141	-2.499**
Number of persons	-.106	-.016	-.404
Shopping list (SL)	-3.636	-.158	-2.097**
SL x TTB	.168	.226	2.770***
Monthly budget	.364	.077	1.946*
Average trip spending (ATS)	.003	.008	.172
Shopping frequency	-.101	-.012	-.279
Familiarity with the shop	.125	.023	.591
Browsing trip	1.639	.063	1.487
Stocking up	.657	.035	.650
Urgent need	.046	.003	.046
Impulsiveness	-.138	-.027	-.711
Drug store (DS)	.073	.004	.053
Organic store (OS)	2.411	.128	1.500
Discounter	3.049	.129	2.717***
NPP x OS	-1.813	-.395	-4.746***
ATS x DS	-.153	-.190	-3.256***
SL x OS	6.514	.152	3.139***
Model R^2	.519***		
F-Statistic	*F*(19, 404) = 21.847		

* $p < .10$; ** $p < .05$; *** $p < .01$

7.3.3 Utilization of In-Store Slack

The regression analysis of the factors influencing the extent to which customers utilize the planned portion of their budget for unplanned spending (Table 18) reveals a series of actionable effects.[13]

Both the motive to browse and the motive to cover an urgent need increase the exploitation of in-store slack, probably due to the low degree of planning for these purchases. Additionally, purchase duration and the impulsiveness of the buyers have a positive influence on the utilization of in-store slack.

Interestingly, the amount of money saved on the itemized portion of the shopping trip budget (e.g., by not buying a planned item) also supports in-store slack utilization. It seems that savings on planned products legitimize more spending on unplanned products. However, this does not apply to the organic food store. Compared to the supermarket, in the organic store, savings on the planned products are accompanied by lower expenditures on unplanned products. On the one hand, this could be due to the comparably limited advertising, the small number of discount campaigns and the high prices in the organic store, all of which make customers less likely to browse. On the other hand, it could be due to the price sensitivity of the customers, which affects the entire budget.

Only paying in cash seems to be able to significantly reduce in-store slack utilization. The degree to which consumers are familiar with the store, can orient themselves in the store, and like the store atmosphere do not play significant roles in the utilization of in-store slack. Hence, the utilization of in-store slack is not due to store-related experiential factors. The store formats themselves have no additional influence.

13 It should be noted here that the negative sign of an effect testifies to its positive influence on the utilization of the in-store slack. This is because we define the utilization on in-store slack as the difference between in-store slack and the amount of money spent on unplanned purchases. Hence, negative values reduce this difference and can even exceed it, meaning that the total budget is also exceeded.

Table 18: Utilization of in-store slack (regression)

	Non-standardized Coef. Beta	Standardized Coef. Beta	*t*-value
Intercept	3.170		.762
Trip duration	-.299	-.205	-4.339***
Itemized savings (IS)	-.407	-.376	-4.548***
Shopping list (SL)	.665	.021	.467
Shopping cart or basket	-.652	-.028	-.596
Cash payment	3.186	.126	3.020***
Browsing trip	-3.364	-.096	-2.001**
Stocking up	-2.313	-.091	-1.545
Urgent need	-3.852	-.163	-2.617***
Familiarity with shop	.352	.048	1.044
Orientation	-.332	-.031	-.652
Atmosphere	.188	.018	.383
Impulsiveness	-.682	-.097	-2.272**
Shopping frequency	.150	.013	.262
Monthly budget	.575	.090	2.022**
Average trip spending (ATS)	.009	.018	.305
Drug store (DS)	-2.429	-.104	-1.371
Organic store (OS)	3.971	.155	1.600
Discounter (D)	.330	.010	.188
IS x OS	.280	.226	2.695***
SL x D	13.089	.114	2.641***
ATS x OS	-.307	-.556	-6.299***
Model R^2		.395***	
F-Statistic		$F(21, 401) = 11.839$	

* $p < .10$; ** $p < .05$; *** $p < .01$

7.4 Conclusions, Limitations, and Discussion

In this replication study, we confirm the existence of in-store slack and demonstrate its generalizability to international markets and product domains other than grocery. Nevertheless, the magnitude of in-store slack varies across different product domains. We established that the customers of discounters tend to plan their shopping trips less precisely and to rely on in-store slack more than do customers of other stores. We suggest that managers of discount stores should exploit this fact and actively stimulate up-selling in their stores by playing with customers' attention through the incorporation of varying promotions and discounts along the shopping route through the store and by hinting at customers regarding products that are likely to be bought impulsively. Managers of other stores should think about organizing regularly changing low-cost areas in their stores to stimulate the exploitation of in-store slack. In order to create a situation that not only serves the stores but also the consumers, the focus should be on promoting healthy, fresh and/or sustainable products.

Furthermore, we confirm the findings of Stilley, Inman, and Wakefield (2010a, 2010b) that the savings that are achieved by underspending on planned items can be transferred into the unplanned portions of budgets. This knowledge can be put into practice in different ways, e.g., by combining promotions for planned products (e.g., bread) with promotions for products that are likely to be unplanned (e.g., seasonal fruits on offer). Moreover, based on our findings, we recommend that store managers offer cashless payments, e.g., by promoting payments made with debit cards or mobile phones.

Because a higher degree of planning for a shopping trip significantly decreases in-store slack, store managers could inspire unplanned purchases by drawing customers' attention to in-store display advertising or special offerings. This conclusion, however, contradicts Stilley, Inman, and Wakefield's (2010a, 2010b) conceptualization of in-store slack as the main driver of unplanned purchases and defends the thesis of prior studies that attribute such purchases to in-store stimuli. Thus, although the presence of in-store slack can be generalized to different product domains, it cannot be generalized to all types of shopping scenarios. Further research has to investigate this in more detail and should also examine the utilization phases of in-store slack more precisely and evaluate the extent to which these phases differ for different store formats.

In general, care should be taken to ensure that the measures also meet the wishes and needs of customers so that the customers' budgets are primarily utilized to satisfy their wishes and support their well-being. In this way, the measures should lead to mutual satisfaction and good customer-provider relationships.

8 Discussion and Take-Aways

At the beginning of this dissertation, three objectives were formulated: (1) to refine and broaden the understanding of FWB and its development; (2) to identify ways in which consumers can be effectively supported in their development and maintenance of FWB; and (3) to show how companies can use the concept of FWB in marketing strategies to achieve a competitive advantage. In the course of the dissertation, six essays have been presented in which these objectives have been pursued. In the following section, the most important findings are presented and discussed, based on which recommendations for research and practice are deduced. The first subchapter contains the findings that contribute to the achievement of the first objective, while the second includes the findings that fulfill the second and third objectives.

8.1 The Concept of Food Well-Being and its Development

In this chapter, first the definition of FWB is refined and extended, after which the central conceptual framework of this dissertation, the hierarchical model of FWB (as presented in Chapter 1.1.2.4), is discussed in light of the findings presented in the course of the dissertation, and enhanced accordingly.

8.1.1 The Extended Definition of Food Well-Being

Block et al. (2011) defined FWB as "a positive psychological, physical, emotional, and social relationship with food at both individual and societal levels" (p. 6). Although this definition of FWB includes important aspects of FWB, it nevertheless lacks precision and completeness, as explained in the first essay. This being so, the first essay presented an extensive literature search on the concept of FWB, as a result of which relevant scientific essays from different research disciplines and areas were identified, sorted, and evaluated. Based on the collected insights, an improved definition of FWB has been put forward: a subjective and objective evaluation of people's physical, emotional, social, intellectual, and spiritual relationship with food.

In contrast to the definition advanced by Block et al. (2011), it is clearly asserted here that FWB should be measured both subjectively and objectively because it has both subjective components, such as emotional responses, and objective components, such as physical effects (Meiselman, 2013; Moons, Budts, and

F. Frentz, *The Pursuit of Food Well-Being*, Handel und Internationales Marketing Retailing and International Marketing,
https://doi.org/10.1007/978-3-658-30366-2_8

De Geest, 2006). Furthermore, the improved definition contains more and different dimensions. The psychological dimension has been removed because it falls under the emotional dimension, and is therefore already included (Roscoe, 2009), while the intellectual and spiritual dimensions were added because the well-being literature suggests that they are relevant (Hettler, 1980; Roscoe, 2009), not only for well-being in general but also for FWB (Ares et al., 2016; King et al., 2015). This led to a final decision to include the physical, emotional, social, intellectual, and spiritual dimensions.

In the second essay, the extended definition was applied by investigating the influence of buying food online on consumers' FWB. Based on three studies that followed a mixed-methods approach, comprehensive and profound insights into the influence of online grocery shopping on FWB were gathered, broadly confirming the applicability of the extended definition of FWB. Only the spiritual dimension had little importance for the participants, at least not consciously; however, spirituality and/or religiousness generally seem to play a comparatively minor role in the food-related lives of our participants, which is why this result could be culture-specific. The literature repeatedly suggests that spirituality can play an important role in food-related life (Casidy and Arli, 2018; Fischer, 2016; Mathras et al., 2016), so further research should be conducted in more and different cultures to investigate the meaning and importance of the spiritual dimension in overall FWB.

Additionally, the findings of the second essay indicate that the definition of FWB should be extended by adding the self-determined dimension. The results suggest that self-determination plays a very important role for consumers, and therefore merits consideration as a separate dimension. Based on Murphey et al. (1963), Mugel, Gurviez, and Decrop (2019), and the study results, a person with a high level of self-determination is regarded as someone "who is able and willing to take decisions that depend neither on others nor on external circumstances and who acts independently and free. Thus, the individual is in control" of their food-related life and well-being (p. 72). With regard to the phenomenon under investigation, this includes making the best possible use of the available resources to reach self-determination, and therefore based on the findings in the second paper, the definition of FWB had to be adapted.

Food well-being: a subjective and objective evaluation of people's physical, emotional, social, intellectual, spiritual, and self-determined relationship with food.

In the fourth essay, this adapted definition was again applied and tested by investigating the influence of stationary grocery shopping on children's FWB. The definition was thus applied to a different phenomenon and another consumer group in a new context. Again, while the physical, emotional, social, and intellectual dimensions were shown to exert an influence, the spiritual dimension did not play a role. However, since this could have been culture-dependent (again, a German sample was used), this dimension should remain part of the definition for the time being. Furthermore, the findings confirmed that the self-determined dimension is highly important, especially for children. One of the main goals of child development is to turn a child into a self-determined and independent adult (Berk, 2011; Deci and Ryan, 2008; McNeal, 2007), and this also applies to food-related life (Hémar-Nicolas and Ezan, 2018). The findings support the adapted definition, and did not indicate any further gaps in the definition. Figure 16 provides an overview of the adapted FWB dimensions.

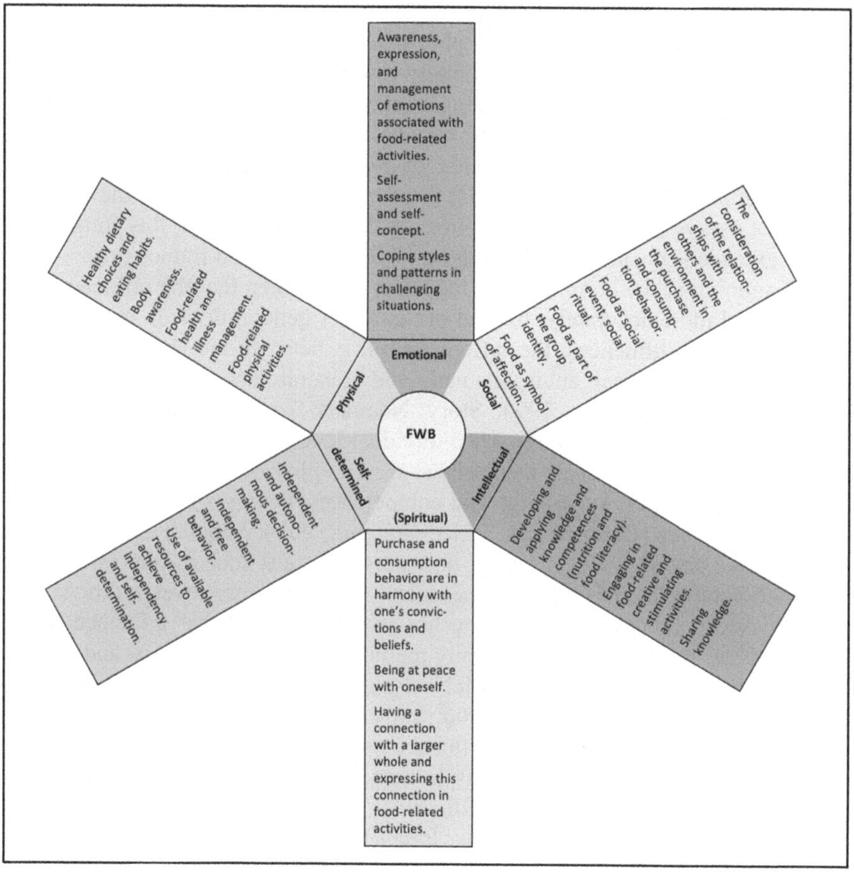

Figure 16: The dimensions of food well-being

8.1.2 The Hierarchical Model of Food Well-Being

The first chapter of this dissertation presented the central conceptual framework, the hierarchical model of FWB (see Chapter 1.1.2.4, Figure 3). This framework is based on the concept of FWB and the corresponding framework (Block et al., 2011), the spillover theory (Lee et al., 2002), and the concept of positive psychology (e.g., Gable and Haidt, 2005).

The hierarchical model of FWB asserts that influences at the individual and societal levels shape the food-related events and experiences that people undergo, and how they perceive these experiences (Block et al., 2011). These experiences that consumers have in their food-related lives in turn affect the various well-being dimensions eudaimonically and/or hedonically (Deci and Ryan, 2008; Diener et al., 1999; Ryff and Keyes, 1995). According to Block et al. (2011), these are made up of psychological, physical, emotional, and social dimensions, and well-being can spill over horizontally to other neighboring dimensions and bottom-up to overall FWB. According to the concept of the vertical top-down spillover, overall FWB can affect the well-being felt at individual dimensions, as well as the experience and perception of food-related experiences and events (Headey et al., 1985; Lee et al., 2002; Sirgy et al., 2001). Based on the findings of the six essays presented in the course of this doctoral thesis, this framework can be extended considerably (see Figure 17 for the extended framework).

Beginning at the bottom of the model, it can be seen that the influences are now divided more accurately; instead of the rather general division into individual and societal influences, the differentiation is between the individual, social environmental, physical environmental, and general environmental levels of influence (Bronfenbrenner, 1994; Story, Neumark-Sztainer, and French, 2002; Lindsström and Eriksson, 2009). The individual level includes all factors that are directly linked to individuals themselves, such as physiological factors, psychological characteristics, knowledge and competences, demographic variables, and personal resources (Bublitz et al., 2013; Góngora, 2014; Sobal et al., 2006). Essays five and six show, for instance, how personal traits such as impulsivity can influence food-related behavior. The social environmental level refers to the personal social relationships that one has with others and that influence one's FWB, such as relationships with family members, friends, educators, and people in one's close community (Blum, McNeely, and Nonnemaker, 2002; Lindström and Eriksson, 2009; Sobal et al., 2006; Story et al., 2002). In this regard, essay two demonstrates how others can influence one's opinion of shopping channels. The settings in which human beings live and consume constitute the physical environmental level of influence (Hill, 1998; Story et al., 2002), including grocery stores, restaurants, and canteens. Essay three provides an example of this, presenting the effects of the digitalization of grocery shopping on consumers. Finally, the general environmental influences refer to the activities of governments, ministries, public institutions, parties, politicians, and non-profit organizations at the local, regional, national, and international level that affect food-related life (e.g., Lindström and Eriksson, 2009; Pearce and Witten, 2010). Essay four, for instance, addresses this level of influences by highlighting the importance of regulations in the grocery retail context to protect children. The general environment also comprises overarching food-related norms and behaviors that are shaped by culture and society (Booth et al., 2001; Story et al., 2008). In the course of this dissertation, it became apparent that these theoretically derived levels of influence all exert influence on the development of FWB, and that it makes sense to consider them separately and formulate recommendations for them.

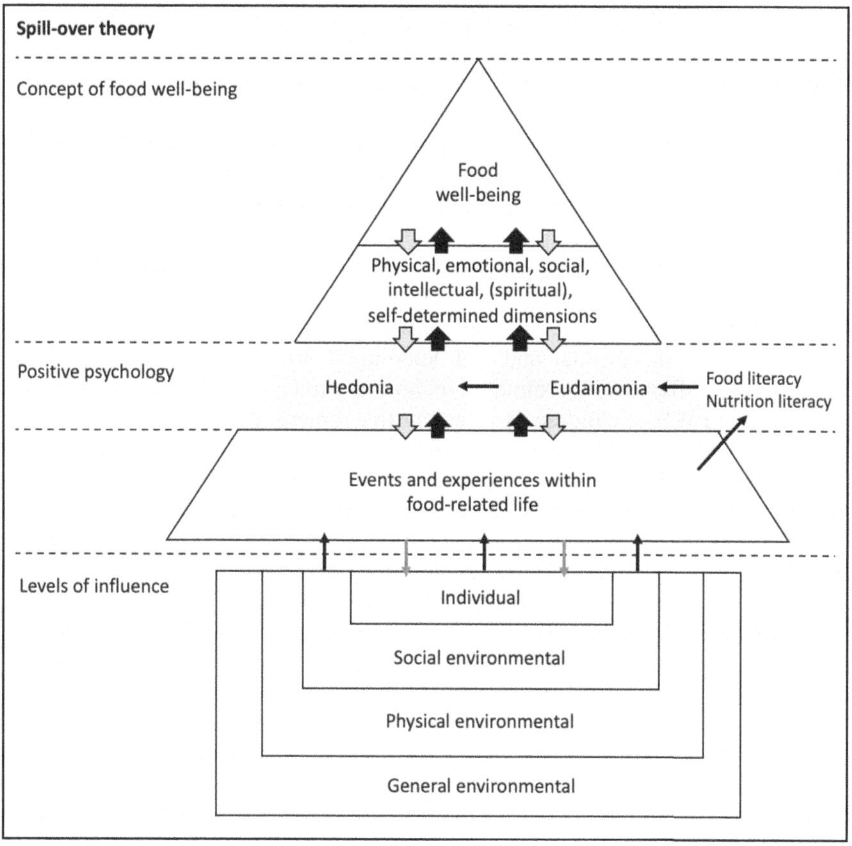

Figure 17: Extended hierarchical model of food well-being

The influences at the various levels shape the experiences one has and how one perceives these experiences, such as a grocery shopping trip (essays two, three, four, and five) or the consumption of food in a specific environment (essay six). These experiences in turn influence the dimensions of FWB in two ways: hedonically and eudaimonically. Hedonia refers to high levels of positive affect and low levels of negative affect, while eudaimonia indicates a sense of fulfillment and meaningfulness in life, based on personal growth and the maximization of one's potential (Deci and Ryan, 2008; Diener et al., 1999; Ryan and Deci, 2001). Based on the theoretical elaborations in the first essay and the findings of essays two, four, and five in particular, it can be assumed that the development of food literacy and nutrition literacy strengthens eudaimonic well-being because it helps consumers to exploit their potential in their food-related life. Food literacy refers to factual and procedural knowledge of how to plan, manage, select, prepare, and consume food in such a way that it supports health and well-being (Vidgen and Gallegos, 2014; Bublitz et al., 2011), while nutrition literacy comprises the ability to gather, interpret, and use nutrition information (Vidgen and Gallegos, 2014). While hedonic and eudaimonic well-being can separately influence the overarching FWB dimensions, eudaimonic well-being can also influence the dimensions by first affecting hedonic well-being (Ryff and Singer, 2008).

While Block et al. (2011) suggested four overarching dimensions (the psychological, physical, emotional, and social dimensions), the findings of this dissertation give rise to six overarching FWB dimensions: the physical, emotional, social, intellectual, spiritual and self-determined dimensions. The second and fourth papers offer useful examples of how a single shopping experience can influence the FWB of children by affecting five dimensions (physical, emotional, social, intellectual, and self-determined). Even though the spiritual dimension was not confirmed by means of the empirical research conducted in this dissertation, this dimension should not be entirely excluded because the literature suggests that it plays an important role in consumers' food-related lives (Casidy and Arli, 2018; Fischer, 2016; Mathras et al., 2016). Furthermore, it can be assumed that spirituality and religiosity are so deeply rooted in people that their effects are often not consciously perceived. Thus, further research should investigate the importance and meaning of the spiritual dimension in more detail to better understand its role within FWB.

Within the framework, the FWB dimensions can influence each other (and thereby spill over horizontally) and indirectly influence overall FWB, or directly feed into FWB (by spilling over vertically). The degree to which individuals score highly on the six dimensions determines their overall FWB, and thereby the top of the hierarchy (Headey et al., 1985; Lee et al., 2002; Sirgy et al., 2001). Based on the concept of a vertical top-down spillover, the overall FWB again influence the lower tiers of the hierarchy (Headey et al., 1985; Lee et al., 2002; Sirgy et al., 2001). This is in line with the life course perspective (Sobal et al., 2006) and the FWB cycle (Chapter 2.5, Figure 5) presented in essay one, because it postulates that people are in an ongoing process of development, and that FWB should not be regarded as an end state, but rather as dynamic and fluent. Accordingly, it makes sense to support consumers in the development of their FWB, regardless of the developmental phase in which they are located.

In summary, this dissertation offers an improved definition of FWB, presents an overarching framework, and strengthens both by means of a number of empirical studies. As the hierarchical model of FWB demonstrates, it is a very complex notion, requiring a societally systematic, population-wide change to bring about fundamental, long-lasting improvements. In the following chapter, suggestions are made as to how this change can be implemented.

8.2 An Integrated Approach towards Food Well-Being

Researchers, policy makers, health authorities, non-governmental organizations, members of the food industry, health professionals, and consumers all benefit from understanding the links between food, health, and well-being. When all these stakeholders understand the concept of FWB and the need to improve it - and, moreover, demonstrate the willingness and opportunities to jointly contribute to the endeavor to enhance FWB in the long run – a stable and high level of individual, group, and societal FWB can be achieved; society, supply chains and governments can and need to perform an entire cultural shift (Lang and Rayner, 2007). The engagement of the various stakeholders, as well as the productive and dynamic interactions between them, are assumed to lead to improved skills and enhanced capacities, a broader and stronger professional network, better understanding for all parties, a knowledge output that is more translatable, a higher societal awareness, and the achievement of positive change that falls in line with the visions of all stakeholders involved (Ozanne et al., 2016). However, the most difficult part is to motivate the stakeholders to take action and engage in the required interactions, create a common action package that can deliver a corrective population-wide shift, and make all stakeholders contribute to the realization of this action in the long term (Lang and Rayner, 2007).

One of the most important recommendations that can be given in the context of this dissertation is the application of the relational engagement approach, which refers to the endeavor to establish long-term co-operation between researchers and other stakeholders, especially those who have the power to induce change, maximize societal impact, and enhance individual and collective well-being (Mick et al., 2012; Ozanne et al., 2016). Following this train of thought, the following section suggests some measures of change to improve FWB at the individual, group, and societal levels and, more specifically, action recommendations are given for the different stakeholders involved to separately and jointly contribute to this endeavor (see Table 19 for an overview).

8.2.1 The Role of Research

The role of research can be divided into two areas. On the one hand, a tool should be developed that measures consumers' FWB in its entirety, while on the other hand, future research should expand knowledge of FWB, as well as its antecedence and consequences.

8.2.1.1 Development of a Measurement Tool for Food Well-Being

Researchers from different disciplines (e.g., nutritionists, consumer behavior researchers, marketing researchers, psychologists, and economists) should work together to develop a comprehensive tool that measures consumers' current state of FWB, as well as their motivation, opportunity, and ability to make changes to progress along the FWB continuum (Bublitz et al., 2011). In order to do so, the currently existing tools that assess (parts of) FWB (e.g., Ares et al., 2016; Grunert et al., 2007; Guillemin et al., 2016; King et al., 2015) should first be reviewed according to their usefulness and applicability, after which useful and applicable scales should be combined with the newest insights from research, and be improved and tested empirically in order to develop a comprehensive, integrated, and valid tool. The tool should comprise all dimensions of FWB that were determined and tested in essays one, two, and four of this dissertation (the physical, emotional, social, intellectual, spiritual, and self-determined dimensions), and objectively and subjectively measure consumers' FWB (Bublitz et al., 2013).

When developing this tool, special attention should be paid to the individual situations of consumers; i.e., the FWB of a student should be assessed differently to that of a senior citizen, due to differences in their physical and mental states, as well as their living circumstances. Furthermore, the cultural and regional backgrounds of consumers need to be considered; essay three shows that both culture and region strongly determine the opportunities that consumers have to develop and maintain high levels of FWB (Ares et al., 2016; Voola et al., 2018). Research suggests that people assess their life satisfaction and well-being by comparing their actual with their ideal life circumstances, which are partly based on cultural construal and regional norms (Zanon et al., 2014). With respect to food in particular, culture is a powerful determinant of attitudes and behaviors (Ares et al., 2016; Cervellon and Dube, 2005; Rozin, 2005), and influences the perception and evaluation of FWB. Previous research has suggested that consumers with different cultural backgrounds tend to use (Likert) scales differently (e.g., Ares et al., 2016; Johnson et al., 2005). This being so, it is necessary to take the cultural and regional backgrounds into account during the development of such a tool, and later, when applying it and analyzing the data.

The tool will help various stakeholders to make informed decisions and to take action according to consumers' current needs and wishes at the individual, group, and societal levels. For instance, the aggregating population and group-level analyses will help policymakers to develop and implement measures at the local, regional, and national level that are tailor-made to the current food-related problems of the population. Paper two, for instance, suggests that people behave differently when shopping for food online than when shopping offline, and that their FWB is influenced differently. Since food information laws are based on the assumption that consumers behave in the same way when shopping for groceries offline and online (EUR-Lex, 2019), it appears necessary to modify these laws in order to protect consumers and their well-being in the online grocery shopping context. Nutritionists and educators could use the information obtained from the tool to adapt their approaches to imparting knowledge and skills, as well as the content they teach. Essay five, for example, shows how nutritionists can positively influence consumers' FWB by integrating contextual classical conditioning in therapy. Furthermore, manufacturers could develop profitable commercial products that support health initiatives, and shape the retail environment in such a way that consumers are led in a positive direction. Essay six demonstrates, for instance, how the retail environment could be changed to encourage consumers to use their in-store slack to make healthy unplanned purchases. Moreover, essays two, three and four offer several suggestions concerning how grocery business operators could provide information and offers that serve the development of specific dimensions of FWB in both the online and offline retail environments.

The tool should not be restricted to researchers, policymakers, and practitioners, but rather made available to consumers so they can assess and track their FWB, such as through mobile phone applications or on regular websites. The tool could also provide consumers with personalized information about their FWB and offer tailor-made recommendations as to how they can improve their individual FWB dimensions, which would help people to become empowered and autonomous consumers. Essays two and four in this dissertation indicate that empowerment and self-determination are essential for the development of long-lasting FWB. When a tool is made freely available for consumers, it is beneficial to pay attention to the needs and preferences of the various consumer groups, and to adapt the tool to their group-specific needs so that all consumer groups are motivated to use it. One example of this would be to offer young consumers a "gamified" version of the tool, while seniors might prefer a clearly structured and easy-to-use app.

8.2.1.2 Further Research on Food Well-Being

This dissertation offers profound insights into the concept of FWB, transfers it to practical and relevant examples, and allows valuable recommendations for practice and research to be derived. However, like any research project, the present dissertation also has a number of limitations that reveal a need for further research. Three particular research strands emerge that merit special attention: (i) theory-oriented research, (ii) process-oriented research, and (iii) consumer-oriented research.

Theory-oriented research should focus on confirming and extending our theoretical knowledge of FWB. For instance, the results of essays two and four, which are based on mainly qualitative studies cannot easily be extrapolated to the general population due to the small sample sizes, revealing a need for further research to confirm the theoretical discoveries. Another issue pertaining to the presented studies is their Western, mainly middle-class context; the theoretical considerations outlined in this thesis should be extended to further phenomena and other contexts, such as how the findings relate to people with different cultures, living conditions, lifestyles, and food-related issues. In this regard, the role of culture should receive special attention because research has shown that culture strongly determines how consumers define and assess FWB (e.g., Ares et al., 2016; Voola et al., 2018). For example, Diener and Suh (2000) found that people of different cultures are likely to assign a different relative importance to the criteria that are used to evaluate subjective well-being, while Rozin (2005) pointed out the pronounced differences that exist between the attitudes, beliefs, and meanings of consumers from different cultural backgrounds with respect to food. In addition, the physical and social environment of consumers, as well as their personal preconditions, should be considered because it has been shown that these factors can strongly influence FWB (Ares et al., 2016; Bublitz et al., 2012; Voola et al., 2018). Perhaps no research illustrates this as strongly as Bublitz et al. (2019), who explored the paradigm of FWB for those who experience hunger. However, both the outcomes and antecedents of FWB should be considered, and it is also worthwhile investigating the objectively and subjectively measurable effects that the shaping of a FWB dimension has on the other dimensions and on consumers' FWB in general, while yet another issue of research interest concerns what changes in consumers' FWB mean for their overall well-being.

Process-oriented research should focus on the realization of the paradigm shift. Future research is required to better understand how to set realistic and achievable FWB-related objectives, which measures are useful to achieve these objectives, and how they should be implemented. Furthermore, future research should investigate which specific stakeholders exert what kind of influence, and how the stakeholders should best join their forces to bring about change. Since it is assumed that policymaking will play a leading role, more policy-oriented research is needed that focuses on how to bring about the required orderly and structured change. It might be useful to start by looking at the approaches and processes already in place across the globe to improve people's health-related and food well-being, and then build on the strengths of these existing structures. For instance, the World Health Organization particularly praises the Dutch system, and recommends following this example (WHO, 2018c). Methods of assessing the outcomes of these endeavors should be researched as well because a lack of solid evidence could otherwise lead to uncertainty over what further action to take (Lang and Rayner, 2007).

Consumer-oriented research should focus on individual consumers and how to bring about a change in thinking and behavior. Even though several papers have been published on how to identify and understand the mechanisms of actions underlying healthy and balanced eating and well-being-oriented decision making, further research is required to better understand the factors that influence consumers' food-related decision making, and their complex relationship to food. Future research would do particularly well to pay close attention to the dimensions of FWB, and how they are influenced by internal and external factors but also by each other; after all, only the fulfillment of and harmonic interplay between all FWB dimensions will lead to a high state of FWB. Furthermore, it should be investigated how food retailers and marketers can positively influence FWB, and what specific effects these activities have on both the FWB of consumers and the success of the businesses involved. The FWB of children and how this can be nurtured and strengthened should also be investigated more comprehensively; recent academic research has focused primarily on adults, but it should be accepted that the cornerstone of FWB is set in childhood, when children start to become consumers (Hémar-Nicolas and Ezan, 2018). Essay four in this dissertation makes it clear that there are many ways to positively influence children's development, but these must first be identified, and appropriate action measures developed and implemented.

8.2.2 The Role of Public Policy

In their "well-being manifesto for a flourishing society," Shah and Marks (2004) state that one of the major goals of any democratic government should be "to promote the good life: a flourishing society, where citizens are happy, healthy, capable and engaged – in other words with high levels of well-being" (p. 2). One of the prerequisites for a high level of general well-being is a high level of FWB, and to this end, several researchers have argued that public policies should be designed and implemented to increase FWB (e.g., Ares et al., 2016, Bublitz et al., 2019). Of course, there have already been a number of efforts on the part of public policymakers to improve the nutrition of overall populations, and to promote physical activity in order to reduce the prevalence of overweight- and obesity-related diseases. For instance, as part of its sustainability strategy, the German federal government has formulated a goal to stop the increase in the proportion of the population with overweight and obesity by 2030 by means of a comprehensive package of measures (BRD, 2018). However, these efforts are seen to be fragmented, and to lack a holistic and coherent approach; changes in individuals' behaviors are needed (which are the subject of many interventions), but in addition, the need for a broad cultural shift is increasingly apparent. People's relationship to food should change radically and manifest itself in culture, but such a paradigm shift is a very complex and challenging undertaking, and necessitates a comprehensive approach. Clear *objectives* should be formulated, while a reshaping of public policy is required at different *levels* and in different *areas*.

I propose three overarching *objectives*: (i) FWB protection, (ii) FWB development, and (iii) FWB education (based on the elements of public health of Lang and Rayner (2007)). *FWB protection* refers to the protection of consumers' FWB through the actions of several bodies such as the Federal Office of Consumer Protection and Food Safety and the Federal Ministry of Health in Germany or the European Food Safety Authority. These bodies seek to enforce rules, laws, and regulations that protect consumers in their food-related lives. The fourth essay of this dissertation illustrates the importance of protecting the FWB of children in food retailing contexts by means of laws and regulations, while essay two demonstrates that not only is it necessary to diligently implement these well-thought-out rules, but also to ensure regular controls of compliance with these rules. *FWB development* (or FWB promotion) concerns the active promotion of the FWB of a population through targeted measures and interventions. To achieve this, local authorities are especially relevant because they can initiate and organize local initiatives that are comparatively easy and quick to establish, and are also quite effective due to the close involvement of local citizens and their direct approach (Lang and Rayner, 2007), which can include the introduction of healthier lunches in schools, or the creation and joint maintenance of vegetable gardens in neighborhoods. Essays one and two of this dissertation confirm the important role of the local community in the development and maintenance of FWB. *FWB education* involves the promotion of food and nutrition literacy to make citizens more well-informed about their FWB, and how to maintain it in the long term. It also includes increasing people's awareness of the external influences that affect their FWB, as demonstrated in essays five and six.

Furthermore, the second and the fourth essays in this dissertation reveal that consumers should not only be sensitized to their own FWB, but also to that of their fellow human beings. Consumers who are responsible for other people, such as children or senior parents, should be aware of the needs of these vulnerable consumer groups. In the long run, successful FWB education would do well to include the redefinition of what is acceptable or not; i.e., the shaping of norms and social rules (Lang and Rayner, 2007).

As described in detail in essay one, public policy activities need to take place at the international, national, regional, and local levels. The activities in different levels should be as integrated and coherent as possible because "coherence and optimism are needed, with firm political leadership across government, supply chains and civil society" (Lang and Rayner, 2007, p. 178). It must be understood that this is an arduous and expensive process because "macroenvironmental structures are essentially beyond the influence of individuals and even governments and nongovernmental organizations usually have difficulty in influencing these sectors because of their size, complexity, and other priorities" (Swinburn, Egger, and Raza, 1999, p. 566). Policymakers should identify the powerful actors in supply chain, society and government who are able to contribute to the required change, and then work with patience and perseverance towards joint co-operation (Lang and Rayner, 2007). Since local policies are comparably easy and quick to implement, and can be designed in such a way that they meet the particular needs and wishes of local citizens, they represent a potentially fruitful area of interest.

Finally, based on the findings of all six essays, it can be concluded that the public policy areas that at least partly require reshaping are manufacturing (including products, ingredients, portion sizes, and packaging), retail (including the accessibility and availability of food), education (including the improvement of food and nutrition literacy), culture (including societal consciousness around food and physical activity), trade (including trading and pricing), and economics (including taxations and subsidies) (Lang and Rayner, 2007; Swinburn, Egger, and Raza, 1999). It will initially be difficult to bring about change in these different areas, given that strong resistance can be expected; for example, many food companies will shy away from integrating FWB into their corporate strategy due to the associated costs and expenses. This makes it all the more important to involve all stakeholders from the beginning, and to create an atmosphere in which everyone feels that they are being taken into account in the search for joint solutions, even if it is not always possible (Mick et al., 2012; Ozanne et al., 2016).

Policymakers may be particularly interested in advancing the FWB of consumers in high-risk groups such as people who are overweight, poor, or who have a genetic predisposition to a certain condition. However, it is also important to address the reasons why people choose to engage in high-risk behavior, and to prevent them from doing so (Lang and Rayner, 2007). Therefore, a holistic strategy must be pursued to promote the FWB of the populations from an early age to ensure that young people develop a positive relationship with food, and that food-related issues such as obesity are prevented from the outset.

8.2.3 The Role of Food Retailers and Marketers

Retailers and marketers are highly influential stakeholders that play an important role in this doctoral thesis. These stakeholders are often perceived as negative influencers because they have contributed strongly to the spread of the overweight and obesity epidemic in recent decades by increasing the availability and accessibility of unhealthy foods, and promoting their purchase and consumption (Charlton et al., 2015; Cobb et al., 2015; Virtanen et al., 2015). However, research also suggests that grocery retailers and marketers can contribute positively to consumers' FWB (Ball et al., 2015; Story et al., 2008; Swinburn, Egger, and Raza, 1999), which is why researchers, policymakers, and international organizations called on them to exert this positive influence, and to support consumers in the development of their FWB (Hawkes, 2013; Hutter, Hoffmann, and Mai, 2016; Schrempf, 2014). In particular, food retailers and marketers are prompted to create a FWB-oriented physical environment by decreasing the number of obesogenic elements that support an unhealthy relationship with food and weight gain, and to instead implement more leptogenic elements that enhance positive and healthy food-related behavior and thinking (Swinburn, Egger, and Raza, 1999).

These measures should serve both consumers and companies. "If consumers perceive that a company is developing strategies and offers that promote consumers' well-being, this will likely result in a more loyal customer, creating a mutually beneficial relationship between the consumer and the firm that generates firm and consumer well-being" (Scott and Vallen, 2019, p. 133). Various strategic approaches confirm this view, such as the concept of positive marketing (Gopaldas, 2015; Mittelstaedt, Killbourne, and Shultz II, 2015), the quality-of-life marketing concept (Lee and Sirgy, 2004; Sirgy, Samli, and Meadow, 1982), and the concept of corporate social responsibility (Garriga and Melé, 2004; Glavas, 2016; Porter and Kramer, 2006). This doctoral dissertation offers a number of suggestions as to how food retailers and marketers can positively influence consumers' FWB. Roughly speaking, these suggestions can be divided into three overarching activities: (i) evaluation, (ii) creation, and (iii) education.

The activities of retailers and marketers should form part of a continuous evaluation and creation process. To contribute to consumers' FWB, retailers and marketers first have to understand the current level of their target groups' FWB, and if applicable, learn how specific products, services, or marketing activities for which they are responsible influence it; in other words, they have to measure consumers' FWB through empirical research, or gather this information via secondary data so that they can create and/or adapt elements of their marketing mix. Paper four of this dissertation, for instance, evaluates the FWB of children in the grocery retail context for the first time, and gives initial suggestions for leptogenic elements that could be implemented in the grocery retail context to help children develop a higher level of FWB. After their creation (and implementation), the new elements of or improvements to the marketing mix should be re-evaluated with regard to their effect on FWB, which may need to be followed by another adjustment. Since the wishes and needs of consumers are constantly changing, as well as the (technical and organizational) possibilities to fulfill them, the overall goal should be continuous progress, which requires a continuous evaluation and creation process.

Retailers and marketers should also educate their customers, which this dissertation shows to be an essential step. Customers need to be informed about (i) their opportunities in the marketplace, (ii) how they can utilize these opportunities, and (iii) how they can exert influence on these opportunities and their physical environment in general. To know the opportunities includes, among others, having an overview of the purchasing channels, stores, assortments, and services that exist. In the second essay, for instance, many participants stated that they have no overview of the online grocery market, and do not know what providers exist, the nature of their delivery area, or what they offer. Such a knowledge asymmetry leads to consumers make sub-optimal decisions due to a lack of background knowledge. The participants in paper two also said that they did not know their rights, and whether and what regulations and laws exist that protect them within the online grocery shopping context. If consumers are educated about their rights and the existing laws and regulations, their trust in food retailers would likely increase. Furthermore, consumers should know where to get support when being in difficult situations. To utilize opportunities in the marketplace, consumers should be helped to develop knowledge (e.g., about food) and skills (e.g., grocery shopping skills), and to use them to the farthest extent (e.g., barrier-free supermarket entrances, and a high ease-of-use in online grocery stores). Another option would be to give consumers the opportunity to co-shape the marketplace and their physical environment, and thereby control the external influences on their FWB. For example, their feedback on specific offers could be obtained through direct interactions on social media, or consumers could be encouraged to actively shape parts of the marketing mix through idea competitions.

8.2.4 The Role of Consumers

Consumers are the most important stakeholders in the endeavor to achieve a higher level of FWB at the individual, group, and societal levels, and they have the potential to function as the driving force in this paradigm shift. On the one hand, consumers exert the greatest influence over themselves and their own FWB, while on the other hand, they can motivate or pressure other stakeholders such as manufacturers and food retailers to rethink their choices.

8.2.4.1 The Empowered Consumer

Consumers exert the strongest influence on their own FWB, and determine to what extent their FWB can and will be improved. Their motivation and readiness to change, as well as their ability to implement changes in their lives that will move them along the FWB continuum, strongly determine their FWB (Block et al., 2011; Bublitz et al., 2011). However, it is often the case that consumers lack the requisite knowledge, skills, awareness of the problem, and urgency to act. Essay three of this dissertation shows, for instance, that consumers rarely have the issue of nutrition uppermost in their mind when they choose a shopping channel. This being so, consumers should be educated from an early age to develop the cognitive and emotional skills and competences needed to independently shape one's own FWB, given that once people have internalized behaviors that do not promote their FWB, it is difficult to change them (Prochaska and Velicer, 1997).

The essays presented in this dissertation offer insights into the process through which consumers can build up a high level of FWB. The first essay theoretically outlines that consumers need to develop conceptual and procedural knowledge with respect to food and nutrition, as well as the ability and motivation to act on this knowledge, while the subsequent essays offer a number of clear recommendations in this regard. The fourth paper emphasizes the importance of food socialization and the need to develop food-related knowledge, skills, and competences from an early age. Essay five shows the need for consumers to possess coping styles and strategies in order to exercise self-control and implement eating and consumption habits that support FWB. The second essay asserts that the learning process never stops, and highlights the need to be able to master the ever-changing retail environment by constantly advancing one's own skills and competences. As essay six emphasizes, consumers need to be especially aware of external stimuli, and how they influence their thinking and behavior. Especially with view on the globalization, region- and country-specific cultural and structural differences also need to be considered in this respect, as demonstrated by the third essay.

Unfortunately, consumers are often not in a position to initiate or continue these necessary learning processes. Especially vulnerable consumer groups often find it difficult to make optimal decisions in the marketplace (Andreasen and Manning, 1990), revealing the importance of positive outside influence. It is necessary to not only give people knowledge and skills, but above all, to awaken a motivation to develop themselves further in their food-related lives, and to enable them to learn and grow independently.

8.2.4.2 Social Responsibility and the Power of the Crowd

Consumers are influential not only with respect to their own FWB, but also concerning that of the people around them. Research has shown that consumers willingly or unwillingly influence other people's relationships with food, and strongly co-determine what others think and do in their food-related life (e.g., Blum, McNeely, and Nonnemaker, 2002; Lindström and Erikkson, 2009; Sobal et al., 2006), so consumers must be aware of their influence and face up to the responsibility that accompanies it. People who have a high level of FWB should help others to achieve this as well, while those with low levels of FWB but a willingness to improve in this regard should join forces and motivate each other. People who have responsibility for others should consider the latter's food-related lives; for example, parents should actively strengthen their children's FWB. Overall, people should work towards creating communities in which mutual support and encouragement are commonplace.

It would be useful if people are able to join their forces to motivate or maybe even pressure powerful stakeholders to contribute to the development of a higher level of FWB. For instance, consumers could put pressure on retailers and other actors by demanding that products, services, and purchasing environments fall in line with the endeavor to improve FWB. This could be done by directly contacting the actors involved, harnessing the support of policymakers (Almy and Wootan, 2015), through intentional non-consumption (Cherrier, Black, and Lee, 2011), or by boycotts that punish businesses for unfavorable behavior and buycotts that reward businesses for favorable behavior (Neilson, 2010). Furthermore, consumers could use the Internet and social media platforms to express their resistance and/or their wishes and needs.

This might be the most effective contemporary approach, given that consumers can exercise influence over the Internet in several ways: This might be the most effective contemporary approach, given that consumers can exercise influence over the Internet in several ways: demand-, information-, network-, and crowd-based power (Labrecque et al., 2013). It is likely that some grocery business operators and marketers will only change if they meet such pressure to change because it is very risky for them to pursue a new approach.

Table 19: General implications for research and practice

Practical implications (divided into levels of influence)				Research implications
Individual	**Social environmental**	**Physical environmental**	**General environmental**	
Individuals should develop the motivation, knowledge, competences, and abilities needed to develop and maintain a high level of FWB. Individuals should learn to understand the internal and external influences that determine their FWB, and the mechanisms that lie behind these influences. Individuals should be aware of the influence they have and positively exert it over other individuals and powerful stakeholders. Individuals should seize opportunities in which they can co-shape their physical environment and the marketplace.	People should create communities that are based on openness and mutual support. FWB and associated topics should not be taboos. People should be aware of their (unintended and intended) influence on others, and actively support each other in making their food-related lives the best they can, and in reaching a high level of FWB. People who are responsible for others should pay attention to their FWB and ensure that all their FWB dimensions are satisfied.	Retailers and marketers should strive for continuous progress in the area of FWB through an ongoing evaluation and creation process. They should evaluate the influences that products, services, and marketing activities have on consumers' FWB, and adapt them if needed. They should create a retail environment, products, and services specifically to support FWB. They should create measures that appeal to different age and consumer groups; vulnerable groups require special attention. They should educate consumers about the opportunities that the marketplace offers, the laws and regulations that protect them, and the knowledge and skills that they need to become empowered.	Actions and interventions at local, regional, national, and maybe even international level should be integrated. Special attention should be paid to interventions at the local and regional level. Policymakers from different policy areas should cooperate to reach an integrated and holistic approach. Strong collaborations should be encouraged between policymakers, industrial players, and researchers. Businesses' compliance with laws and regulations should be monitored more closely. Consumers should be educated about laws and regulations that protect their FWB, as well as the internal and external factors that influence it. Vulnerable consumers should receive special attention and support.	The theoretical foundation (the elements of FWB and their interrelationships) should be investigated further. The theoretical findings of this dissertation should be transferred to different phenomena, contexts, and cultures to test their robustness. A measurement tool should be developed that measures FWB in its entirety. Research should be conducted on how to bring about change at the individual, group, and societal level to achieve higher FWB. Interdisciplinary exchanges and cooperation should be extended. Closer cooperation is necessary between research, government, NGOs, and industrial players.

8.3 Conclusions

In this dissertation, six essays have been presented that are intended to increase our understanding of consumers' FWB, and identify ways in which the various stakeholders involved can exert a positive influence on improving and maintaining this well-being. The essays encompass various methodological approaches from literature reviews and theoretical elaborations to think-aloud protocols, interviews, focus groups, field studies, surveys, and experiments. Based on these studies, (i) our understanding of FWB and its development is refined and broadened, (ii) the ways in which consumers can be effectively supported in their development and maintenance of FWB have been identified, and (iii) recommendations are given that can help companies to use the concept of FWB in their marketing strategies. In this way, the findings allow for an expansion of knowledge in the field of FWB, and the derivation of comprehensive and valuable recommendations for research and practice. They also showcase a positive outlook for the future because they indicate that a paradigm shift "to an integrated, positive approach to understanding food as a key contributor to individual and societal well-being" has already begun (Block et al., 2011; p. 11), but must now be continued.

References

Adams, T., Bezner, J., & Steinhardt, M. (2016). The conceptualization and measurement of perceived wellness: Integrating balance across and within dimensions. *American Journal of Health Promotion, 11*(3), 208-218.

Ágh, T., Kovács, G., Supina, D., Pawaskar, M., Herman, B. K., Vokó, Z., & Sheehan, D. V. (2016). A systematic review of the health-related quality of life and economic burdens of anorexia nervosa, bulimia nervosa, and binge eating disorder. *Eating and Weight Disorders – Studies on Anorexia, Bulimia and Obesity, 21*(3), 353-364.

Alam, I. (2005). Fieldwork and data collection in qualitative marketing research. *Qualitative Market Research, 8*(1), 97-112.

Al-Debei, M. M., Akroush, M. N., & Ashouri, M. I. (2014). Consumer attitudes towards online shopping: The effects on trust, perceived benefits, and perceived web quality. *Internet Research, 25*(5), 707-733.

Allen-O'Donnell, M., Cottingham, M. D., Nowak, T. C., & Snyder, K. A. (2011). Impact of group settings and gender on meals purchased by college students. *Journal of Applied Social Psychology, 41*(9), 2268–2283.

Allirot, X, Maiz, E., & Urdaneta, E. (2017). Shopping for food with children: A strategy for directing their choices toward novel foods containing vegetables. *Appetite, 120,* 287-296.

Allison, B. N., and Schultz, J. B. (2004). Parent-adolescent conflict in early adolescence. *Adolescence, 39*(153), 101-120.

Almy, J., & Wootan, M. G. (2015). Temptation at checkout: The food industry's sneaky strategy for selling more. Center for Science in the Public Interest. https://cspinet.org/sites/default/files/attachment/report.pdf, Last accessed 31.07.19.

Andersson, I., & Sidenvall, B. (2001). Case studies of food shopping, cooking and eating habits in older women with Parkinson's disease. *Journal of Advanced Nursing, 35*(1), 69-78.

Andreasen, A., & Manning, J. (1990). The dissatisfaction and complaining behavior of vulnerable consumers. *Journal of Consumer Satisfaction, Dissatisfaction and Complaining Behavior, 3*(1), 12-20.

Andrews, J. C., Burton, S., & Kees, J. (2011). Is simpler always better? Consumer evaluations of front-of-package nutrition symbols. *Journal of Public Policy & Marketing, 30*(2), 175-190.

Andrews, F. M., & Withey, S. B. (1976). *Social indicators of well-being: American's perceptions of life quality.* New York: Plenum.

F. Frentz, *The Pursuit of Food Well-Being*, Handel und Internationales Marketing Retailing and International Marketing,
https://doi.org/10.1007/978-3-658-30366-2

Anesbury, Z., Nenycz-Thiel, M., Dawes, J., & Kennedy, R. (2016). How do shoppers behave online? An observational study of online grocery shopping. *Journal of Consumer Behaviour, 15*(3), 261-270.

Antonovsky, A. (1996). The salutogenic model as a theory to guide health promotion. *Health Promotion International, 11*(1), 11-18.

Appelhans, B. M., Lynch, E. B., Martin, M. A., Nackers, L. M., Cail, V., Woodrick, N. (2013). Feasibility and acceptability of internet grocery service in an urban food desert, Chicago, 2011-2012. *Preventing Chronic Disease, 10*: E67.

Ares, G., Giménez, A., Vidal, L., Zhou, Y., Krystallis, A., Tsalis, G., Symoneaux, R., Cunha, L. M., Pinto de Moura, A., Claret, A., Guerrero, L., Cadello, A. V., Wright, A., Jefferies, L., Lloyd, M., Oliveira, D., & Deliza, R. (2016). Do we all perceive food-related wellbeing in the same way? Results from an exploratory cross-cultural study. *Food Quality and Preference, 52*, 62-73.

Ares, G., de Saldamando, L., Giménez, A., Claret, A., Cunha, L. M., Guerrero, L., Pinto de Moura, A., Oliveira, D., Symoneaux, R., & Deliza, R. (2014). Consumers' associations with wellbeing in a food-related context: A cross-cultural study. *Food Quality and Preference, 40*(B), 304-315.

Ares, G., De Saldamando, L., Giménez, A., & Deliza, R. (2013). Food and wellbeing. Towards a consumer-based approach. *Appetite, 74*, 61-69.

Arner, P., Arner, E., Hammerstedt, A., Smith, U. (2011). Genetic predisposition for type 2 diabetes, but not for overweight/obesity, is associated with a restricted adipogenesis. *PLoS ONE, 6*(4), e18284, 1-5.

Arnould, E. J., Price, L., & Zinkhan, G. M. (2002). *Consumers*. New York: McGraw-Hill.

A.T. Kearney. (2012). A fresh look at online grocery. https://www.atkearney.de/documents/10192/582867/A+Fresh+Look+at+Online+Grocery.pdf/f62c2bb7-d874-42b9-9a0c-07e1054f93f5, Last accessed 11.09.19.

Atkin, C. K. (1978). Observation of parent-child interaction in supermarket decision-making. *Journal of Marketing, 42*(4), 41-45.

Babin, B., Darden, W. R., & Griffin, M. (1994). Work and/or fun: Measuring hedonic and utilitarian shopping value. *Journal of Consumer Research, 20*(4), 644-656.

Bacha, F., & Gidding, S. S. (2016). Cardiac abnormalities in youth with obesity and type 2 diabetes. *Current diabetes reports, 16*(7), 62-71.

Baker, J., Grewal, D., & Parasuraman, A. (1994). The influence of store environment on quality inferences and store image. *Journal of the Academy of Marketing Science, 22*(4), 328-339.

Balcarová, T., Pokorná, J., & Pilar, L. (2014). The influence of children on the parents' buying behavior: Food purchase in the Czech Republic. *Agris on-line Papers in Economics and Informatics, 6*(2), 11-19.

Ball, K., McNaughton, S. A., Le, H. N., Gold, L., Ni Mhurchu, C., Abbott, G., Pollard, C., & Crawford, D. (2015). Influence of price discounts and skill-building strategies on purchase and consumption of healthy food and beverages: Outcomes of the Supermarket Healthy Eating for Life randomized controlled trial. *The American Journal of Clinical Nutrition, 101*(5), 1055–1064.

Batat, W., Peter, P. C., Moscato, E. M., Castro, I. A., Chan, S., Chugani, S., & Muldrow, A. (2018). The experiential pleasure of food: A savoring journey to food well-being. *Journal of Business Research, 100*, 392-399.

Baur, L. A., & Garnett, S. P. (2019). Early childhood – a critical period for obesity prevention. *Nature Reviews Endocrinology, 15*, 5-6.

Benn, Y., Webb, T. L., Chang, B. P. I., & Reidy, J. (2015). What information do consumers consider, and how do they look for it, when shopping for groceries online? *Appetite, 89*(C), 265-273.

Berk, L. E. (2011). *Entwicklungspsychologie*, (5th ed.). Munich: Pearson Studium.

Berrett, M. E., Hardman, R. K., & Richards P. S. (2010). The role of

spirituality in eating disorder treatment and recovery. In M. Maine, B. Hartman McGilley, & D. W. Bunnel (Eds.), *Treatment of eating disorders: Bridging the research-practice gap*, London: Academic Press, 367-385.

Berry, B., & McMullen, T. (2008). Visual communication to children in the supermarket context: Health protective or exploitive? *Agriculture and Human Values, 25*(3), 333-348.

Bessenoff, G. R., & Snow, D. (2006). Absorbing society's influence: Body image self

discrepancy and internalized shame. *Sex Roles, 54*(9-10), 727-731.

Biltekoff, C. (2010). Consumer response: The paradoxes of food and health. *Annals of the New York Academy of Sciences, 1190*(1), 174-178.

Birch, L. L., McPhee, L., Sullivan, S., & Johnson, S. (1989). Conditioned meal initiation in young children. *Appetite, 13,* 105-113.

Block, L. G., Grier, S. A., Childers, T. L., Davis, B., Ebert, J. E. J., Kumanyika, S., Laczniak, R. N., Machin, J. E., Motley, C. M., Peracchio, L., Pettigrew, S., Scott, M., & Van Ginkel Bieshaar, M. N. G. (2011). From Nutrients to nurturance: A conceptual introduction to food well-being. *Journal of Public Policy & Marketing, 30*(1), 5-13.

Blum, R. W., McNeely, C., and Nonnemaker, J. (2002). Vulnerability, risk, and protection. *Journal of Adolescent Health, 31*(1), 28–39.

Boelsma, E., Brink, E. J., Stafleu, A., Hendriks, H. F. J. (2010). Measures of postbrandial wellness after single intake of two protein-carbohydrate meals. *Appetite, 54*, 456-464.

Boggiano, M. M., Dorsey, J. R., Thomas, J. M., & Murdaugh, D. L. (2009). The Pavlovian power of palatable food: Lessons for weight-loss adherence from a new rodent model of cue-induced overeating. *International Journal of Obesity, 33,* 693-701.

Booth, S. L., Sallis, J. F., Ritenbaugh, C., Hill, J. O., Birch, L. L., Frank, L. D., Glanz,

K., Himmelgreen, D. A., Mudd, M., Popkin, B. M., Rickard, K. A., St. Jeor, S., & Hays, N. P. (2001). Environmental and societal factors affect food choice and physical activity: Rationale, influences, and leverage points. *Nutrition Reviews, 59*(3), 21-36.

Borgers, N., De Leeuw, E., & Hox, J. (2000). Children as respondents in survey research: Cognitive development and response quality. *Bulletin of Sociological Methodology, 66*(1), 60-75.

Botella, C. M., Juan, M. C., Baños, R. M., Alcañniz, M., Guillén, V., & Rey, B. (2005). Mixing realities? An application of augmented reality for the treatment of cockroach phobia. *CyberPsychology & Behavior, 8,* 162-17.

Bouton, M. E. (2002). Context, ambiguity, and unlearning: Sources of relapse after behavioral extinction. *Biological Psychiatry, 52,* 976-986.

Breugelmans, E., Campo, K., & Gijsbrechts, E. (2007). Shelf sequence and proximity effects on online grocery choices. *Marketing Letters, 18*(1/2), 117-133.

Bronfenbrenner, U. (1994). Ecological Models of Human Development. In M. Gauvin & M.

Cole (Eds.), *Readings on the development of children* (2nd ed., pp. 37–43). NY: Freeman.

Brown, R. (2004). Children's eating attitudes and behaviour: A study of the modelling and control theories of parental influence. *Health Education Research, 19*(3), 261–271.

Broyles, S. T., Denstel, K. D., Church, T. S., Chaput, J.-P., Fogelholm, M., Hu, G., Kuriyan, R., Kurpad, A., Lambert, E. V., Maher, C., Maia, J., Matsudo, V., Olds, T., Onywera, V., Sarmiento, O. L., Standage, M., Tremblay, M. S., Tudor-Locke, C., Zhao, P., & Katzmarzyk, P. T. (2015). The epidemiological transition and the global childhood obesity epidemic, *International Journal of Obesity Supplements, 5*(2), 3-8.

Bublitz, M. G., Hansen, J., Peracchhio, L. A., & Tussler, S. (2019). Hunger and food well-being: Advancing research and practice. *Journal of Public Policy and Marketing, 38*(2), 136-153.

Bublitz, M. G., Peracchino, L. A., Andreasen, A. R., Kees, J., Kidwell, B., Miller, E. G., Motley, C. M., Peter, P. C., Rajagopal, P., Scott, M. L., & Vallen, B. (2011). The quest for eating right: advancing food well-being. *Journal of Research for Consumers, 19,* 1-12.

Bublitz, M. G., Peracchino, L. A., Andreasen, A. R., Kees, J., Kidwell, B., Miller, E. G., Motley, C. M., Peter, P. C., Rajagopal, P., Scott, M. L., & Vallen, B. (2013). Promoting positive change: Advancing the food well-being paradigm. *Journal of Business Research, 66,* 1211-1218.

Bublitz, M. G., Peracchio, L. A., & Block, L. G. (2010). Why did I eat that? Perspectives on food decision making and dietary restraint. *Journal of Consumer Psychology, 20,* 239-258.

Bucher, T., Collins, C., Rollo, M. E., & McCaffrey, T. A. (2016). Nudging consumers towards healthier choices: A systematic review of positional influences on food choice. *British Journal of Nutrition, 115*(12), 2252-2263.

Buhrmester, M., Kwang, T., & Gosling, S. D. (2011). Amazon's mechanical Turk: A new source of inexpensive, yet high-quality, data? *Perspectives on Psychological Science, 6*(1), 3-5.

Buijzen, M., & Valkenburg, P. M. (2008). Observing purchase-related parent-child communication in retail environments: A developmental and socialization perspective. *Human Communication Research, 34*(1), 50-69.

Bundesregierung Deutschland (2016). Deutsche Nachhaltigkeitsstrategie Aktualisierung 2018. https://www.bundesregierung.de/resource/blob/975292/1559082/a9795692a667605f652981aa9b6cab51/deutsche-nachhaltigkeitsstrategie-aktualisierung-2018-download-bpa-data.pdf?download=1, Last accessed 17.08.19.

Burnkrant, R. E., & Cousineau, A. (2018). Informational and normative social influence in buyer behavior. *Journal of Consumer Research*, *2*(3), 206–215.

Burns, C., Cook, K., & Mavoa, H. (2013). Role of expendable income and price in food choice by low income families. *Appetite, 71,* 209-217.

Burton, P., Smit, H. J., & Lightowler, H. (2007). The influence of restrained and external eating patterns on overeating. *Appetite, 49,* 191-197.

Caburnay, C. A., Graff, K., Harris, J. K., McQueen, A., Smith, M., Fairchild, M., & Kreuter, M. W. (2015). Evaluating diabetes mobile applications for health literate designs and functionality. *Preventing Chronic Disease, 12*, E61, 1-13.

Caleyachetty, R., Thomas, G. N., Kengne, A. P., Echouffo-Tcheagui, J. B., Schilsky, S., Khodabocus, J., & Uauy, R. (2018). The double burden of malnutrition among adolescents: Analysis of data from the Global School-Based Student Health and Health Behavior in School-Aged Children surveys in 57 low- and middle-income countries. *American Journal of Clinical Nutrition, 108*(2), 414-424.

Calderon, J., Ayala, G. X., Elder, J. P., Belch, G. E., Castro, I. A., Weibel, N., & Pickrel, J. (2017). What happens when parents and children go grocery shopping? An observational study of Latino dyads in Southern California, USA. *Health Education & Behavior, 44*(1), 5-12.

Calloway, E. E., Ranjit, N., Sweitzer, S. J., Roberts-Gray, C., Romo-Palafox, M. J., McInnis, K. A., & Briley, M. E. (2016). Exploratory cross-sectional study of factors associated with the healthfulness of parental responses to child food purchasing requests. *Maternal Child Health Journal, 20*(8), 1569-1577.

Campbell, C. (2016). The craft consumer: Culture, craft and consumption in a postmodern society. *Journal of Consumer Culture*, *5*(1), 23–42.

Campbell, S., James, E. L., Stacey, F. G., Bowman, J., Chapman, K., and Kelly, B. (2012). A mixed-method examination of food marketing directed towards children in Australian supermarkets. *Health Promotion International*, *29*(2), 267-277.

Campo, K., & Breugelmans, E. (2015). Buying groceries in brick and click stores: Category allocation decisions and the moderating effect of online buying experience. *Journal of Interactive Marketing*, *31*, 63-78.

Caraher, M., and Lang, T. (1999). Can't cook, won't cook: A review of cooking skills and their relevance to health promotion. *International Journal of Health Promotion and Education*, *37*(3), 89–100.

Cash, T. F. (2004). Body image: Past, present, and future. *Body Image, I*, 1-5.

Casidy, R., & Arli, D. (2018). Spirituality, religion and consumption: Introduction to a special issue. *International Journal of Consumer Studies, 42*, 583-585.

Cervellon, M. C., and Dube, L. (2005). Cultural influences in the origins of food likings and dislikes. *Food Quality and Preference, 16*(5), 455-460.

Chang, V. W., & Christakis, N. A. (2003). Self-perception of weight appropriateness in the United States. *American Journal of Preventive Medicine, 24*(4), 332–339.

Charlton, E. L., Kähkönen, L. A., Sacks, G., Cameron, A. J. (2015). Supermarkets and unhealthy food marketing: An international comparison of the content of supermarket catalogues/circulars. *Preventive Medicine, 81*, 168-173.

Chatzitheochari, S., & Class, A. S. (2012). Class, gender and time poverty: A time-use analysis of British workers' free time resources. *British Journal of Sociology, 63*(3), 451-71.

Chazin, E. (2013). *If You Can't Beat 'Em, Eat 'Em Like Junk Food.* Retrieved from http://www.crystal.kitchen/wp-content/uploads/2014/03/Baby_Carrots.pdf, Last accessed 22.07.19

Cherrier, H., Black, I. R., & Lee, M. (2011). Intentional non-consumption for sustainability: Consumer resistance and/or anti-consumption? *European Journal of Marketing, 45*(11/12), 1757-1767.

Cho, J. Y., & Lee, E.-H. (2014). Reducing confusion about grounded theory and qualitative content analysis: Similarities and differences. *The Qualitative Report, 19*(32), 1-23.

Christakis, N., & Fowler, J. H. (2007). The spread of obesity in a large social network over 32 years. *The New England Journal of Medicine, 357*, 370-379.

Cicourel, A. V. (1982). Interviews, surveys, and the problem of ecological validity. *The American Sociologist, 17*(1), 11-20.

Clark, L., & Wright, P. (2007). Off their trolley – Understanding online grocery shopping behaviour. In A. Venkatesh, T. Gonsalves, A. Monk, & K. Buckner (Eds). *Home Informatics and Telematics: ICT for the Next Billion* (pp. 157-170), Boston: Springer.

Clayton, M. C., Boron, J. B., & Mattila, L., (2014). Child safety in grocery stores: The impact of verbal prompts and reinforcement on safety strap use in shopping carts. *Journal of Organizational Behavior Management, 34*(1), 52-58.

Cobb, L. K., Appel, L. J., Franco, M., Jones-Smith, J. C., Nur, A., & Anderson, C. A. (2015). The relationship of the local food environment with obesity: A systematic review of method, study quality, and results. *Obesity, 23*(7), 1331-1344.

Conrad, F. G., & Blair, J. (2009). Sources of error in cognitive interviews. *Public Opinion Quarterly, 73*(1), 32-55.

Conway, N., Campbell, I., Forbes, P., Cunningham, S., & Wake, D. (2016). mHealth applications for diabetes: User preference and implications for app development. Health Informatics Journal, *22*(4), 1111-1120.

Cohen, D. A., Collins, R., Hunter, G., Ghosh-Dastidar, B., & Dubowitz, T. (2015). Store impulse marketing strategies and body mass index. *American Journal of Public Health*, *105*(7), 1446-1452.

Cornil, Y., & Chandon, P. (2016). Pleasure as an ally of healthy eating? Contrasting visceral and epicurean eating pleasure and their association with portion size preference and wellbeing. *Appetite*, *104*, 52-59.

Corr, P. J., Pickering, A. D., & Gray, J. A. (1995). Personality and reinforcement in associative and instrumental learning. *Personality and Individual Differences, 19,* 47-71.

Corr, P. J. (2001). Testing problems in J. A. Gray's personality theory: A commentary on Matthews and Gilliland (1999). *Personality and Individual Differences, 30,* 333-352.

Crose, R., Nicholas, D. R., Gobble, D. C., & Frank, B. (1992). Gender and wellness: A multidimensional systems model for counseling. *Journal of Counseling & Development*, *71*(2), 149-156.

Daniels, S., Glorieux, I., Minnen, J., & van Tienoven, T. P. (2012). More than preparing a meal? Concerning the meanings of home cooking. *Appetite*, *58*(3), 1050–1056.

Dallinger, U., Oberndorfer, R., & Rupp, M. (2001). Informationen für Eltern von Babys und Kleinkindern (ifb-Materialien, 6-2011). Bamberg: Staatsinstitut für Familienforschung an der Universität Bamberg (ifb)

Darmon, N., & Drewnowski, A. (2008). Does social class predict diet quality?. *The*

American Journal of Clinical Nutrition, *87*(5), 1107-1117.

Dawe, S., Gullo, M. J., & Loxton, N. J. (2004). Reward drive and rash impulsiveness as dimensions of impulsivity: Implications for substance misuse. *Addictive Behaviors, 29,* 1389-1405.

Dean, M, Grunert, K. G., Raats, M. M., Nielsen, N. A., Lumbers, M., Food in Later Life Team (2008). The impact of personal resources and their goal relevance on satisfaction with food-related life among the elderly. *Appetite*, *50*, 308-315.

Deci, E. L., & Ryan, R. M. (2008). Hedonia, eudaimonia, and well-being: An introduction. *Journal of Happiness Studies*, *9*(1), 1-11.

DeJesus, J. M., Shutts, K., & Kinzler, K. D. (2018). Mere social knowledge impacts children's consumption and categorization of foods. *Developmental Science, 21*(5), 1-8.

Deloitte (2018). *Global Powers of Retailing 2018.* https://www2.deloitte.com/content/dam/Deloitte/at/Documents/about-deloitte/global-powers-of-retailing-2018.pdf, Last accessed 15.07.19.

Denzin, N. K. (2012). Triangulation 2.0. *Journal of Mixed Methods Research, 6*(2), 80-88.

de Ruyter, K., & Scholl, N. (1998). Positioning qualitative market research: Reflections from theory and practice. *Qualitative Market Research*, 1(1), 7-14.

Devine, C. M., & Jastran, M., Jabs, J. A., Wthington, E., Farrell, T. J., & Bisogni, C. A. (2009). A lot of sacrifices: "Work-family spillover and the food choice coping strategies of low wage parents. *Social Science and Medicine*, *62*(10), 2591-2603.

de Vries, R., Jager, G., Tijssen, I., & Zandstra, E. H. (2018). Shopping for products in a virtual world: Why haptics and visuals are equally important in shaping consumer perceptions and attitudes. *Food Quality and Preference, 66,* 64-75.

de Zwaan, M., Mitchell, J. E., Seim, H. C., Specker, S. M., Pyle, R. L., Raymond, N. C., & Crosby R. B. (1994). Eating related and general psychopathology in obese females with binge eating disorder. *International Journal of Eating Disorders, 15,* 43-52.

Diener, E., & Ryan, K. (2009). Subjective well-being: A general overview. *South African Journal of Psychology*, *39*(4), 391-406.

Diener, E., & Suh, E. M. (2000). *Culture and subjective well-being.* Cambridge, MA: MIT Press.

Diener, E., Suh, E. M., Lucas, R. E., & Smith, H. L. (1999). Subjective well-being: Three decades of progress. *Psychological Bulletin*, *125*(2), 276-302.

Diener, E., Suh, E., & Oishi, S. (1997). Recent findings on subjective wellness. *Indian Journal of Clinical Psychology*, *24*, 25-41.

Diener, E., Emmons, R. A., Larsen, R. J., & Griffin, S. (1985). The satisfaction with life scale. *Journal of Personality Assessment*, *49*, 71-75.

Dodge, R., Daly, A. P., Huyton, J., Sanders, L. D. (2012). The challenge of defining well-being. *Journal of Wellbeing*, *2*(3), 222-235.

Donini, L. M., Scardella, P., Piombo, L., Neri, B., Asprino, R., Proietti, A. R., Carcaterra, S., Cava, E., Cataldi, S., Cucinotta, D., Di Bella, G., Barbagallo, M., & Morrone, A. (2013). Malnutrition in elderly: Social and economic determinants. *The Journal of Nutrition, Health, & Ageing, 17*(1), 9-15.

Draganich, C., & Erdal, K. (2014). Placebo sleep affects cognitive functioning. *Journal of Experimental Research: Learning, Memory, and Cognition*, *40*(3), 857-864.

Drummond, D. C. (2001). Theories of drug craving, ancient and modern. *Addiction, 96,* 33-46.

Ebster, C., Wagner, U., & Neumueller, D. (2009). Children's influences on in-store purchases. *Journal of Retailing and Consumer Services, 16*(2), 145-154.

Engel, G. L. (1977). The need for a new medical model: A challenge for biomedicine. *Science*, 196, 129-136.

Elder, R. S., & Krishna, A. (2009). The effects of advertising copy on sensory thoughts and perceived taste. *Journal of Consumer Research, 36*(5), 748-756.

Elms, J., de Kervenoael, R., & Hallsworth, A. (2016). Internet or store? An ethnographic study of consumers' internet and store-based grocery shopping practices. *Journal of Retailing and Consumer Services, 32,* 234-243.

Epstein, L. H., Finkelstein, E. A., Katz, D. L., Jankowiak, N., Pudlewski, C., & Paluch, R. A. (2015). Effects of nutrient profiling and price changes based on NuVal® scores on food purchasing in an online experimental supermarket, *Public Health Nutrition*, *19*(12), 2157-2164.

Ericsson, K. A., & Simon, H. A. (1998). How to study thinking in everyday life: Contrasting think-aloud protocols with descriptions and explanations of thinking. *Mind, Culture, and Activity, 5*(3), 178-186.

Eriksson, M., & Lindström, B. (2008). A salutogenic interpretation of the Ottawa charter. *Health Promotion International, 23*(2), 361-370.

Escaron, A. L., Martinez-Donate, A. P., Riggall, A. J., Meinen, A., Hall, B., Nieto, F. J., & Nitzke, S. (2016). Developing and implementing "Waupaca Eating Smart." *Health Promotion Practice, 17*(2), 265–277.

EUR-Lex. (2019). Verordnung (EU) Nr. 1169/2011 des Europäischen Parlaments und des Rates. https://eur-lex.europa.eu/legal-content/DE/TXT/?uri=celex%3A32011R1169, Last accessed 21.09.2019.

European Commission. (2018). *EU platform for action on diet, physical activity and health - European Commission.* https://ec.europa.eu/health/nutrition_physical_activity/platform_en, Last accessed 13.09.19.

Fan, Y., & Li, Y. (2010). Children's buying behavior in China. *Marketing Intelligence & Planning, 28*(2), 170-187.

Fischer, J. (2016). Markets, religion, regulation: Kosher, halal and Hindu vegetarianism in global perspective. *Geoforum, 69*, 67-70.

Flaherty, S.-J., McCarthy, M., Collins, A., McAuliffe, F. (2017). Can existing mobile apps support healthier food purchasing behaviour? Content analysis of nutrition content, behaviour change theory and user quality integration. *Public Health Nutrition, 21*(2), 288-298.

Flegal, K. M., Carroll, M. D., Ogden, C. L., & Curtin, L. R. (2010). Prevalence and trends in obesity among US adults, 1999-2008. *JAMA: the Journal of the American Medical Association, 303,* 235-241

Forrester (2018). *Forrester Data: Online Grocery Retail Forecast, 2017 To 2022 (Global),* https://www.forrester.com/report/Forrester+Data+Online+Grocery+Retail+Forecast+2017+To+2022+Global/-/E-RES143132, Last accessed 9.04.19.

Forsythe, S., Liu, C., Shannon, D., Gardner, L. C. (2006). Development of a scale to measure the perceived benefits and risks of online shopping. *Journal of Interactive Marketing, 20* (2), 55-75.

Francis, J. E., & Davis, T. (2014). Exploring children's socialization to three dimensions of sustainability. *Young Consumers, 15*(2), 125-137.

Gable, S. L., & Haidt, J. (2005). What (and why) is positive psychology? *Review of General Psychology, 9*, 103-110.

Garcia, D. (2014). La vie en Rose: High levels of well-being and events inside and outside autobiographical memory. *Journal of Happiness Studies, 15*(3), 657-72.

Garcia, A. L., Vargas, E., Lam, P. S., Shennan, D. B., Smith, F., & Parrett, A. (2013). Evaluation of a cooking skills programme in parents of young children – a longitudinal study. *Public Health Nutrition, 17*(05), 1013–1021.

Garriga, E., & Melé, D. (2004). Corporate social responsibility theories: Mapping the territory. *Journal of Business Ethics*, *53*, 51-71.

Gaumer, C. J., Arnone, C. S., & Ashley-Cotleur, C. (2013). Child influence: Depth interviews with pre-operational child consumers and their parents. *Journal of Food Products Marketing, 19*(3), 219-235.

Gaumer, C. J., & Arnone, C. (2010). Grocery store observation: Parent-child interaction in family purchases. *Journal of Food Products Marketing, 16*(1), 1-18.

Glavas, A. (2016). Corporate social responsibility and organizational psychology: An integrative review. *Frontiers in Psychology*, *7*, 144, 1-13.

Goettler, A., Grosse, A., & Sonntag, D. (2017). Productivity loss due to overweight and obesity: A systematic review of indirect costs. *BMJ Open, 7*(10), 1-9.

Gómez-Pinilla, F. (2008). Brain foods: the effects of nutrients on brain function.

Nature Reviews Neuroscience, *9*, 568-578.

Góngora, V. C. (2014). Satisfaction with life, well-being, and meaning in life as protective

factors of eating disorder symptoms and body dissatisfaction in adolescents. *Eating*

Disorders, *22*(5), 435–449.

Goodman, J. K., Cryder, C. E., & Cheema, A. (2012). Data collection in a flat world: The strengths and weaknesses of mechanical Turk samples. *Journal of Behavioral Decision Making*, *26*(3), 213-224.

Gopaldas, A. (2015). Creating firm, customer, and societal value: Toward a theory of positive marketing. *Journal of Business Research*, *68*(12), 2446-2451.

Gorin, A. A., Raynor, H. A., Niemeier, H. M., & Wing, R. R. (2007). Home grocery delivery improves the household food environments of behavioral weight loss participants: Results of an 8-week pilot study. *International Journal of Behavioral Nutrition and Physical Activity*, *4*:58.

Gram, M., & Grønhøj, A. (2016). Meet the good child. 'Childing' practices in family food co-shopping. *International Journal of Consumer Studies, 40*(5), 511-518.

Gram, M. (2015). Buying food for the family: Negotiations in parent/child supermarket shopping: An observational study from Denmark and the United States. *Journal of Contemporary Ethnography, 44*(2), 169-195.

Gram, M. (2011). The death of 'pester power': Intergenerational food shopping. *European Advances in Consumer Research, 9,* 479-480.

Grant, D. B., Fernie, J., & Schulz, B. (2014). Enablers and barriers in German online food retailing. *Supply Chain Forum: An International Journal, 15*(3), 4-11.

Grier, S. A., Mensinger, J., Huang, S. H., Kumanyika, S. K., & Stettler, N. (2007). Fast-food marketing and children's fast-food consumption: Exploring parents' influences in an ethnically diverse sample. *Journal of Public Policy & Marketing, 26*(2), 221-35.

Griffiths, C., Harnack, L., & Pereira, M. A. (2018). Assessment of the accuracy of nutrient calculations of five popular nutrition tracking applications. *Public Health Nutrition, 21*(8), 1495-1502.

Grover, S. A., Kaouache, M., Rempel, P., Joseph, L., Dawes, M., Lau, D. C. W., & Lowensteyn, I. (2015). Years of life lost and healthy life-years lost from diabetes and cardiovascular disease in overweight and obese people: a modelling study. *The Lancet Diabetes & Endocrinology, 3*(2), 114-122.

Grunert, K. G. (2017). Consumer trends and new product opportunities in the food sector. Wageningen: Wageningen Academic Publishers.

Grunert, K. G., Dean, M., Raats, M. M., Nielsen, N. A., & Lumbers, M. (2007). A measure of satisfaction with food-related life. *Appetite, 49*(2), 486-493.

Grzeskowiak, S., Sirgy, M. J., Foscht, T., & Swoboda, B. (2016). Linking retailing experiences with life satisfaction: The concept of store-type congruity with shopper's identity. *International Journal of Retail & Distribution Management, 44*(2), 124-138.

Guerrieri, R., Nederkoorn, C., & Jansen, A. (2008). The effect of an impulsive personality on overeating and obesity: Current state of affairs. *Psychological Topics,* 17(2), 265-286.

Guh, D. P., Zhang, W., Bansback, N., Amarsi, Z., Birmingham, C. L., & Anis, A. H. (2009). The incidence of co-morbidities related to obesity and overweight: a systematic review and meta-analysis. *BMC Public Health, 9*, 1-20.

Guillemin, I., Marrel, A., Arnould, B., Capuron, L., Dupuy, A., Ginon, E., Layé, S., Lecerf, J., Prost, M., Rogeaux, M., Urdapilleta, I., & Allaert, F. (2016). How French subjects describe well-being from food and eating habits? Development, item reduction and scoring definition of the Well-Being related to Food Questionnaire (Well-BFQ©). *Appetite, 96*, 333-346.

Gupta, S., & Shukla, A. P. (1989). Verbal operant conditioning as a function of extraversion and reinforcement. *British Journal of Psychology, 80*(1), 39-44.

Hand, C., Dall'Olmo Riley, F., Harris, P., Singh, J., & Rettie, R. (2009). Online grocery shopping: The influence of situational factors. *European Journal of Marketing, 43*(9/10), 1205–1219.

Handelsverband Deutschland (2018). *Handel digital. Online-Monitor 2018*, https://einzelhandel.de/images/HDE-Publikationen/HDE_Online_Monitor_2018_WEB.pdf, Last accessed 15.04.19.

Harris, P., Dall'Olmo, F., Riley, D., & Hand, C. (2017). Online and store patronage: A typology of grocery shoppers. *International Journal of Retail & Distribution Management, 45*(4), 419-445.

Harris, J. L., Schwartz, M. B., & Brownell, K. D. (2009). Marketing foods to children and adolescents: Licensed characters and other promotions on packaged foods in the supermarket. *Public Health Nutrition, 13*(3), 409-417.

Harter, S. (2006). The Self, in *Handbook of child psychology*: Vol. 3. Social, emotional, and personality development, 6th edition, N. Eisenberg (Eds.). Hoboken, NJ: Wiley, 505-570.

Hartmann, C., Dohle, S., & Siegrist, M. (2013). Importance of cooking skills for balanced food choices. *Appetite*, *65*(C), 125–131.

Harvey, J., Smith, A., Goulding, J., & Illodo, I. B. (2019). Food sharing, redistribution, and waste reduction via mobile applications: A social network analysis. *Industrial Marketing Management*, in Press.

Haselhoff, V., Faupel, U., & Holzmüller, H. H. (2014). Strategies of children and parents during shopping for groceries. *Young Consumers, 15*(1), 17-36.

Havas Group (2017). Meaningful Brands. https://jamanetwork.com/journals/jama/articlepdf/2678018/jama_mokdad_2018_oi_180029.pdf, Last accessed 07.03.19.

Havermans, R. C., & Jansen, A. T. M. (2003). Increasing the efficacy of cue exposure treatment in preventing relapse of addictive behavior. *Addictive Behaviors,* 28, 989-994.

Hawkes, C. (2013). *Promoting healthy diets through nutrition education and changes in the food environment: an international review of actions and their effectiveness.* Nutrition Education and Consumer Awareness Group, Food and Agriculture Organization of the United Nations. www.fao.org/ag/humannutrition/nutritioneducation/69725/en/, Last accessed 15.03.19.

Hawks, S. (1994). Spiritual health: Definition and theory. *Wellness Perspectives*, *10*(4), 3-13.

Hawks, S. R., Goudy, M. B., & Gast, J. A. (2003). Emotional eating and spiritual well-being: A possible connection? *American Journal of Health Education*, *34*(1), 30-33.

Hays, N. P., & Roberts, S. B. (2007). Aspects of eating behaviors disinhibition and restraint are related to weight gain and BMI in women. *Obesity, 16*(1), 52-58.

Headey, B., Glowacki, T., Holmstrom, E., & Wearing, A. (1985). Modelling change in perceived quality of life (PQOL). *Social Indicators Research,* 17(3), 267-298.

Heath, C., & Soll, J. B. (1996). Mental budgeting and consumer decisions. *Journal of Consumer Research*, *23*, 40-52.

Hedhli, K. E., Chebat, J.-C., Sirgy, M. J. (2013). Shopping well-being at the mall: Construct, antecedents, and consequences. *Journal of Business Research*, *66*, 856-863.

Hémar-Nicolas, V., & Ezan, P. (2018). How do children make sense of food well-being? Food for thought for responsible retailers. *International Journal of Retail & Distribution Management, 19*(3), 419-433.

Herman, C. P., & Polivy, J. (2008). External cues in the control of food intake in humans: The sensory-normative distinction. *Physiology & Behavior*, *94*(5), 722–728.

Hettler, B. (1980). Wellness Promotion on a University Campus. *Family Community Health, 3*(1), 77-95.

Hill, J. O. (1998). Environmental Contributions to the Obesity Epidemic. *Science, 280*(5368), 1371–1374.

Hoffman, H. G., Hollander, A., Schroder, K., Rousseau, S., & Furness, T. (1998). Physically touching and tasting virtual objects enhances the realism of virtual experiences. *Virtual Reality,* 3(4), 226-234.

Hoffman, H. G., Richards, T., Coda, B., Richards, A., & Sharar, S. R. (2003). The Illusion of presence in immersive Virtual reality during an fMRI brain scan. *CyberPsychology & Behavior*, *6*(2), 127-134.

Hogarth, L., Dickinson, A., Hutton, S. B., Bamborough, H., & Duka, T. (2006). Contingency knowledge is necessary for learned motivated behaviour in humans: Relevance for addictive behaviour. *Addiction, 101*, 1153-1166.

Holt, C. L., Haire-Joshu, D. L., Lukwago, S. N., Lewellyn, L. A., & Kreuter, M. W.

(2005). The role of religiosity in dietary beliefs and behaviors among urban African American women. *Cancer Control*, *12*(2), 84-90.

Horsley, J. A., Absalom, K. A. R., Akiens, E. M., Dunk, R. J., and Ferguson, A. M. (2014). The proportion of unhealthy foodstuffs children are exposed to at the checkout of convenience supermarkets. *Public Health Nutrition, 17*(11), 2453-2458.

Howlett, E., Davis, C., & Burton, S. (2015). From food desert to food oasis: The potential influence of food retailers on childhood obesity rates. *Journal of Business Ethics, 139*(2), 215-224.

Hou, R., Mogg, K., Bradley, B. P., Moss-Morris, R., Peveler, R., & Roefs, A. (2011). External eating, impulsivity and attentional bias to food cues. *Appetite, 56*, 424-427.

Hsieh, H. F., & Shannon, S. E. (2005). Three approaches to qualitative content analysis. *Qualitative Health Research*, *15*(9), 1277-88.

Huang, C. Y., Reisch, L. A., Gwozdz, W., Molnár, D., Konstabel, K., Michels, N., Tornaritis, M., Eiben, G., Siani, A., Fernández-Alvira, J. M., Ahrens, W., Pigeot, I., & Lissner, L. (2016). Pester power and its consequences: Do European children's food purchasing requests relate to diet and weight outcomes? *Public Health Nutrition, 19*(3), 2392-2403.

Huang, R., & Yang, M. (2013). But what is advertised on television? Evidence from bans on child-directed food advertising. *Journal of Public Policy & Marketing, 32*(2), 207-222.

Huber, O. (1993). Beobachtung. In E. Roth. *Sozialwissenschaftliche Methoden. Lehr- und Handbuch für Forschung und Praxis* (pp. 130-132). Salzburg: R. Oldenbourg Verlag.

Huck, C. W., Pezzei, C. K., & Huck-Pezzei, V. A. C. (2016). An industry perspective of food fraud. *Current Opinion in Food Science, 10*, 32-37.

Huskisson, E. C. (1974). Measurement of pain. *The Lancet,* 304, 1127-1131.

Hutter, K., Hoffmann, S., & Mai, R. (2016). Carrotmob: A win-win-win approach to creating benefits for consumers, business, and society at large. *Business and Society, 55*(7), 1059-1077.

Huyghe, E., Verstraeten, J., Geuens, M., & Van Kerckhove, A. (2017). Clicks as a healthy alternative to bricks: How online grocery shopping reduces vice purchases. *Journal of Marketing Research, 54*(1), 61-74.

IGD (2018). *Shoppers of the future.* https://www.igd.com/Portals/0/Shoppers-of-the-Future.pdf, Last accessed 07.03.19

Ilyuk, V. (2018). Like throwing a piece of me away: How online and in-store grocery purchase channels affect consumers' food waste. *Journal of Retailing and Consumer Services, 41*, 20-30.

Jabs, J., & Devine, C. M. (2006). Time scarcity and food choices: an overview. *Appetite. 47*(2), 196-204.

Jansen, A. (1998). A learning model of binge eating: Cue reactivity and cue exposure. *Behaviour Research and Therapy, 36*(3), 257-272.

Jansen, A., Havermans, R. C., & Nederkoorn, C. (2011). Cued overeating. In V. R., Preedy, R. R. Watson & C. R. Martin. *Handbook of Behavior, Food and Nutrition* (pp. 1431-1443). New York: Springer.

Jansen, A., Klaver, J., Merckelbach, H., & van den Hout, M. (1989). Restrained eaters are rapidly habituating sensation seekers. *Behaviour Research and Therapy*, *27*(3), 247-252.

Jansen, A., Stegerman, S., Roefs, A., Nederkoorn, C., & Havermans, R. C. (2010). Decreased salivation to food cues in formerly obese successful dieters. *Psychotherapy and Psychosomatics, 79*, 257-258.

Janssen, I., Boyce, W. F., Simpson, K., & Pickett, W. (2006). Influence of individual- and area-level measures of socioeconomic status on obesity, unhealthy eating, and physical inactivity in Canadian adolescents. *The American Journal of Clinical Nutrition, 83*(1), 139–145.

Jayasankaraprasad, C., & Kathyayani, G. (2014). Cross-format shopping motives and shopper typologies for grocery shopping: A multivariate approach. *The International Review of Retail, Distribution and Consumer Research*, *24*(1), 79-115.

Johnson, T., Kulesa, P., Cho, Y. I., & Shavitt, S. (2005). The relation between culture and response styles: Evidence from 19 countries. *Journal of Cross-Cultural Psychology, 36*, 264-277.

Karahsanovic, A., Holm, K. T., & Nejad, A. (2017). Design for trust - Online grocery shopping. *International Conference Interfaces and Human Computer Interaction* 2017, 239-243.

Kashdan, T. B., Biswas-Diener, R., & King, L. A. (2008). Reconsidering happiness: The costs of distinguishing between hedonics and eudaimonia. *Journal of Positive Psychology, 3*(4), 219-233.

Kahneman, D., Diener, E., & Schwarz, N. (1999). *Well-being: The foundations of hedonic psychology.* New York: The Russell Sage Foundation.

Kahneman, D., & Tversky, A. (1984). Choices, values, and frames. *American Psychologist, 39*(4), 341-350.

Kang, C., Moon, J., Kim, T., & Choe, Y. (2016). Why consumers go to online grocery: Comparing vegetables with grains. *Proceedings of the 49th Hawaii International Conference on System Sciences* (HICSS), 3604-13.

Keski-Rahkonen, A., & Mustelin, L. (2016). Epidemiology of eating disorders in Europe: Prevalence, incidence, comorbidity, course, consequences, and risk factors. *Current Opinion in Psychiatry, 29*(6), 340-345.

Keyes, C. L. M. (1998). Social Well-Being. Social Psychology Quarterly, 61(2), 121-140.

Khan, U., & Dhar, R. (2007). Where there is a way, is there a will? The effect of future choices on self-control. *Journal of Experimental Psychology, 136*(2), 277-288.

Kharuhayothin, T., & Kerrane, B. (2018). Learning from the past? An exploratory study of familial food socialization processes using the lens of emotional reflexivity. *European Journal of Marketing, 52*(12), 2312-2333.

King, S. C., Snow, J., Meiselman, H. L., Sainsbury, J., Carr, B. T., McCafferty, D., Serrano, D., Gilette, M., Millard, L., & Li, Q. (2015). Development of a questionnaire to measure consumer wellness associated with foods: The WellSense Profile™. *Food Quality and Preference,* 39, 82-94.

Kolbe, R. H., & Burnett, M. S. (1991). Content-analysis research: An examination of applications with directives for improving research reliability and objectivity. *Journal of Consumer Research, 18*(2), 243-250.

Köster, E. P., & Mojet, J. (2015). From mood to food and from food to mood: A psychological perspective on the measurement of food-related emotions in consumer research. *Food Research International, 76*(2), 180–191.

Kotler, P. (1986). *Principles of Marketing*, 3rd ed., Englewood Cliffs, NJ: Prentice-Hall.

Krueger, R. A., & Casey, M. A. (2000). *Focus groups: A practical guide for applied researchers* (3rd.). Thousand Oaks, CA: Sage.

Kuczynski, L., and Kochanska, G. (1990). Development of children's noncompliance strategies from toddlerhood to age 5. *Developmental Psychology, 26*(3), 398-408.

Labrecque, L. I., vor dem Esche, J., Mathick, C., Novak, T. P., & Hofacker, C. F. (2013). Consumer power: Evolution in the digital age. *Journal of Interactive Marketing, 27*(4), 257-269.

Lakerveld, J., Mackenbach, J. D., Rutter, H., & Brug, J. (2018). Obesogenic environment and obesogenic behaviours. In C. Hankey, & K. Whelan (Eds.), *Advanced Nutrition and Dietetics in Obesity* (pp. 132-138). London: John Wiley & Sons.

Lang, T. & Caraher, M. (2012). Influencing International Policy. In C. Guest, I. Kawachi, I. Lang, & W. Ricciard (Eds.), *Oxford Handbook of Public Health*, Edition: 3rd, Oxford University Press.

Lang, T., Barling, D., Caraher, M. (2001). Food, social policy and the environment: Towards a new model. *Social Policy & Administration, 35*(5), 538-558.

Lang, T., & Rayner, G. (2007). Overcoming policy cacophony on obesity: An ecological public health framework for policymakers. *Obesity reviews, 8*(1), 165-181.

Larson, R., & Richards, M. (1998). Waiting for the weekend: Friday and Saturday night as the emotional climax of the week. *New Directions for Child and Adolescent Development, 82*, 37-52.

Lawlor, M.-A., & Prothero, A. (2011). Pester power – A battle of wills between children and their parents. *Journal of Marketing Management, 27*(5/6), 561-581.

Leech, N. L., & Onwuegbuzie, A. J. (2007). A typology of mixed methods research designs. *Quality & Quantity, 43*(2), 265-75.

Lee, D.-J., & Sirgy, J. (2004). Quality-of-Life (QOL) Marketing: Proposed antecedents and consequences. *Journal of Macromarketing, 24*(1), 44-58.

Lee, D.-J., Sirgy, M. J., Larsen, V., & Wright, N. D. (2002). Developing a subjective measure of consumer wellbeing. *Journal of Macromarketing, 22*(2), 158-169.

Leelakulthanit, O., Day, R., & Walters, R. (1991). Investigating the relationship between marketing and overall satisfaction with life in a developing country. *Journal of Macromarketing, 11*(1), 3-23.

Lennon, S. J., Ha, Y., Johnson, K. K. P., Jasper, C. R., Damhorst, M. L., & Lyons, N. (2009). Rural consumers' online shopping for food and fiber products as a form of outshopping. *Clothing & Textiles Research Journal, 27*(1), 3-30.

Lindström, B., & Eriksson, M. (2009). The salutogenic approach to the making of HiAP/healthy public policy: Illustrated by a case study. *Global Health Promotion, 16*(1), 17-28.

Lovibond, P. F., & Shanks, D. R. (2002). The role of awareness in Pavlovian conditioning: Empirical evidence and theoretical implications. *Journal of Experimental Psychology, Animal Behavior Processes, 28*(1), 3-26.

Lumeng, J. C., Taveras, E. M., Birch, L., & Yanovski, S. Z. (2015). Prevention of obesity in infancy and early childhood: A National Institutes of Health workshop, *JAMA Pediatrics*, March, E1-E7.

Luppino, F. S., de Wit, L. M., Bouvy, P. F., Stijnen, T., Cuijpers, P., Penninx, B. W., & Zitman, F. G. (2010). Overweight, obesity, and depression: A systematic review and meta-analysis of longitudinal studies. *Archives of General Psychiatry, 67*(3), 220-229.

MacInnis, D. J., Moorman, C., & Jaworski, B. J. (1991). Enhancing and measuring consumers' motivation, opportunity, and ability to process brand information from ads. *Journal of Marketing, 55*(4), 32-53.

Malik, F., & Marwaha, R. (2018). *Development, stages of social emotional development in Children.* https://www.ncbi.nlm.nih.gov/books/NBK534819/, Last accessed 19.07.19.

Marshall, D. (2014). Co-operation in the supermarket aisle: Young children's accounts of family food shopping. *International Journal of Retail & Distribution Management, 42*(11/12), 990-1003.

Martin, K. D., & Hill, R. P. (2012). Life satisfaction, self-determination, and consumption adequacy at the bottom of the pyramid. *Journal of Consumer Research, 38*(6), 1155-1168.

Martinez, O., Tagliaferro, B., Rodriguez, N., Athens, J. A., Abrams, C., & Elbel, B. (2018). EBT payment for online grocery orders: A mixed-methods study to understand its uptake among SNAP recipients and the barriers to and motivators for its use. *Journal of Nutrition Education and Behavior, 50*(4), 396-402.

Mathras, D., Cohen, A. B., Mandel, N., & Mick, D. G. (2016). The effects of religion on consumer behavior: A conceptual framework and research agenda. *Journal of Consumer Psychology, 26*(2), 298-311.

Mau, G., Schramm-Klein, H., Schuhen, M, Steinmann, S. (2019). What helps children resist distracting marketing stimuli? Implementation intentions and restrictions alter food choice. *Appetite, 140*, 159-168.

Mau, G., Schuhen, M. Steinmann, S., & Schramm-Klein, H. (2016). How children make purchase decisions: Behavior of the cued processors. *Young Consumers, 17*(2), 111-126.

Mayo, E., & Nairn, A. (2009). *Consumer Kids. How Big Business is Grooming Our Children for Profit*, Constable: London.

McFerran, B., Dahl, D. W., Fitzsimons, G. J., & Morales, A. C. (2010). I'll have what she's having: Effects of social influence and body type on the food choices of others. *Journal of Consumer Research, 36*(6), 915–929.

McKie, L. (1999). Older people and food: Independency, locality and diet. *British Food Journal, 101*(7), 528-536.

McMahon, A.-T., Williams, P., & Tapsell, L. (2010). Reviewing the meanings of wellness and well-being and their implications for food choice. *Perspectives in Public Health, 130*(6), 282-286.

McNeal, J. U. (2007). *On becoming a consumer: Development of consumer behavior in patterns in childhood.* Woburn, MA: Butterworth-Heinemann.

McNeal, J. U., & Yeh, C.-H. (1993). Born to shop. *American Demographics, 15*(6), 34-39.

Meadow, H. L. (1983). *The relationship between consumer satisfaction and life satisfaction for the elderly*. Blacksburg, VA: Virginia Polytechnic Institute and State University.

Meena, S., Swerdlow, F., & Kumar, S. (2018). The state of global online grocery retail, 2018. https://www.forrester.com/report/The+State+Of+Global+Online+Grocery+Retail+2018/-/E-RES143057, Last accessed 12.06.19.

Mehta, K., Phillips, C., Ward, P., Coveney, J., Handsley, E., & Carter, P. (2012). Marketing foods to children through product packaging: prolific, unhealthy and misleading. *Public Health Nutrition, 15*(9), 1763-1770.

Meiselman, H. L. (2016). Quality of life, well-being and wellness: Measuring subjective health for foods and other products. *Food Quality and Preference, 54*, 101-109.

Meiselman, H. L. (2013). The future in sensory/consumer research: ..... evolving to a better science. *Food Quality and Preference, 27*, 208-214.

Melis, K., Campo, K., Lamey, L., & Breugelmans, E. (2016). A bigger slice of the multichannel grocery pie: When does consumers' online channel use expand retailers' share of wallet? *Journal of Retailing,* 92(3), 268-286.

Meldrum, D. R., Morris, M. A., & Gambone, J. C. (2017). Obesity pandemic: Causes, consequences, and solutions – but do we have the will? *Fertility and Sterility, 107*(4), 833-839.

Metcalfe, J., & Mischel, W. (1999). A hot/cool-system analysis of delay of gratification: Dynamics of willpower. *Psychological Review, 106*(1), 3-19.

Meyer, C., & Waller, G. (1999). The impact of emotion upon eating behavior: The role of subliminal visual processing of threat cues. *International Journal of Eating Disorders, 25*(3), 319-326.

Meyer-Höfer, von, M., Wense, von der, V., & Spiller, A. (2013). Characterising convinced sustainable food consumers. *GlobalFood Discussion Papers, 28,* 1–24.

Mick, D. G., Pettigrew, S., Pechmann, C., and Ozanne, J. L. (2012). *Transformative Consumer Research for Personal and Collective Well-Being.* New York: Routledge.

Mick, D. G. (2006). Meaning and mattering through transformative consumer research, *Advances in Consumer Research, 33,* 1-4.

Milkman, K. L., Rogers, T., & Bazerman, M. H. (2010). I'll have the ice cream soon and the vegetables later: A study of online grocery purchases and order lead time. *Marketing Letters, 21*(1), 17-35.

Miller, G., & Foster, L. T. (2010). *Critical synthesis of wellness literature.* University of Victoria, Faculty of Human and Social Development & Department of Geography.

Ministère des Solidarités et de la Santé (2017). *Deux textes visant à prévenir les troubles du comportement alimentaire et en particulier l'anorexie, notamment chez les jeunes, sont publiés au Journal Officiel.* https://solidarites-sante.gouv.fr/archives/archives-presse/archives-communiques-de-presse/article/deux-textes-visant-a-prevenir-les-troubles-du-comportement-alimentaire-et-en, Last accessed 15.03.19.

Mischel, W., and Ebbesen, E. B. (1970). Attention in delay of gratification. *Journal of Personality and Social Psychology, 16*(2), 329-337.

Mittelstaedt, J. D., Kilbourne, W. E., & Shultz II, C. J. (2015). Macromarketing approaches to thought development in positive marketing: Two perspectives on a research agenda for positive marketing scholars. *Journal of Business Research, 68*(12), 2513-2516.

Mitterschiffthaler, M. T., Fu, C. H. Y., Dalton, J. A., Andrew, C. M., & Williams, S. C. R. (2007). A functional MRI study of happy and sad affective states induced by classical music. *Human Brain Mapping, 28,* 1150-1162.

Mochis, G. P. (1985). The role of family communication in consumer socialization of children and adolescents. *Journal of Consumer Research, 11,* 898-913.

Mohana, S., Tapp, H., McWilliams, A., & Dulin, M. (2014). Obesity and asthma: Pathophysiology and implications for diagnosis and management in primary care. *Experimental Biology and Medicine, 239*(11), 1531-1540.

Monaghan, L. (2001). Looking good, feeling good: The embodied pleasures of vibrant physicality. *Sociology of Health and Illness*, *23*(3), 330–356.

Monteiro, C. A., Moubarac, J. C., Cannon, G., Ng, S. W., & Popkin, B. (2013). Ultra-processed products are becoming dominant in the global food system. *Obesity reviews: an official journal of the International Association for the Study of Obesity, 2*, 21-28.

Montoya-Weiss, M. M., Voss, G. B., & Grewal, D. (2003). Channel use and overall satisfaction with a relational, multichannel service provider. *Journal of the Academy of Marketing Science*, *31*(4), 448-458.

Moons, P., Budts, W., and De Geest, S. (2006). Critique on the conceptualization of quality of life: A review and evaluation of different conceptual approaches. *International Journal of Nursing Studies*, *43*(7), 891-901.

Moore, E., Wilkie, W., & Lutz, R. (2002). Passing the torch: Intergenerational influences as a source of brand equity. *Journal of Marketing, 66*, 17-37.

Morrison, K. M., Shin, S., Tarnopolsky, M., & Taylor, V. H. (2015). Association of depression & health related quality of life with body composition in children and youth with obesity. *Journal of Affective Disorders, 172*(1), 18-23.

Mugel, O., Gurviez, P., & Decrop, A. (2019). Eudaimonia around the kitchen: A hermeneutic approach to understanding food well-being in consumers' lived experiences. *Journal of Public Policy & Marketing, 38*(2), 1-16.

Murphey, E. B., Silber, E., Coelho, G. V., Hamburg, D. A., & Greenberg, I. (1963). Development of autonomy and parent-child interaction in late adolescence. *American Journal of Orthopsychiatry, 33*(4), 643-652.

Muzellec, L. Feenstra, F., Faultrier (de), B. and Boulay, J. (2016). Children's experiences and parents' perceptions of retailers' mobile applications. *International Journal of Retail & Distribution Management*, *44*(11), 1118-1131.

Nakano, N., MacDonald, M., & Douthitt, R. (1995). Toward consumer wellbeing: Consumer socialization effects of work experience. In M. J. Sirgy, & A. Coskun Samli (Eds.). *New Dimensions in Marketing/Quality-of-Life Research* (pp. 107-111). Westport, CT: Quorum Books.

Nasser, J. A., Gluck, M. E., & Geliebter, A. (2004). Impulsivity and test meal intake in obese binge eating women. *Appetite, 43*, 303-307.

Nederkoorn, C., Smulders, F., & Jansen, A. (2000). Cephalic phase responses, craving and food intake in normal subjects. *Appetite, 35*, 45-55.

Nederkoorn, C., Braet, C., Van Eijs, Y., Tanghe, A., & Jansen, A. (2006a). Why obese children cannot resist food: The role of impulsivity. *Eating Behaviors, 7*, 315-322.

Nederkoorn, C., Smulders, F. T. Y., Havermans, R. C., Roefs, A., & Jansen, A. (2006b). Impulsivity in obese women. *Appetite, 47*, 253-256.

Nederkoorn, C., Jansen, E., Mulkens, S., & Jansen, A. (2007). Impulsivity predicts treatment outcome in obese children. *Behaviour Research and Therapy, 45*, 1071-1075.

Nederkoorn, C., Guerrieri, R., Havermans, R. C., Roefs, A., & Jansen, A. (2009). The interactive effect of hunger and impulsivity on food intake and purchase in a virtual supermarket. *International Journal of Obesity, 33*, 905-912.

Nekitsing, C., Hetherington, M. M., & Blundell-Birtill, P. (2018). Developing healthy food preferences in preschool children through taste exposure, sensory learning, and nutrition education. *Current Obesity Reports, 7*(1), 60-67.

Neilson, L. A. (2010). Boycott or boycott? Understanding political consumerism. *Journal of Consumer Behavior*, *9*, 214-227.

Nicklas, T. A., Baranowski, T., Baranowski, J. C., Cullen, K., Rittenberry, L., & Olvera, N. (2009). Family and child-care provider influences on preschool children's fruit, juice, and vegetable consumption. *Nutrition Reviews*, *59*(7), 224–235.

Nielsen (2015). The future of groceries – E-commerce, digital technology and changing shopping preferences around the world. https://www.nielsen.com/wp-content/uploads/sites/3/2019/04/nielsen-global-e-commerce-new-retail-report-april-2015.pdf, Last accessed 11.09.19.

Nutbeam, D. (2008). The evolving concept of health literacy. *Social Science and Medicine*, *67*(12), 2072-2078.

O'Brien, M. C., McConnon, A., Hollywood, L. E., Cuskelly, G. J., Barnett, J., Raats, M., & Dean, M. (2014). Let's talk about health: Shoppers' discourse regarding health while food shopping. *Public Health Nutrition, 18*(6), 1001-1010.

O'Dougherty, M., Story, M., & Strang, J. (2006). Observations of parent-child co-shoppers in supermarkets: Children's involvement in food selections, parental yielding, and refusal strategies. *Society for Nutrition Education, 38*(3), 133-138.

Onwuegbuzie, A. J., & Dickinson, W. B. (2009). A qualitative framework for collecting and analyzing data in focus group research. *International Journal of Qualitative Methods, 8*(3), 1-21.

Ozanne, J. L., Davis, B., Murray, J. B., Grier, S., Benmecheddal, A., Downey, H., Ekpo, A. E., Garnier, M., Hietanen, J., Le Gall-Ely, M., Seregina, A., Thomas, K. D., & Veer, E. (2016). Assessing the societal impact of research: The relational engagement approach. *Journal of Public Policy & Marketing, 36*(1), 1-14.

Page, B., Sharp, A., Lockshin, L., & Sorensen, H. (2018). Parents and children in supermarkets: Incidence and influence. *Journal of Retailing and Consumer Services, 40*, 31-39.

Paisey, T. J. H., & Mangan, G. L. (1988). Personality and conditioning with appetitive and aversive stimuli. *Personality and Individual Differences, 9*(1), 69-78.

Palinkas, L. A., Horwitz, S. M., Green, C. A., Wisdom, J. P., Duan, N., & Hoagwood, K. (2013). Purposeful sampling for qualitative data collection and analysis in mixed method implementation research. *Administration and Policy in Mental Health and Mental Health Services Research, 42*(5), 533-544.

Papachristou, H., Nederkoorn, C., Beunen, S., & Jansen, A. (2013). Dissection of appetitive conditioning. Does impulsivity play a role? *Appetite, 69*, 46-53.

Patton, J. H., Stanford, M. S., & Barratt, E. S. (1995). Factor structure of the Barratt impulsiveness scale. *Journal of Clinical Psychology, 51*(6), 768-774.

Paul, J., & Rana, J. (2012). Consumer behavior and purchase intention for organic food. *Journal of Consumer Marketing, 29*(6), 412–422.

Pearce, J., & Witten, K. (2010). *Geographies of obesity: Environmental understandings of the obesity epidemic*. Oxon, New York: Routledge.

Petrovich, G. D., Ross, C. A., Gallagher, M., & Holland, P. C. (2007). Learned contextual cue potentiates eating in rats. *Physiology & Behavior, 90*(2-3), 362-367.

Piacentini, M., Mac Fadyen, L., & Eadie, D. (2000). Corporate social responsibility in food retailing. *International Journal of Retail & Distribution Management, 28*(11), 459-472.

Picot-Coupey, K., Huré, E., Cliquet, G., & Petr, C. (2009). Grocery shopping and the Internet: Exploring French consumers' perceptions of the 'hypermarket' and "cybermarket" Formats. *The International Review of Retail, Distribution and Consumer Research, 19*(4), 437-455.

Pike, K. M., Hoek, H. W., & Dunne, P. E. (2014). Cultural trends and eating disorders.

Current Opinion in Psychiatry, 27(6), 436-442.

Pitts, S. B. J., Ng, S. W., Blitstein, J. L., Gustafson, A., & Niculescu, M. (2018). Online grocery shopping: Promise and pitfalls for healthier food and beverage purchases. *Public Health Nutrition, 21*(18), 3360-3376.

Polivy, J., Herman, C. P., & Howard, K. (1988). The restraint scale: Assessment of dieting. In M. Hersen & S. Bellack (Eds.). *Dictionary of behavioural assessment techniques* (pp. 377-380). New York, NY: Pergamon.

Pólya, É., & Földi, K. (2014). Role of children in the case of parental food store choice. *Economica, 7*(2), 180-187.

Porter, M. E., & Kramer, M. R. (2006). Strategy & society: The link between competitive advantage and corporate social responsibility. *Harvard Business Review*, December, 78-93.

Powley, T. L. (1977). The ventromedial hypothalamic syndrome, satiety, and a cephalic phase hypothesis. *Psychological Review, 84*(1), 89-126.

Prochaska, J. O., & DiClemente, C. C. (1982). Transtheoretical therapy: Toward a more integrative model of change. *Psychotherapy: Theory, Research and Practice, 19*(3), 276-288.

Prochaska, J. O., & Velicer, W. F. (1997). The transtheoretical model of health behavior change. *American Journal of Health Promotion, 12*(1), 38-48.

Prochaska, J. O., Wright, J. A., Velicer, W. F. (2008). Evaluating theories of health behavior change: A hierarchy of criteria applied to the transtheoretical model. *Applied Psychology, 57*(4), 561-588.

Quigley, M. (2013). Nudging for health: On public policy and designing choice architecture. *Medical Law Review, 21*(4), 588–621.

Raggiotto, F., Mason, M. C., & Moretti, A. (2018). Religiosity, materialism, consumer environmental predisposition. Some insights on vegan purchasing intentions in Italy. *International Journal of Consumer Studies*, *42*(6), 613-626.

Raju, S., Rajagopal, P., & Gilbride, T. J. (2010). Marketing healthful eating to children: The effectiveness of incentives, pledges, and competitions. *Journal of Marketing*, *74*(3), 93-106.

Ramachandran, K. K., Karthick, K. K., & Kumar, M. S. (2011). Online shopping in the UK. *International Business & Economics Research Journal*, *10*(12), 23-36.

Ranadive, A. (2015). An empirical study on the online grocery shopping intentions of consumers in Vadodara City. *International Journal of Management and Social Sciences Research*, *4*(3), 8-14.

Ratzan, S. C. (2001). Health literacy: Communication for the public good. *Health Promotion International*, *16*(2), 207-214.

Ravanbakht, S. N., Skinner, A. C., Perrin, E. M. (2017). Early prevention and treatment interventions for childhood obesity. *Current Pediatrics Reports*, *5*(4), 199-203.

Ravussin, E., & Ryan, D. H. (2017). Three new perspectives on the perfect storm: What's behind the obesity epidemic? *Obesity, 26*(1), 9-10.

Renger, R. F., Midyett, S. J., Mas, F. G., Erin, T. E., McDermott, H. M., Papenfuss, R. L., Eichling, M. D., Baker, D. H., Johnson, K. A., Hewitt, M. J. (2000). Optimal living profile: An inventory to assess health and wellness. *American Journal of Health Behavior*, *24*(6), 403-412.

Richards, T. J., Hamilton, S. F., & Allender, W. (2016). Search and price dispersion in online grocery markets. *International Journal of Industrial Organization, 47*, 255-281.

Rivlin, G. (2016). *Rigged: Supermarket Shelves for Sale*,

https://cspinet.org/sites/default/files/attachment/CSPI_Rigged_4_small.pdf, Last accessed 07.03.19.

Robertson, T. S. (1967). The process of innovation and the diffusion of innovation. *Journal of Marketing*, *31*, 14-19.

Robinson, H., Dall'Olmo Riley, F., Rettie, R., & Rolls-Willson, G. (2007). The role of situational variables in online grocery shopping in the UK. *The Marketing Review*, *7*(1), 89–106.

Rodin, J., & Slochower, J. (1976). Externality in the nonobese: Effects of environmental responsiveness on weight. *Journal of Personality and Social Psychology, 33*(3), 338-344.

Rodríguez-Arauz, G., Ramírez-Esparza, N., & Smith-Castro, V. (2016). Food attitudes and well-being: The role of culture. *Appetite*, *105*, 180–188.

Rogers, E. M. (1995). *Diffusion of Innovations* (4th ed.), New York: Free Press.

Rook, D. W., & Fisher, R. J. (1995). Normative influences on impulse buying behavior. *Journal of Consumer Research*, *22*, 305-313.

Roscoe, L. J. (2009). Wellness: A review of theory and measurement for counselors. *Journal of Counseling & Development, 87*(2), 216-22.

Rosen, S. J. (2011). *Food for the Soul: Vegetarianism and Yoga.* Oxford: ABC-CLIO.

Rozin, P. (2005). The meaning of food in our lives: A cross-cultural perspective on eating and wellbeing. *Journal of Nutrition and Behavior, 37*(2), 107-112.

Rust, L. (1993). Parents and children shopping together: A new approach to the qualitative analysis of observational data. *Journal of Advertising Research, 33*(4), 65-71.

Rutter, M. (2012). Resilience as a dynamic concept. *Development and Psychopathology,*

24(2), 335-344.

Ryan, R. M., & Deci, E. L. (2000). Self-determination theory and the facilitation of intrinsic motivation, social development, and well-being. *American Psychologist, 55*(1), 68-78.

Rydén, A., Sullivan, M., Torgerson, J. S., Karlsson, J., Lindroos, A. K., & Taft, C. (2003). Severe obesity and personality: A comparative controlled study of personality traits. *International Journal of Obesity and Related Metabolic Disorders, 27*, 1534-1540.

Ryff, C. D., & Keyes, C. L. M. (1995). The structure of psychological well-being revisited. *Journal of Personality and Social Psychology, 69*(4), 719-727.

Ryff, C. D., & Singer, B. H. (2008). Know thyself and become what you are: A eudaimonic approach to psychological well-being. *Journal of Happiness Studies, 9*(1), 13-39.

Sacks, G., Tikellis, K., Millar, L., & Swinburn, B. (2011). Impact of 'traffic-light' nutrition information on online food purchases in Australia. *Australian and New Zealand Journal of Public Health, 35*(2), 122-126.

Salvy, S.-J., la Haye, de, K., Bowker, J. C., & Hermans, R. C. J. (2012). Influence of peers and friends on children's and adolescents' eating and activity behaviors. *Physiology & Behavior, 106*(3), 369–378.

Scharff, R. L. (2012). Economic burden from health losses due to foodborne illness in the United States. *Journal of Food Protection, 75*(1), 123-131.

Schienkiewitz, A., Mensink, G. B. M., Kuhnert, R., & Lange, C. (2017). Übergewicht und Adipositas bei Erwachsenen in Deutschland. *Journal of Health Monitoring, 2*(2), 21-28.

Schnellbächer, C., Behr, J., & Leonhäuser, I.-U. (2015). Potential of online food shopping. *Ernährungs Umschau, 62*(11), 178–187.

Schnettler, B., Miranda-Zapata, E., Sánchez, M., Grunert, K. G., Lobos, G., Adasme-Berríos, C., Orellana, L., Sepúlveda, J., & Hueche, C. (2016). Measurement invariance in the satisfaction with food-related life scale: A comparison of Chilean and Spanish university students. *Food Quality and Preference, 57*, 79-86.

Schoonenboom, J., & Johnson, R. B. (2017). How to construct a mixed methods research design. *Kölner Zeitschrift für Soziologie und Sozialpsychologie, 69*(2), 107-131.

Schramm-Klein, H., Zentes, J., Steinmann, S., Swoboda, B., & Morschett, D. (2016). Retailer corporate social responsibility is relevant to consumer behavior. *Business & Society*, *55*(4), 550-575.

Schrempf, J. (2014). A social connection approach to corporate responsibility. The case of the fast-food industry and obesity. *Business & Society, 53*(2), 300-332.

Schuhen, M., Mau, G., Schramm-Klein, H., & Hartig, J. (2017). When children become purchasers: A qualitative study for describing the purchasing literacy of children. *Zeitschrift für ökonomische Bildung, 6*, 171-192.

Scott, M. L., & Vallen, B. (2019). Expanding the lens of food well-being: An examination of contemporary marketing, policy, and practice with an eye on the future. *Journal of Public Policy and Marketing, 38*(2), 127-135.

Seitz, C. (2014). Psychological evaluation of grocery shopping. *Proceedings of the 13th International Conference Improving Performance of Agriculture and the Economy*, 348-354.

Seitz, C., Pokrivčák, J., Tóth, M. & Plevný, M. (2017). Online grocery retailing in Germany: An explorative analysis. *Journal of Business Economics and Management, 18*(6), 1243-1263.

Shah, H., & Marks, N. (2004). *A well-being manifesto for a flourishing society.* London: The New Economics Foundation.

Sheth, J. N. (1983). An integrative theory of patronage preference and behavior. In W. R. Darden & R. F. Lush (Eds.), *Patronage Behavior and Retail Management* (pp. 9-28). Orlando: Elsevier.

Sobal, J., Bisogni, C. A., Devine, C. M., & Jastran, M. (2006). A conceptual model of the food choice process over the life course. In R. Shepherd & M. Raats, (Eds.). *The Psychology of Food Choice* (pp. 1–18). Oxfordshire, England: CABI.

Silverman, D. (2006). *Interpreting Qualitative Data.* 3rd Ed. London: Sage Publications Ltd.

Simonin, B. L., & Ruth, J. A. (1998). Is a company known by the company it keeps? Assessing the spillover effects of brand alliances on consumer brand attitudes. *Journal of Marketing Research, 35*(1), 30-42.

Sinkovics, R. R., Penz, E., & Ghauri, P. N. (2005). Analysing textual data in international marketing research. *Qualitative Market Research: an International Journal*, *8*(1), 9-38.

Sirgy, M. J. (2008). Ethics and public policy implications of research on consumer well-being. *Journal of Public Policy & Marketing*, *27*(2), 207-12.

Sirgy, M. J., Efraty, D., Siegel, P. and Lee, D.-J. (2001). A new measure of quality of work life (QWL) based on need satisfaction and spillover theory. *Social Indicators Research, 55*(3), 241-302.

Sirgy, M. J., Hansen, D. E., & Littlefield J. E. (1994). Does hospital satisfaction affect life satisfaction? *Journal of Macromarketing, 14*, 36-46.

Sirgy, M. J., & Lee, D.-J. (1996). Setting socially responsible marketing objectives. A quality-of-life approach. *European Journal of Marketing, 30*(5), 20-34.

Sirgy, M. J., Lee, D.-J., & Rahtz, D. (2007). Research on consumer well-being (CWB): Overview of the field and introduction to the special issue. *Journal of Macromarketing, 27*(4), 341-349.

Sirgy, M. J., & Lee, D.-J. (1996). Setting socially responsible marketing objectives: A quality-of-life approach. *European Journal of Marketing, 30*(5), 20-34.

Sirgy, M. J., Samli, A. C., Meadow, L. (1982). The Interface between Quality of Life and Marketing: A Theoretical Framework. *Journal of Marketing & Public Policy*, 1(1), 69-84.

Spiggle, S. (1994). Analysis and Interpretation of Qualitative Data in Consumer Research. *Journal of Consumer Research*, 21(3), 491-503.

Sreeram, A., Kesharwani, A., & Desai, S. (2017). Factors affecting satisfaction and loyalty in online grocery shopping: An integrated model. *Journal of Indian Business Research, 9*(2), 107-132.

Stilley, K. M., Inman, J. J., & Wakefield, K. L. (2010a). Spending on the fly: Mental budgets, promotions, and spending behavior. *Journal of Marketing*, *74*(3), 34-47.

Stilley, K. M., Inman, J. J., & Wakefield, K. L. (2010b). Planning to make unplanned purchases? The role of in-store slack in budget deviation. *Journal of Consumer Research, 37*(2), 264-278.

Stitt, S. (1996). An international perspective on food and cooking skills in education. *British Food Journal*, *98*(10), 27–34.

Story, M., Neumark-Sztainer, D., & French, S. (2002). Individual and environmental influences on adolescent eating behaviors. *Journal of the American Dietetic Association*, *102*(3), 40-51.

Sturm, R. (2002). The effects of obesity, smoking, and drinking on medical problems and costs. *Health Affairs*, *21*(2), 245-253.

Swan, E., Bouwman, L., Aarts, N., Rosen, L., Hiddink, G. J., & Koelen, M. (2018). Food stories: Unraveling the mechanisms underlying healthful eating. *Appetite, 120*, 456-463.

Swinburn, B., Egger, G., & Raza, F. (1999). Dissecting obesogenic environments: The development and application of a framework for identifying and prioritizing environmental interventions for obesity. *Preventive Medicine, 29*(6), 563-570.

Teller, C., Kotzab, H., & Grant, D. B. (2012). The relevance of shopper logistics for consumers of store-based retail formats. *Journal of Retailing and Consumer Services, 19*(1), 59-66.

Tetley, A. C., Brunstrom, J. M., & Griffiths, P. L. (2010). The role of sensitivity to reward and impulsivity in food-cue reactivity. *Eating Behaviors, 11*(3), 138-143.

Thaler, R. (1985). Mental accounting and consumer choice. *Marketing Science, 4*(3), 199-214.

Thaler, R.H., & Sunstein, C.R. (2008). *Nudge. Improving Decisions About Health, Wealth, and Happiness*. New Haven, London: Yale University Press.

Thewissen, R., Van Den Hout, M., Havermans, R. C., & Jansen, A. (2005). Context-dependency of cue-elicited urge to smoke. *Addiction, 100*(3), 387-396.

Thomson, D., & Hassenkamp, A.-M. (2008). The social meaning and function of food rituals in healthcare practice: An ethnography. *Human Relations*, *61*(12), 1775–1802.

Tiggemann, M. (2014). The status of media effects on body image research: Commentary on articles in the themed issue on body image and media. *Media Psychology*, *17*(2), 127–133.

To, P.-L., Liao, C., & Lin, T. H. (2007). Shopping motivations in the Internet: A study based on utilitarian and hedonic value. *Technovation*, *27*, 774-787.

Tonkin, E., Coveney, J., Webb, T., Wilson, A. M., & Meyer, S. B. (2017). Consumer concerns relating to food labeling and trust – Australian governance actors respond. *The Journal of Consumer Affairs, 52*(2), 349-372.

Tukkinen, P., & Lindqvist, J. (2015). Understanding motivations for using grocery shopping applications. *IEEE Pervasive Computing, 14*(4), 38-44.

Valkenburg, P. M., & Cantor, J. (2001). The development of a child into a consumer. *Journal of Applied Developmental Psychology, 22*(1), 61-72.

van den Akker, K., Jansen, A., Frentz, F., & Havermans, R. C. (2013). Impulsivity makes more susceptible to overeating after contextual appetitive conditioning. *Appetite*, *70*(C), 73–80.

van de Poel, I. (2013). Translating values into design requirements. In D. Michelfelder, N. McCarthy, D. Goldberg (Eds.). *Philosophy and Engineering: Reflections on Practice, Principles and Process. Philosophy of Engineering and Technology*, 15, 253-266. Dordrecht: Springer.

van der Veer, L. (2017). *Food Online. PhD thesis on food legal and civil law requirements for digital contracts regarding food purchases by consumers in the Netherlands.* Wageningen University and Research Center.

Van Droogenbroeck, E., & Van Hove, L. (2017). Adoption of online grocery shopping: Personal or household characteristics? *Journal of Internet Commerce, 16*, 255-286.

Van Gucht, D., Baeyens, F., Hermans, D., & Beckers, T. (2013). The inertia of conditioned craving. Does context modulate the effect of counterconditioning? *Appetite, 65*, 51-57.

Van Gucht, D., Baeyens, F., Vansteenwegen, D., Hermans, D., & Beckers, T. (2010). Counterconditioning reduces cue-induced craving and actual cue-elicited consumption. *Emotion, 10*(5), 688-695.

Van Gucht, D., Vansteenwegen, D., Beckers, T., & Van den Bergh, O. (2008a). Return of experimentally induced chocolate craving after extinction in a different context: Divergence between craving for and expecting to eat chocolate. *Behaviour Research and Therapy, 46*(3), 375-391.

Van Gucht, D., Vansteenwegen, D., Van den Bergh, O., & Beckers, T. (2008b). Conditioned craving cues elicit an automatic approach tendency. *Behaviour Research and Therapy, 46*(10), 1160-1169.

Van Strien, T., Schippers, G. M., & Cox, W. M. (1995). On the relationship between emotional and external eating behavior. *Addictive Behaviors, 20*(5), 585–594.

Vartanian, L. R. (2015). Impression management and food intake: Current directions in research. *Appetite, 86*(1), 74-80.

Vartanian, L. R., Herman, C. P., & Polivy, J. (2007). Consumption stereotypes and impression management: How you are what you eat. *Appetite, 48*(3), 265-77.

Vidgen, H. A., & Gallegos, D. (2014). Defining food literacy and its components. *Appetite, 76*, 50-59.

Virtanen, M., Kivimäki, H., Ervasti, J., Oksanen, T., Pentti, J., Kouvonen, A., Halonen, J., Kivimäki, M., & Vaherta, J. (2015). Fast-food outlets and grocery stores near schools and adolescents' eating habits and overweight in Finland. *European Journal of Public Health, 25*(4), 650-655.

Voola, A. P., Voola, R., Wyllie, J., Carlson, J., & Sridharan, S. (2018). Families and food: Exploring food well-being in poverty. *European Journal of Marketing, 52*(12), 2423-2448.

Wallendorf, M., & and Arnould, E. J. (1991). "We gather together": Consumption

rituals of Thanksgiving Day. *Journal of Consumer Research, 18*(1), 13-31.

Wang, C. Y., McPherson, K., Marsh, T., Gortmaker, S. L., & Brown, M. (2011). Health and economic burden of the projected obesity trends in the USA and the UK. *The Lancet, 378*(9793), 815–825.

Wang, H., Tong, L., Takeuchi, R., & George, G. (2016). Corporate social responsibility: An overview and new research directions, *Academy of Management Journal, 59*(2), 534-544.

Wansink, B., & Sobal, J. (2016). Mindless eating. *Environment and Behavior, 39*(1), 106–123.

Ward, S. (1974). Consumer socialization. *Journal of Consumer Research, 1*(2), 1-14.

Wardle, J. (1990). Conditioning processes and cue exposure in the modification of excessive eating. *Addictive Behaviors, 15*(4), 387-393.

Weischer, C. & Gehrau, V. (2017). *Die Beobachtung als Methode in der Soziologie.* Konstanz, Germany: UVK Verlagsgesellschaft mbH.

Williams, E. P., Mesidor, M., Winters, K., Dubbert, P. M., & Wyatt, S. B. (2015). Overweight and obesity: Prevalence, consequences, and causes of a growing public health problem. *Current Obesity Reports, 4*(3), 363-370.

Wilson, N. L., & Blackhurst, A. E. (2011). Food advertising and eating disorders: Marketing body dissatisfaction, the drive for thinness, and dieting in women's magazines. *The Journal of Humanistic Counseling, Education and Development, 38*(2), 111–112.

Wingert, K., Zachary, D. A., Fox, M., Gittelsohn, J., & Surkan, P. J. (2014). Child as change agent. The potential of children to increase healthy food purchasing. *Appetite, 81*, 330-336.

Witmer, B. G., & Singer, M. J. (1998). Measuring presence in virtual environments: A presence questionnaire. P*resence: Teleoperators and Virtual Environments, 7*(3), 225-240.

WHO (2018a). *Obesity and overweight.* https://www.who.int/news-room/fact-sheets/detail/obesity-and-overweight, Last accessed 15.03.19.

WHO (2018b). *World Health Statistics 2018: Monitoring health for the SDGs.* https://apps.who.int/iris/bitstream/handle/10665/272596/9789241565585-eng.pdf, Last accessed 15.03.19.

WHO (2018c). Integrated health promotion: The Dutch experience. http://www.euro.who.int/en/countries/netherlands/news2/news/2018/04/integrated-health-promotion-the-dutch-experience, Last accessed 21.09.19.

WHO (2017). *Tenfold increase in childhood and adolescent obesity in four decades: New study by Imperial College London and WHO.* http://www.who.int/news-room/detail/11-10-2017-tenfold-increase-in-childhood-and-adolescent-obesity-in-four-decades-new-study-by-imperial-college-london-and-who, Last accessed 15.03.19.

Wu, B. T. W., & Petroshius, S. M. (1987). The halo effect in store image measurement. *Journal of the Academy of Marketing Science, 15*(3), 044-051.

Zentes, J., Morschett, D., & Schramm-Klein (2016). Corporate social responsibility. In J. Zentes (Ed.). *Strategic Retail Management* (pp. 207-226). Wiesbaden: Springer Gabler.

Zanon, C., Bardagi, M. P., Layous, K., and Hutz, C. (2014). Validation of the satisfaction with life scale to Brazilians: Evidence of measurement noninvariance across Brazil and US. *Social Indicators Research, 119*, 443-453.

Zhu, Q., & Semeijn, J. (2014). Antecedents of customer behavioral intentions for online grocery shopping in Western Europe. In T. Foscht, D. Morschett, T. Rudolph, P. Schnedlitz, H. Schramm-Klein, & B. Swoboda. (Eds). *European Retail Research* (pp. 1-19). Wiesbaden: Springer Gabler.

Zinbarg, R. E., & Mohlman, J. (1998). Individual differences in the acquisition of affectively valanced associations. *Journal of Personality and Social Psychology, 74*(4), 1024-1040.

The manufacturer's authorised representative in the EU is Springer
Nature Customer Service Centre GmbH, Europaplatz 3, 69115 Heidelberg,
Germany. If you have any concerns regarding our products, please
contact ProductSafety@springernature.com

Printed and bound by CPI Group (UK) Ltd, Croydon, CR0 4YY
30/09/2026
02225597-0001